WALKING FROM EAST TO WEST

GOD IN THE SHADOWS

WALKING FROM EAST TO WEST

RAVI ZACHARIAS

ZONDERVAN™

GRAND RAPIDS, MICHIGAN 49530 USA

ZONDERVAN.COM/
AUTHORTRACKER

We want to hear from you. Please send your comments about this book to us in care of zreview@zondervan.com. Thank you.

ZONDERVAN™

Walking from East to West
Copyright © 2006 by Ravi Zacharias

This title is also available as a Zondervan ebook product.
Visit www.zondervan.com/ebooks for more information.

This title is also available as a Zondervan audio product.
Visit www.zondervan.com/audiopages for more information.

Requests for information should be addressed to:

Zondervan, *Grand Rapids, Michigan 49530*

Library of Congress Cataloging-in-Publication Data

Zacharias, Ravi K.
  Walking from east to west : God in the shadows / Ravi Zacharias
with R. S. Sawyer — 1st ed.
    p. cm.
  ISBN – 13: 978-0-310-25915-2
  ISBN – 10: 0-310-25915-0
  1. Zacharias, Ravi K. 2. Christian biography — India. 3. Christian
biography — Canada. I. Sawyer, Scott. II. Title.
  BR1725.Z33A3 2006
  269'.2'092 — dc22

                                                              2005020433

This edition printed on acid-free paper.

Published in association with the literary agency of Wolgemuth and Associates, Inc.

Part 3 title page photos by Tigert Communications, Nashville, TN, USA

Interior design by Beth Shagene

Printed in the United States of America

06 07 08 09 10 11 12 • 21 20 19 18 17 16 15 14 13 12 11 10 9 8 7 6 5 4 3 2 1

To Beverly and Rick,
Bill and Kathalleyne
Because of their love and friendship,
this story continues in a worldwide reach.

Truth forever on the scaffold,
Wrong forever on the throne, —
Yet that scaffold sways the future,
And, behind the dim unknown,
Standeth God within the shadow,
Keeping watch above his own.

James Russell Lowell,
from The Present Crisis *(1844)*

CONTENTS

Acknowledgments   9

Preface   11

PART 1: EAST

1. A Life Out of Nothing   15

2. Long Shadows   29

3. Hidden Gold   41

4. My Father's House   51

5. The Cricket Field   63

6. Wedding Crashers and Ashes   75

7. The Raj Path and the Assigned Way   85

8. The Longest Shadow   101

9. A Book on the Ash Heap   109

10. Extraordinary Men   123

PART 2: EAST TO WEST

11. The Girl in the Church   139

12. "I Am Called to This"   151

13. The Longest Journey   173

14. Veritas   195

15. One Destination   211

PART 3: WEST TO EAST

16. Returning: God in the Shadows   227

acknowledgments

My sincere thanks go first and foremost to my family for the memories, both good and bad, that in the end taught me the value of home and culture. In the telling of this story, the one most deserving of my appreciation is Scott Sawyer, who framed the entire narrative and told it in the simplest but most reflective terms. He worked hard to make this book a reality. We traveled together through the cities of my youth so that he could feel the heartbeat of my years growing up in India. I could tell when he wrote it that he well understood what I was trying to recall of those years.

A special word of thanks to Zondervan's John Sloan, who patiently nursed this book along until it came to the place that it is now. As always, my agent and representative Robert Wolgemuth was my best cheerleader, encouraging and affirming me along the way. But the best of all that I can say is to Margie, my wife, who not only *understood* the challenge I had before me but helped edit in a way that kept my voice yet smoothened the rough spots. The final edits were done by Dirk Buursma, and I deeply appreciate his work to complete the task.

PREFACE

SOME BOOKS ARE DIFFICULT TO WRITE; OTHERS BORDER ON THE ALMOST impossible. This one is in the latter category. Many friends and even strangers over the years have asked if I would pen such a story, and when Zondervan asked me to write a book of my memoirs, I concluded that the time had come. The difficulty lies on many fronts. First is that of accurate recall. How does one piece together all of the past? How does one be truly objective when one's own feelings are locked in to the situation? Then arises a very personal matter. How do you tell a story of such intimate issues and not at the same time make someone else look unduly bad or good? That was the toughest challenge of all. It is one thing for an individual to disclose his or her own heart, but to do so for someone else runs an unfortunate risk. If I have erred here, I sincerely hope it is not because of any personal ill will but only because I know the story did not end as it had begun.

As I struggled with these issues, the publisher agreed to have me tell the story to another writer, who would spend hours with me and others to cull the material and then write it in the way it unfolded. I took the narrative he penned and wrote the story line in my own words, along with his. Throughout this process, the publisher asked if I would keep it at a simple level of reach and not make it inaccessible in content and depth. The goal was simple: "Tell us your story in the simplest terms with your heart on your sleeve." I suppose being accustomed to writing on philosophical themes, this was a reminder to me as "a word to the wise."

So that has been the approach. Much more could have been said and said at a lofty level portraying all my philosophical struggles and so on. But we avoided that. Maybe some instances in the narrative

need not have been shared, but were in order to show the backdrop
of what was shaping me all along. What I do know is that as I retraced
steps and memories, some of them were hard to relive, while others
brought a renewed sense of happiness; some memories brought the
depth of tears to the surface, and yet others brought to mind cherished
moments long forgotten. I have concluded that it is an exercise that
is well undertaken by everybody—to journal and write down one's
thoughts at shorter intervals. Memories are good reminders of what
God has done and where we could have done better. I remember the
time an older man asked me when I was young, "Do you know what
you are doing now?" I thought it was some kind of trick question.

"Tell me," I said.

"You are building your memories," he replied, "so make them good
ones."

If each reader would glean just that from the book, then it will
have been worth it.

But there is something greater here, and it is this: as life progresses,
you wish there were some safeguards you had taken along the way,
and even some different decisions you had made along the way. For
one, I wish I had talked more to my parents about their past and about
my ancestors. What did they know? What were the stories of their
lives? What made each one the way they were? Now it is too late for
that, for my parents have both passed away. I nevertheless come away
with the absolute certainty that God has ordered my steps and that
God was there, even in the darkest moments of my life. I know this
as surely as I know I exist. He never abandoned me and has brought
me by His grace and mercy this far. This is the most certain truth I
possess, and it is truly liberating.

One other great enrichment was to think back on my youth in
India, even as now the West has become home. India gave me much
that I can never repay. It really is an intriguing culture—weaknesses
and ironies notwithstanding. Now living first in Canada and then in
America, these countries have become home. I am so grateful to God
for the privilege of living here. Beyond my residences, the heart has
found its home in my faith and love for Jesus Christ. I sincerely hope
and pray that as you read these pages, you will feel Him near to you
and that you will be guided by His wisdom and kept by His grace.

Without Him, this story would not be worth telling or reading.

CHAPTER 1

A LIFE OUT OF NOTHING

ONE OF MY EARLIEST MEMORIES IS OF THE OLD MAN ON MY STREET, A MYSTIC who wore only a loincloth. He was tall, with matted hair and piercing eyes, quite fearsome to look at. Mud was caked all over his bony frame, his face was scarred by deep gashes that were self-inflicted from his religious devotion, and his skin was burned by constant exposure to the torrid heat of the midday sun. "How did he come to look like this?" I wondered as a boy. "What had he done to himself?"

I found out soon enough. Two or three times each week he would appear on our street; then, almost like a coiled rope unwinding, he would lie down on that filthy road and begin his routine. Cow dung and dog droppings littered the path, to say nothing of the stones or sharp objects that cluttered it as well, yet he would roll down the length of the street with a howl that sounded as if it came from the depths of a cavern.

"Govinda! Govinda! Govinda!"

I had no clue what his cry was about—I only knew it terrified me.

It was an astonishing sight to a five-year-old, and I recall scampering to my mother and asking her, "What is he doing? What is he doing?"

"He's OK," she replied. "Just ignore him."

"But what is he doing?" I would implore. "Why is he doing it?"

"He's calling to his god!" she said.

That did not quench my curiosity. But I did not pursue it as long as he continued to roll away from me, and his voice became a faint but haunting sound in the distance: "Govinda!"

The old mystic was only one of the striking sights on our street, a place that teemed with life in my eyes. On that street, I believed I saw everything that living represented. The world there was filled with sounds and screams and, yes, smells of different kinds. Silence was at a premium. Every morning at sunrise, any seeming quietness was broken by the shouts of the street vendors, hawking the items they were selling. "Onions! Milk! Vegetables! Knife sharpeners!" When these sellers came to our door, they would look through our open but barred windows. There was no privacy to speak of. We stepped outside onto the street, and the road itself was so narrow that a car couldn't pass through but only hand-pulled or cycle rickshaws. Outside were stray animals and people, each about some pursuit. Sometimes it was a beggar at the door, sometimes a leprous hand reaching for a handout with a plea for compassion. Life with all its hurts and pains squinted at you, squatted before you, and stared you down daily. This was the street where I grew up.

Life in our neighborhood was lived out amid this jumble of sounds, sights, and scents. There, on the street every day, friends played soccer or cricket. Laughter, cries, angry outbursts—all the emotions were in evidence. Around the corner, a small shop sold potato-crisp snacks and spicy Indian treats, and the best thing you could do was go into the shop and have your uncle or your friend buy you a treat of some kind. Flavors were in the air—the smell of oil heated to its peak, frying food of some kind—and taking it all in was an all-day activity, with someone buying a morsel or two and munching on it as they went on their way. From sunrise to sunset, people of every stripe and need passed by.

Then at dusk, when the streetlamps came on, students came out of their homes to continue their studies under lamplight. In some homes, there was no electricity; in others, parents sent their children outside to study under the streetlamps to conserve electricity. There was often a tussle as to who claimed a lamppost first. Once that was settled, the fortunate student sat with his back resting against the post. Most of his scalp was shaved except for an area called the *bodi*, and he tied this part to the lamppost behind him. That way, whenever he began to doze off and nod forward, the pull on his hair kept him awake. This was the discipline of study in those days.

Now, more than a half century later, as I again walk the street where I was born, memories come alive with a wave of nostalgia. I find it hard to believe this is where I had my beginnings.

The narrow lane has been widened and paved. Still, it would be an adventure to try to wedge a larger car in here. Yet taxi drivers do it regularly and intrepidly, and as you watch you wonder if the metal shrinks when they approach an object that seems too close to avoid a scrape. An Indian friend of mine says that whenever he's asked if India has a Disney World, he answers, "No, we just take a taxi ride. That is breathtaking enough."

The first time I brought my wife here, we couldn't get to the door of the house on this street where I was born and to which we returned to spend our vacations. A water buffalo had stopped in front of the door. That was twenty years ago, and I was completely overwhelmed then. The memories come flooding back so quickly and sharply: the neem tree in the backyard that we used as a wicket for our cricket games; the window to the room where my whole family slept; a kitchen with a clay coal fire in which to do all the cooking—the hot Indian flat-breads that would come out of the oven puffing fresh and make you hungry just by their smell, the curries that were lip-smacking good, the delicacies that to this day charm my imagination.

What a world that was for me as a youngster!

THIS HOUSE WHERE I SPENT MANY A SUMMER BELONGED TO MY UNCLE and was like our second home. It used to be number 7, but now it is number 13, and above the doorpost a large eye has been painted to ward off evil spirits. A Hindu family lives here now, a lovely couple with two young daughters, and I've made it a practice to visit them whenever I come back to Chennai (the historic city formerly known to the world as Madras in the state of Tamil Nadu, next to Kerala). The little girls have fallen in love with my Canadian wife, Margie. Every time she accompanies me, they giggle excitedly. They love her sandy-blonde hair and delightedly say, "Oh, Auntie, Auntie, I love your blue eyes!"

This simple little house is like most others on the street, very small, made up of four rooms, each measuring about ten feet by ten. Even these small rooms are carefully compartmentalized. There may be a stove next to a bed, that sort of thing. In fact, when my family returned here to visit, your bed was a chair, a desk, or whatever you wanted to make it for the moment. During those long summer stays, there were twelve of us altogether, including our relatives, squeezed into this tiny place. But we never once thought of complaining. This was life, and this is the way we grew up.

I am sitting with the present owners in a room that has been further divided into two. He and his brother have had a falling-out and have divided the house into these two compartments. Each family now uses two rooms. The girls probably sleep on the floor, just as my siblings and I did fifty years ago. Their mother offers me tea — there is always the beautiful custom of tea in India. This, too, takes me back. It is a marvel to sit here drinking tea with this family in the house that was my uncle's years ago. They plead with me to stay for a meal, but much to their disappointment I have an appointment elsewhere, a speaking engagement.

It is an August evening, and it is hot — around 100 degrees. I remember having ceiling fans that kept the air circulating, but there was little else to cool you. You simply got used to it. And there were various other ways to manage. We had thatched-straw drapes — called *khus-khus* — that were woven together. You could water these home-spun creations with a hose to moisten them, and then, as the breeze blew through the thatched straw, it cooled things somewhat.

I have brought the two girls of this family a bag full of gifts. Margie and I always prepare something for them at home before we come. And they're always appreciative that we think of them.

The father asks, "How was your trip? Why are you here this time?"

"I'm speaking in various places here in Chennai. Then I'll be going up to Delhi in a few days."

This man is a marketing director for a small firm, with a master's degree that he attained by going to night school. His English is broken, as is my Tamil, but between the two of us we make a sensible conversation. The girls do fairly well with English; the mother speaks none at all. They know I live in the United States, and one of the girls ventures to ask what city I live in.

"In Atlanta," I say.

They begin to tell me their dreams. One wants to be a teacher, the other a doctor.

"A doctor," I think, for I also was a premed student at one time.

The father tells me, in so many words, that his greatest burden is for his children to get an education, because none of his family did. Yet he doesn't have the wherewithal to send the two girls to college.

"Anything you can do to help them get the best education in America or Canada is my heart's deepest desire."

I tell him we could help. Our ministry provides scholarships toward education for families in need. His eyes get moist, hoping that this dream for his children might come true.

The last time I was here I tried to give the father some money, but he wouldn't take it. He said, "You gave to me last time, sir. I am just honored you have come. That is enough for me, to see your face."

So I handed it to one of the girls instead, telling her, "I want you each to have a bicycle to ride to school." They beamed with gratitude, and now they ride those bikes to school every day.

Later, the father and I discover in our conversation that this house was sold to his father by one of my uncles. Family ties run deep here, coloring virtually every detail of life. I tell him that just a few doors down is the home that my mother's family owned, the house where I was born.

That house was called "Dalmejiem." The name was an acronym that included every member of my mother's family: Devaram, the father; Agnes, the mother; Leela, the oldest daughter; Margaret; Elizabeth; James; my mother, Isabella; Ebenezer; and Manickam, the surname.

Now the girls are begging to show me the tree in their backyard. With their mother's permission, they lead me to the very same neem tree that my cousins and I used as the wicket for our cricket games. The girls tell me they worship that tree for its antibiotic qualities. Every now and then, the mother lights a fire, and they hold a ceremony to pay homage. They tell me that she goes to the temple every day. "Every day, Uncle, she goes there," they assure me, calling me by the affectionate term that Indian youths use to address their familiar elders.

Their mother's eyes reveal the inner quest for piety, and my heart longs to tell her that God does not live in temples made with human hands. I trust that the time we spend together during my trips here will present the right moment.

※

IT IS NOT FOR SENTIMENTAL REASONS THAT I VISIT THIS FAMILY IN MY UNCLE'S former home. They are simply more of the beautiful people of my homeland with whom God has chosen that I cross paths. The truth is,

I'm happiest when I'm with people such as these, people with whom I'm at ease. Here in my homeland I am most free to be me, with no one to recognize me because of my profession. And I get to do what I love best—simply to be with people. It reminds me of my youth when I surrounded myself with friends.

But the reality is, in the next month I will be speaking before the United Nations on the opening day of their assembly. I have been asked to address the ambassadors on the subject of "Navigating with Absolutes in a Relativistic World." The contrasts between where I am now, in this humble house, and where I am going to be in a matter of weeks are too vast to fully process. Yet, there is no doubt that God prepared me for this life I now lead, connecting the varied and ironic threads of my experience into a beautiful tapestry as He would see fit.

It is not a natural drive within me to appear in such a prominent place as the United Nations. Yes, it is a privilege I hold dear, and a sacred trust. But I never would have wanted to engineer something like this. That was my father's life. Because of the position to which he rose in the government of India, my siblings and I shook hands with prime ministers and presidents. We met and mixed with international leaders; we even entertained ambassadors and their entourages. The wealthy and the powerful are one side of India. Yet, I can't explain why today I shrink from such a public life. I can only say that it has to do with the way the Lord has framed me. I truly do feel for a world in need. And I relate with ease to the ordinary person.

Even so, the last time I came here to Chennai, to the very street of my birth, a man came running out of his house and called me by name. "Raviji! Raviji!" he cried, using a term of reverence. "What are you doing here?" He had heard me speak in Amsterdam some years before and now as I passed in front of him, speaking to someone in Tamil, he was shocked to know that I understand his language, indeed, that this was the very street where I was born.

INDIA IS A NATION WITH POLARITIES OF INCREDIBLE PROPORTIONS. SOME OF the world's greatest minds come from here, making great advances in medicine, philosophy, and in the world of the Internet and high technology. Yet in the midst of this, of course, is dire deprivation and longing for a better way of life.

In this subcontinent, the raw reality of life stares you in the face. For that very reason, it has always been easy for me to see Jesus on these streets. Any time I read the accounts in the Gospels, I can envision the Lord with the lame man in all his bare need on the side of the road, or the leprous body longing for a touch. After all, that's what I saw growing up, every day. Moreover, each time I read of the Lord walking in the streets of Bethany or Jerusalem and telling a parable, I see my Indian culture, which also deals in parables.

I see the tailor who sets up his machine in the open air on the street corner, wedged between other craftsmen and craftswomen, shoe shiners, fabric menders—all businesspeople who eke out a living from wherever they can find a small, square space. The people here know how to manage with very little. Yet, sometimes I wonder how they make a living out of it. Theirs are lives full of burdens and chores, and they're so very hard-pressed for money just to get by. Some are forced to set up home on the side of the road in a little shack. Others live on the streets in poverty, without even the advantage of a roof. And it's virtually impossible for the lower classes to rise upward.

This unvarnished reality must be one reason why India is the largest producer of movies in the world. The movies that are made here are the best barometer of humanity's gnawing need for an escape hatch. Through movies, you can escape to romance, to justice, to the fulfilling marriage you never had, to upholding the cause of the poor. Yet, in spite of the escapism that movies promise, you can never escape the sharp edges of life in India. It's always there to greet you as you exit the theater.

At the same time, there is also evident on these streets the very real resilience of the human spirit. People make a go of things with what they have. As I look from one side of the street to the other, I see those who will survive against all odds and who have learned to cope. India also is a deeply artistic culture. You see it even in this muddled-up, mixed-up, mishmash of a marketplace, in the way a merchant hangs beads or arranges his cushions with a pleasing aesthetic.

Each time I walk the streets in my homeland now, it's a matter of good news/bad news to me. The good news is, I am able to see clear-eyed here—to behold life and all its pain. The bad news is, the pain is so overwhelming that I can get desensitized to it, and one has to be careful of that. It's why I keep telling my children to never forget from whence they ultimately came.

As I walk my home street now, I'm hit with the reality that my own life came out of nothing. By the time I was a teenager, when my family returned here on vacations to my mother's home in Chennai, in the South, from our home in Delhi in northern India, I realized how small her family's house was and how little my cousins had. I would ask my mother, "Why are they so poor?" By then, coming to Chennai always reminded me of the meager side of our existence.

Now, whenever I return, I have a yearning in my soul to be a solution to this. How can I help the very people whose blood is in my veins? Their food, their language, their ragtag existence from day to day, their struggle to survive—all of that is in me.

I always bring an envelope with money I've saved up or set aside. At the beginning of the week, that envelope is open to various needs. By the time I leave, everything in it will be gone. In a little over a week from now, I will go home to a steady income and a comfortable home, and, yes, a kind of sanitized life. But the ones I see struggling here I know cannot make it on their own. Sharing with these people some of what I have, and seeing the small bit of happiness it brings into their lives, is the privilege of a native son.

Sometimes we can convince ourselves that the answer to everything lies in economic well-being. Obviously, this is a very important facet of life. When you can afford a meal, a bed, a home for your family, you can be content. But it does not ultimately solve the deepest questions that haunt you. That is where religion is supposed to help, to offer answers.

Whether we like to admit it or not, many religions of the world are concocted to hold fear and control over people. Nobody likes to talk about this, but it's the way it is. The human psyche is vulnerable because of its built-in fear of failure, and becomes an easy prey.

That's the way I remember first experiencing religion—as something involving fear: A man rolling down the street, chanting the name of his god. Men and women with deep gashes in their faces. Tales of goats being sacrificed in temples to procure answers to prayers. Each time I asked my mother about these things, she explained, "They do it to worship their god."

Worship? It was an empty word to me, steeped in some mysterious expression that didn't make ordinary sense. It was a magic wand to ward off tragedy. The one thing I learned from observing such rituals was a palpable sense of fear. Everything had to follow a certain sequence. If you didn't do it right, something bad was going to happen to you. If I didn't make my offering, what would befall me? If I didn't do this one thing correctly, what price would I have to pay to some sharp, implacable divine being? Was all that just superstition born out of fear, dressed up into a system, and embedded into a culture?

There was one wonderful aspect of the religious world I grew up in that held my fascination — and that was its stories. I loved the pictures; the mythologies; and the ideas of rescue, of winning wars, of magical potions, of how your mother could be saved by some god who came down and carried her away from harm. It was a bit of folklore here, a bit of drama there, a bit of religion, a bit of historical fact, all mixed together.

I used to go with my friends and their families to watch the religious plays at the festivals, and I became quite fond of them. To me, it wasn't so much religious as that it was part of a family's annual routine. Each year, when the Hindu god Ram's birthday came around, I went with my friends to see the plays that reenacted stories about Ram. I loved these dramas, because my little brother Ramesh was named after Ram.

My siblings and I got our first taste of Western religion when two Jehovah's Witnesses came knocking on our door one day. A Mr. and Mrs. Smith appeared, telling my father they wanted to teach us children to read and to know the Bible. They assured our dad how very important this was.

So the Smiths came to our home once a week, and for the next year and a half they sat in our living room and taught us for an hour or two at a time. I remember reading the Witnesses' book *Let God Be True* and the magazines *The Watchtower* and *Awake*. Most impressive, though, were the assemblies where they gathered groups and showed movies. One of these movies featured tens of thousands of people attending a Jehovah's Witnesses rally at Yankee Stadium in New York City. When my siblings and I saw that spectacle, we couldn't help being awed by it.

Yet, in retrospect, it shows how easily the human mind and heart can be manipulated. Ours was a small family with very little in comparison to most families in the West. And seeing that movie, with all those highly successful-looking people gathered in a magnificent stadium, my siblings' hearts must have raced as my heart did. I'm sure they also thought, "This has to be true." It made us want to be part of such a great event, in a great city like New York.

So we continued to study with the Smiths until the day Mr. Smith came to the chapter on heaven in the book of Revelation. He stopped there and told us that, according to Jehovah's Witnesses' teaching, only 144,000 people were going to make it to paradise.

That hit me like a ton of bricks. Here my siblings and I had thought we were becoming very spiritual. These Western missionaries had sat with us each week, giving us homework and encouraging our studies. But now I scratched my head over this news. I asked Mr. Smith, "Only 144,000?"

"That's right," he said.

"Sir, how many people are there in your organization?"

"Oh, we have many."

"Do you have more than 144,000?"

"Oh yes."

"So even all of *your* people aren't going to make it to heaven?"

I thought of the Smiths' constant praying, of all their efforts to reach more and more people — and yet even *they* had no way of knowing where they were going after death. So they certainly couldn't assure me of where I might be going.

"Mr. Smith, before you came, I didn't know where I was going after I died," I said. "But now, after all this study, I *still* don't know where I'm going after I die."

They probably sensed they were up against something difficult at that point. Or perhaps my outright shock over this curious point of doctrine registered with them more deeply than normal. But not long afterward, the Smiths were succeeded by another couple, and when they sensed they were getting nowhere, they stopped coming to our house. Who knows, in another six or eight months, maybe we would have been convinced by them. But at that stage, I told myself, "I don't much care for this. I'm done with Christianity."

I didn't know that it wasn't Christianity I was rejecting, but I really had no idea how to distinguish one sect from another. At best, each of us was only thinking pragmatically, "What is it that's going to work for *me*?"

LIKE MOST OF INDIA, MY MOTHER WAS VERY SPIRITUAL AND AT THE SAME time very superstitious. In our home hung a picture of Saint Philomena, a Catholic saint, because of a commitment my mom had made after my sister Shyamala (Sham to us) was diagnosed with polio at five days old. The doctor gave Sham no hope of surviving, and in desperation my mother decided to send a gift to the Saint Philomena shrine in South India. She pledged that if my sister would get through this, my mother would give money to the shrine faithfully.

Sham survived. In her younger years she wore a crude knee brace from just above the knee to her ankle and walked with a bit of a hop. (Today, after a surgery, she has only a slight limp that is virtually undetectable.) But what was most important to my mother was that her daughter's life was spared. That is why, almost until the day Mom died, she faithfully sent money to the Saint Philomena shrine. It is also why my sister Sham was given the middle name Philomena.

After that ordeal, our family was brought to the brink again years later over our baby brother Ramesh. I especially was very close to him, so it struck me hard when little Ramesh, only six or seven years old, became ill with double pneumonia and typhoid. Very little could be done in those days for someone in his condition, and the doctors offered us no hope.

I remember the evening my parents decided to take us to the hospital to visit our brother in what we sensed might be our last time to see him. I was deeply shaken when I witnessed what had happened to Ramesh. He was shriveled down to a bag of bones. I barely recognized him; he looked like a picture of a starved child. After seeing him, we all expected that this would be the night he would die.

My mother stayed at the hospital with my brother while my dad took us home. We gathered for prayer in my parents' bedroom around a picture of Jesus that hung on the wall beside the picture of Saint Philomena. I recall that night clearly, on our knees in that room, my father's voice cracking as he prayed. I couldn't believe we were losing him. My little brother was really dying.

One of the people my dad had called to come and pray with us was a certain Pentecostal minister. Mr. Dennis had come to our house occasionally on his motorbike to talk with my dad and pray with him. We used to make a lot of fun of Mr. Dennis and to joke behind his back because he always sang when he prayed. He simply broke out into song, and it sounded so odd to us. We were unkind because we had no clue what this was all about, and our Hindu servants in the house reprimanded us for making fun.

But now, with my brother dying, I prayed as I never had, alongside Mr. Dennis and the others in the room that night. In a voice of deep reverence, this man asked God for a touch of healing, for a miracle. There was nothing funny now. I was moved to tears as he called on the Lord to have mercy on my brother.

Meanwhile, the doctor had come to my mother soon after we left the hospital. He uttered to her the worst news of her life. "Sometime between midnight and 5:00 a.m.," he said, "it will be over."

My mother had not slept for several days. She had sat by Ramesh's side the entire time. Now, as she faced the torturous hours ahead, she was overcome with exhaustion. She simply couldn't keep her eyes open. As the night wore on, she fell sound asleep at my brother's bedside.

Hours later, my mother suddenly shocked herself awake. When she realized what had happened, she feared the worst. The hour had long passed at which Ramesh was to have gone. Yet when she looked at my brother, she saw that he was still breathing. In fact, his chest now rose and fell with a stronger rhythm than before. Something had happened during the night.

When morning came, my mom sent a message to us that Ramesh was looking stronger and better. None of us were sure what this meant. But the same message came to us on the second day, then the third day, then the fourth. Our brother had made the turn, and his strength was restored.

In our family's collective memory, this was one of our most defining moments. I don't know to what degree Mr. Dennis's prayer consciously played a role in this monumental episode of our history. But to me, there was something of God in it.

I don't recall ever seeing Mr. Dennis again, though I have often thought of him. He was a missionary living on a meager salary, a living saint. Somebody must have supported him. Why did he pick our family to visit? Was this not God in the shadows, keeping watch over His own? I did not think of it then, but I see it now. I made an association with the life of prayer and calling in that man, and with the miracle we all had witnessed—my brother's life had been spared.

BEING BACK HERE IN MY MOTHER'S BROTHER'S HOME BRINGS ME CLOSER, I
sense, to the reality of a sovereign God. I can never forget that sovereignty behind my life, and it brings to mind a great Indian custom.

If you travel to the north of India, you will find the most magnificent saris ever made, and Varanasi is where the wedding saris are
handwoven. The gold, the silver, the reds, the blues—all the marvelous colors threaded together are spectacular. These saris are usually
made by just two people—a father who sits on a platform and a son
who sits two steps down from him. The father has all the spools of
silk threads around him. As he begins to pull the threads together, he
nods, and the son responds by moving the shuttle from one side to the
other. Then the process begins again, with the dad nodding and the
son responding. Everything is done with a simple nod from the father.
It's a long, tedious process to watch. But if you come back in two or
three weeks, you'll see a magnificent pattern emerging.

This is an image I always remind myself of: we may be moving the
shuttle, but the design is in the mind of the Father. The son has no
idea what pattern is emerging. He just responds to the father's nod.

Back here in my homeland, I see the threads. My family, my home
city, my spartan beginnings, a life having come out of nothing—I'm
reminded again that the threads are all being pulled together.

This is the only explanation for the great irony in my being here
now. You see, of all five siblings in my family, I had the unhappiest
childhood. Yet I am the one who is most drawn to come back.

It's unexplainable. All of my siblings are natural leaders, and all
live in Toronto today. Each had the beginnings of his or her success
and happiness sown here, in India. Ajit, the oldest, was an engineer
with IBM in the 1970s who later went on to his own commercial success as an entrepreneur. You would think he'd want to come back to
the place where his mind was shaped, where all his dreams and hopes
and promises were formed. You would think the same of my younger
brother, Ramesh, now a successful surgeon, and my two sisters, Sham
and Prem. I have no doubt they have this desire, but not one shares
the deep, soul-wrenching, unshakable tug that I feel. Ramesh does
tell me, "I want to go back sometime. But I want to do it with you,
Ravi."

I'm the one who keeps coming back—and who wants to keep coming back. I have maintained the language and the contacts, mainly by
walking these streets. When I return and see the buildings and the

beauty and the people, I reminisce, "This is where my life was shaped. This is where my calling began. And this is where I very nearly ended it all, out of my own despair."

The sound of a voice crying out to God, a voice that once spelled terror in my heart, is now the very cry to which I respond with a sense of privilege all over the world. Still, to me, coming back is a dip into an ocean too deep for me to fully fathom. The full story only the tapestry can explain.

chapter 2

Long shadows

When it was first published, you could walk into any bookstore in Kerala and purchase a massive red volume titled *The Malayalam-English Dictionary*. Malayalam, which is one of the world's most difficult languages, is the language of Kerala, the most southern state of India. Kerala is also the region that has birthed some of the nation's greatest philosophers.

On the spine of that Malayalam-English dictionary, the first of its kind, you would have read two authors' names: Zacharias and Zacharias—my grandfather and great-grandfather. Both were very prominent linguists, and for Malayalam and English this dictionary is the equivalent of *Webster's Dictionary*. A compilation of such magnitude could be designated the work of two lifetimes, pioneering in its effort for its time and a landmark in its effect to date. I am told it was an enormous help to missionaries and to businessmen and women trading in that part of the world. When the Bible was translated into Malayalam, the translators borrowed from the genius of this work. I was so thrilled when I held the massive volume in my hand for the first time—to see the incredible accomplishment of my grandfather and great-grandfather. Linguistically, they paved the way for the British to reach India's intellectual elite.

Of all the many language groups in India, Malayalis take particular pride in their language. When it is spoken, it sounds like a person with a mouth full of marbles, head thrown back and gargling in abandon with mellifluous tones. The polysyllables just roll off the tongue, and you may find yourself wondering whether this is for real or just a game to see who can outsound the other! The person who engages in palindromes will appreciate that the name of the language itself,

Malayalam, is the same spelled backward or forward. I have often wondered if that's why its very sounds are mesmerizing.

The defenders of this language will tell you passionately that it is the most beautiful and descriptive tongue in the world. I shall let them argue it out with others who lay the same claim for their own language. To speak it well is considered to be quite an accomplishment, much the same way that Arabs view the beauty of Arabic or the academics of old viewed Latin. They bemoan the fact that the world doesn't know their tongue.

Although my dad wasn't a linguist like his forebears, he was naturally very fluent in Malayalam. I learned other languages as a boy—English and Hindi—and I understand and can speak some Tamil. But Malayalam was not commonly used where I grew up in Delhi, and I regret that I never learned it. I often quip now that the only words I learned in Malayalam were the words my father used to chastise me, and those are not fit to be heard in public!

I never knew my grandfather, Oliver Zacharias. With the exception of my mother's mother, Agnes Manickam, all of my grandparents died before I was born. Yet, Grandfather Zacharias provided me with an important legacy that still touches me very tangibly today.

He was the first Indian to be appointed by the British as professor of English at a university in India, Madras Christian College in Madras (which, I remind you, is now Chennai). The college was founded by the British and remains one of the country's best-known schools. His appointment was a historic honor.

That my grandfather was near the top in his field has been confirmed many times by several of his former students I've met in their later years. To a person, they have said he was very gifted in both his native tongue and English, and a delight to be with. But mostly what they've wanted to tell me about was his way with words and his ready wit.

About ten years ago, I had just spoken to a large audience in Chennai when an elderly man approached me. He asked, "Does the name Oliver Zacharias mean anything to you?"

"Yes, sir, it does," I answered smiling. "He was my grandfather."

With a twinkle in his eye, the man said, "I thought so. I was one of your grandfather's students."

I was momentarily caught off guard. "You studied under my grandfather?" I asked.

"Yes, son," he said, "and as soon as I heard you speak, I leaned over to my wife and said, 'He must be Oliver Zacharias's grandson. He *has* to be.'"

Then this man told me something that amazed and delighted me. "Listening to you," he said, "I see you have the same sense of humor your grandfather had."

In the brief moments we had, he noted something else: "Obviously, you are of a different stripe spiritually from your grandfather."

"Why do you say that?"

"Well, he was very much the maverick," he began. Then a grin formed. "He was also very attached to snuff."

"Snuff? You mean tobacco that is inhaled?"

"Yes. And the reason I mention this to you," he said, "is that on the day he retired, he was presented with a silver walking stick and a silver snuff box. That was over half a century ago now, yet I'll never forget it.

"When the presentation was made, with a long speech commemorating his accomplishments, your grandfather simply approached the lectern to receive the gifts. Then, with a sarcastic grin on his face, he said, 'Those who smoke tobacco look like pigs. Those who chew tobacco act like pigs. And those who snort tobacco *are* pigs. Thank you very much.' And he sat down to roaring laughter and applause!

"That was it. No protracted speech, just that single line of humor. Your grandfather was brief, witty, and very self-effacing. All of those traits were captured in that one moment. I will never forget him for his way with words and his love for his students."

My eyes moistened with a longing to have met my grandfather as I heard this all too brief description. We were surrounded at that moment by hundreds of people, yet what I would have given to be able to talk with this man for the rest of the night! It was a wondrous moment, all too fleeting. I marveled at how this stranger could recognize a trait I shared with a man I'd never met. It was a moment when God seemed to peek out from behind the shadows, revealing in the very makeup of my family a glimpse of His tapestry.

But this man's description of my grandfather struck home for another reason. The moment he told me the story, I thought, "Boy, that was exactly the way my dad was with *his* wit!"

My father was always fussy about "dotting his i's and crossing his t's." Language was important to him. His entire family had a touch

of irony and sarcasm in their humor. Like my grandfather, my dad
was a very brilliant man in his own right. And I believe his type of
humor bordered on genius—that rare ability to caricature reality in
the moment and to play on words, adding a creative twist to a situation that reveals a different dimension to its reality.

All of this only makes me wish I had known more of my ancestry.
That evening in Chennai, I had to acknowledge that whatever the
elderly gentleman recognized in me from my grandfather was evidently a transgenerational trait.

Kerala, where my father grew up, is a beautiful place. It is known
as the "fruit basket of India" because it's full of banana plantations,
coconut groves, and acres of well-irrigated orchards. The miles and
miles of green everywhere contrast beautifully against the rich tur-
quoise waters of the Indian Ocean. Some years ago, I enjoyed basking
in the sun one summer afternoon with the famed astronaut James
Irwin. He and I were sharing some meetings together in Kerala. He
said to me, "When I was in space, I well remember the unique blue of
these waters and always wanted to come here. From space and from
here, this is a luxurious reflection of God's beauty." This part of the
country is very different from the north, which is known for being
the center of government, Delhi, and also India's cosmopolitan hub.

It is said that India's brains come from the South, and, as I mentioned, many well-known philosophers have emerged from here. This
was home to Sankara, the Socrates of Indian philosophy. He was a
pantheist who believed there was one ultimate impersonal reality
called "Brahma," of which we are all part and parcel. To him, any
effort to define God in personal terms was a beggar's refuge. In the
beginning was Reality, impersonal and absolute without attribute,
and you and I are part of that reality. Sankara's name is writ large in
philosophy today, and he is revered as the best exponent of this strain
of Hinduism.

Ramanuja, also from the South, was by contrast a Hindu "theist."
To him, God could be defined in personal terms and was manifested
in a multiplicity of incarnations. Worship, hymns, and all the expression that assumed a significant other were God-ward devotion. To
him, God was describable.

In terms of modern Indian thinkers, Sarvapelli Radhakrishnan is
probably the most quoted and prolific. He, too, hailed from the South
and at one time held the prestigious chair of Eastern philosophy at

Oxford University in England. He later became India's second president following its independence in 1947. As a little boy, I had the
privilege of meeting him when my father was invited to his home.
Little did I know then that I was shaking the hand of one of India's
seminal thinkers and writers and would later study Hindu philosophy
under one of his students. He was also a very humble man and much
beloved by Indian people.

I cannot resist adding to this list of distinguished southern figures
a contributor whose intellectual origins were foreign—the apostle
Thomas. He came to India and paid with his life to bring a new message to the upper crust of India's cradle of philosophy. One of the largest church groups in India today, nine million members and a thousand
parishes strong—called the Mar Thoma Church ("Lord Thomas," a
title of honor, not comparing Thomas to the Lord Jesus)—originated
in Kerala and is named after the apostle. Thomas's contribution,
both to the philosophical landscape and to my own path, has been
incalculable.

My father's side of the family certainly had its share of brainpower.
They came from what can only be described as the upper echelon of
Indian society. My father's brother-in-law, my uncle, was a prominent
pharmacologist who wrote a well-known textbook used for decades
in India's medical schools. This distinguished gene pool often showed
in his attitude and self-confidence and, sadly, many times in his dis-
position to those not from such privileged roots.

My dad applied his intellect to studies in industrial labor relations
at Nottingham University in England. Sometime after he returned to
India, the government transferred him from Madras in the South to
Delhi in the North, so my family bid good-bye to southern life and
became, in effect, northerners in our tongue and culture. I was quite
young at the time, probably around four or five years old, and we lived
in Delhi until I was twenty. During that period, my father ascended
government ranks to hold a very powerful portfolio as deputy secretary in the State Department, which in India is called the Home
Ministry.

Being born in the South and raised in the North has presented
unique challenges. My name and coloring are southern, but my language and accent are northern. Often when I speak in India, I am

asked, "Are you a *Dilliwallah?*" which means, "Are you a Delhi-ite?" This is like asking in England, "Are you from London?" Or, if I may mix geographies a little, it is a bit like being Atlanta born and New York raised. I always answer, "Yes, I am a *Dilliwallah,*" but then explain that my roots are southern. In that way I am a product culturally and psychologically of both the North and the South. My language is northern, but my philosophical bent is southern.

It's somewhat funny that when I am given any introduction in India, what is said of me depends on where I am being introduced. If in Delhi, I am introduced as "a native son." In Chennai, I am said to be "a child of Chennai's soil." In Kerala, I am described as the "product of Keralite blood." All these things are very important there. And I am happy to cater to each setting, appreciative of all the many teary-eyed elderly persons who want to come and stroke my face when I'm finished, each endearingly laying claim to my roots.

Most people I have met who have grown up in a Western culture don't seem to be nearly as aware of their ancestry as those from the East. I have lived in North America for almost forty years now, and I've experienced the differences between cultures. In Western culture, we are so pragmatically and entrepreneurially driven that we tend to overlook the lines throughout history that have fallen into place for us to arrive at where we are today. We think it has just "happened."

It hasn't. And those from Eastern cultures never forget that. They always know their ancestry. I remember such a moment when I was still in my twenties and, for the first time, had returned to India to preach. My wife and I were the honored guests at a very prestigious cricket club where I was to speak, and the introduction caught Margie completely off guard. To begin with, it was about ten minutes long. Beyond that, it was all about my father, and, in typical Eastern fashion, no part of his credits and accomplishments was left unembellished. Finally, after a pause, the hostess said, "And we will now hear from his son."

I understood what was happening. And I smiled, also understanding what was behind the stunned look on my wife's face. I knew she was thinking, "What? Couldn't you say anything about Ravi? His father isn't even here!" But in their minds, they had. What greater compliment could they give me than that I was the son of my father?

This was driven home to me again just a few months ago. I had finished writing a book about a conversation between two Muslim young men, one a rigid Muslim and the other a convert to Christ. It was an imaginary debate between Jesus and Mohammed being argued by these two young men. Before I sent it to the publisher, I asked a Muslim scholar to review the manuscript. After reading it, his first comment was, "You can't do this. I know nothing about these two men, except what they're conversing about here. How can you tell me so little about their roots? There is no way I can enter into this conversation without knowing something about their ancestry."

So he set to work. He labored for hours and created by sheer imagination an extensive family tree: what the father did; what the grandfather did; who killed whom, when, and why; which school each boy attended; the name of the street they lived on as children; how many children in each family had been lost due to violence. In fact, he traced their ancestries all the way back to the Ottoman Empire. On and on it went.

After two full days, he returned the manuscript to me, along with a complex diagram of two family trees. I was overwhelmed and absorbed by the detail, and yet I knew he was right. Suddenly the characters were brought to life in a context. "Now your conversation makes sense," he said. "Keep this, because you may someday do a sequel, and you don't want to forget who came from where and from whom." I felt justifiably rebuked.

It is an amazing piece of work. What that Muslim scholar did for me in critiquing my manuscript in this way was incredibly generous. Yet he didn't do it just for me; it was as much for his own benefit. You see, to an Easterner, one cannot pass judgments or make evaluations on the present without equally taking the past into consideration, in a very linear fashion. This, of course, is a tendency that has its good and bad side, for in the East history and ancestry never die. The very life you live is a debt from the past.

I was once speaking in Cambridge, England, when a young Pakistani student came up to me quite deeply troubled. "I came to hear you because I learned you were from India and had become a Christian. The same is true for me, except that I am from Pakistan and was a Muslim before I became a Christian. I am troubled, very troubled. My father paid for my education. But while I've been studying here, I have found Jesus Christ and committed my life to Him. I don't know how to deal with this.

"My father died last year. I was his pride and joy. Now I have decided that after I receive my degree, I will take it and bury it in his grave as my honor to him and as the only way to express that in my conversion I intended no disrespect to him. Let it mingle with the soil that carries his bones. Do you think I will have done enough?"

He was too choked up to finish his thoughts. That speaks of the deep etchings of culture upon the Eastern soul. In a proverbial sense, soil and soul define the "I" and the "U," and if we do not understand this, we will never understand the East. Religion, language, and ancestral indebtedness are carved into the consciousness of every child of the East. And this is precisely what makes conversion to any other faith an upheaval of titanic proportions.

I thank God for the Eastern part of me. My upbringing in India gave me a true understanding of how the Easterner thinks. I don't have to struggle to figure it out. Likewise, having lived in the West since I was twenty, I believe I've come to understand how a Westerner thinks. I've been given a unique opportunity to learn to think in different languages, to be shaped by different cultures, to have a completely different way of measuring values in order to decipher the between-the-lines hints of the world and, if I may dare say it, the breaking points within each.

God makes an incredible investment in you when He combines two worlds into your mind. Christians see the great value of such convergence in the life of the apostle Paul, who was Hebrew by birth but deeply conversant in both the Greek and Roman cultures. Being able to speak in two languages from opposite ends of the world helps you to be sympathetic and, I believe, effective in not just hearing but *listening*; in responding not just to the question but to the questioner. For this, language and shared tragedy are indispensable. You really only learn to think like the other when you speak their language and share a cultural DNA. With the world increasingly becoming a crossroads between East and West, being bicultural helps to answer the crucial question, "How can I connect with the soul of this man or this woman?"

I understand very well what is being said by a fellow Indian, even when the words he's using may be very different from what he actually means to convey. In Eastern culture, appearance and essence are implicitly accepted as two different parts of reality and can oppose one another. Indeed, it is very common in many Eastern cultures to live a bifurcated life. For instance, your religious life and your moral life are not necessarily connected. It is perfectly acceptable for a man to light holy candles, walk out of the temple, and then lie through his teeth about what he's selling you. The incredible thing is that it may not even qualify as hypocrisy, because he genuinely believes that the rules of engagement in commercial enterprises are different from his life of ceremony and superstition. The theorist from the East may challenge what I am saying, but he or she can never deny its accepted reality. Life is a bargain, and you negotiate the best deal for yourself. That's just the way it is. In fact, there is a Middle Eastern proverb that says, "The lie is the salt of man." You season everything you do with a lie. Everyone ends up finding how to skirt around the truth and appear honorable.

This disconnection stared me in the face very early in life. I saw vividly that things were not right in many of the families we knew, a fact that struck very close to home. On hot summer nights in Delhi, our entire family used to sleep on the lawn in front of our flat. A thick hedge of jasmine plants ringed the frontage of the home, giving us a degree of privacy, and after dark the servants would carry the beds outside and ready them for the night. That way we could enjoy the cooler fresh air outdoors rather than the stifling heat indoors. It was a lot of fun for us, and it usually involved plenty of laughter and pillow fights with my brothers and sisters, as we had more room to horse around than we had inside.

But while lying on our outdoor beds on some of those nights, we often heard the abuse that took place in the flat above us. Every now and then, the silence of the night would be broken by the horrific sounds of the husband beating his wife, even chasing her from room to room as she would try to flee his wrath. Yes, I could hear the thud of his hand landing on her as she would run and sometimes stumble. This is a horrible memory for me. I would take my pillow and cover my head, unable to block out her pleadings for him to stop.

And nobody did a thing about it—not us, not the other neighbors, no one. It was just not done within the cultural ethos. I would lie there silent, like my brothers and sisters, and terrified. I realized, "This isn't right. Where does one go to complain? What does one do to make it stop?"

The next morning, at the crack of dawn, we would be awakened by the same couple singing together in worship, as if nothing had happened. Like a nightmare, it had come and gone, and the new morning was another day in which to just carry on living as if all was well. I fought it on the inside, but such dissonance is kept private in an otherwise very public culture. I would avoid even looking the man in the eye if I ever crossed his path.

Sadly, it was a disconnection I learned all too well, even in my own household.

One of the most emphasized lessons I learned from listening all around and observing was that you had to succeed professionally. Keep your private heartache private; keep your collapsing world propped up. Professional appearances are all that you could take with you. And one dare not wash the family "dirty linen" in public. I could understand that to a degree, but it left a residual heartache in private. That's what life is all about: Become a doctor or lawyer or military officer. Become part of society's influential lot. This was passed along to each of us, both explicitly and implicitly.

In this sense, Ajit, the oldest of us, was the mirror image of my dad. He was confident, poised—and I wanted so much to be like him. Ajit was very sharp and professionally driven, like our father. I think that's why the two of them got along very well. My dad apparently saw Ajit as the one who was going to carry the family's accolades. To this day we each see my dad differently.

My two sisters, Prem and Sham, were gifted in music and in many other qualities that I didn't have. And my little brother, of course, was the darling of the family, being the youngest. Somewhere in the middle was me.

My dad was very affirming toward my siblings—not to the degree that a typical father would have been, but he did affirm them. He always affirmed Ajit. In fact, my father and brother were so much alike that on the rare occasions they butted heads, my heart would beat faster as I watched Ajit stand his ground, which is something I never could have done. My dad knew that Ajit was a "toe to toe" kind of person, like himself, and that he couldn't be pushed too far.

On one occasion when we were all at the dining room table for dinner, my dad did something that upset Ajit. My brother said something in response, and there followed a very long, tense moment. I shivered in my shoes. I did not know what would happen. After a tense moment between them that seemed like an eternity, each staring the other down, my dad backed down, and the tension slowly deflated in silence. My dad knew he was up against his own kind.

Our father had very endearing terms for my sisters and my younger brother, and he had a very affectionate way with them and with other young children. But for whatever reason, he had no such term of endearment for me. He always called me by my name.

That was a small thing compared to knowing that I was also the one consistently on the receiving end of his rather violent temper. I never could figure out why his wrath was reserved for me in ways that carried over even into my middle teens. None of the rest of our family ever have, either. Maybe I cowered in his presence, and it was just his nature to go for the weak one. I was certainly the weakest of the bunch. Whatever it was, something developed in which I became the brunt of all his anger. My brothers and sisters knew it. My mother certainly knew it. Even Margie came to know it, in our married years, from the stories that were told and by the way I held myself in my father's presence, even as an adult.

I've often wondered if this was because my dad didn't even see me until more than a year after I was born. He was in England, studying at Nottingham, when my mother gave birth to me, and he didn't return until well after I was a year old. That may or may not have had some bearing on the tension I always felt from him.

As soon as he came home from work each night, my whole demeanor would change. If he were going out for the evening, for me it was good news. If he and I were alone in a room, I would find an excuse to leave to get something. I am sure it was not all his fault. I feared him and therefore could not make conversation.

As time went on, his fears of my failure and my fear of him met in some very painful memories. I simply never performed at the level my siblings did. My life seemed purposeless, without direction; I could never live up to his expectations, nor could I bridge the distance that existed between us. It was an impasse neither of us was able to solve on our own.

Like his father and grandfather before him, my father certainly made his own contribution to Indian culture. He did this especially in his support of Indian sports, spending a lot of his energies procuring funds for the training of Indian athletes and sportsmen and women. Interestingly enough, when he left India for Canada, a newspaper article was headlined, "Good Samaritan of Indian Sports Moves to Canada." I have no doubt that his work as a government leader was somewhere lining the fabric of the recognition people gave me the first few times I returned to India. So there was that side to him that was giving and caring.

And it was my mother's heart that shaped my soul. She always cared for the poor. When we were young and our family had very little money, she would come home from a tea party or a dinner bringing little pastries or cookies wrapped in a napkin for us, her purse full of crumbs from the goodies. After we moved to Canada, and I began traveling to India, she always sent with me clothes and jewelry or little household items to give to the servants who had worked in our home when we lived there. These people held her in the highest esteem.

I see her also in the etchings of my own conscience. I have brought into being a division of our ministry — RZIM Wellspring International — that reaches out to Asian women, the destitute and the poor, and particularly to women who have been sexually abused or forced into prostitution. It is a privilege for me to see my middle daughter, Naomi, directing its reach and its touch.

My southern Indian heritage, grounded in the philosophical and intellectual, has surely informed the scholarly programs our ministry sponsors. And my love of words and the use of language to generate wonder may have been the bequest of my grandfather. My opportunity to move to Canada was a gift from my father's belief that if his children had the opportunity in the West, then I might succeed. And my mother's gift was a tender heart.

It strikes me that as I pen these acknowledgments, I am minutes away from landing in Chennai on a visit. It also happens to be my birthday today — quite fitting, I think. As I set foot on my native soil again, I am reminded in its sights and sounds and smells and everything else this land represents to me, whether of pain or in the brain, that the marvel of the work of God in all this is that He planted in me the roots of order for my calling. But my hungers went unfulfilled until I found *Him*.

Sometimes in the shadows of one's self lie the problems, and in the shadows of one's shaping lie the answers.

hidden gold

I HAVE OFTEN WONDERED HOW MUCH WE REALLY KNOW ABOUT OUR OWN particular individuality and if, when the veil is finally lifted some day, we may marvel at how we missed so much of it. We know that physical attributes are transferred from generation to generation through DNA, but is it also possible that some of our spiritual sympathies and religious inclinations may be carried over in our very biochemical makeup?

This thought was suggested to me by a friend, who wondered if our subconscious awareness of certain prior events may well be the cumulative bequest of ancestry. I have thought of this often and believe she may be on to something. I'm not speaking merely of cultural influences, which are substantial enough; I'm talking about the collective memory of generations deposited deep in our being that can surface in ways we would never imagine.

Each time I visit a Hindu temple in India, I am conscious that the religious lives of the people worshiping there have been shaped and transferred to them around these temples for literally thousands of years. Their songs, their chants, their superstitions, their commitments, and their fear of spirits have all come to them across the centuries in the womb of their heritage. Can it be that the "beliefs of the forefathers are visited for generations"?

If that is so, how does one casually dismiss centuries of belief in his or her own religious lineage? How can one impulsively decide one day to disbelieve what one's ancestors, those who have come from the same root, have believed since their culture's inception? As my friend suggested, is there something "spiritual" in our biochemical makeup that comes from previous generations? Could this explain

41

experiences of déjà vu, the thought of having been somewhere before or of having previously experienced something before?

This connection with past generations and centuries is one reason why it is very hard for anyone from the East to convert to Christianity. It is a much more intricate matter than in the West where, generally speaking, one thinks individually. In the East, one's thinking is collective. As I see it, if it is true that heredity plays a role in the spiritual dispositions that are imprinted on our souls, Jesus' declaration that each of us needs to be born again is even more profound. The DNA of generations past marks itself very deeply in us, and it takes a new birth for us to be able to see through new eyes.

My own DNA goes back to the very heart of my homeland's religion. My ancestors were Nambudiris, the highest caste of the Hindu priesthood. They belong to the dominant caste of the South and regard themselves as the repositories of the ancient Vedic religion. Through marriage to the Nayars, the warrior caste, the Nambudiris enjoy a combination of power in doctrinal prerogative and in might of propagation. These two castes provided the bedrock of my ancestry.

But that pride of birth was dramatically broken in my lineage five generations ago, on my paternal grandfather's side, in Kerala. There, in 1858, a young Nambudiri woman who had five brothers came into contact with Christian belief and was fascinated by what she heard. Evidently, she had been speaking with the missionaries at the Basel Mission, a German-Swiss Christian mission in her village. When the rest of the family learned of her interest, she was strongly rebuked, threatened, and warned not to visit the mission compound anymore.

As I understand it—and as was told to me by my grandaunt who lived to the age of 103—on the day after this reprimand, as soon as her brothers left for work, my ancestor went to the missionaries to tell them she could no longer come. But while she was there, news arrived that a cholera epidemic was spreading rapidly throughout the village, which meant that everyone was ordered to be quarantined—wherever they were at the moment.

She could not leave the mission compound, and her brothers were not permitted inside to take her home. So she had to remain there for several weeks, much to her family's displeasure. During that quarantined period, the young Nambudiri asked all her questions about Jesus Christ, and before she left that compound once the quarantine was lifted, she had made her heart's commitment to follow Christ.

That woman was my great-great-great-grandmother, and her conversion started my ancestors on the road to the Christian faith. There was no question that hers was an extraordinary conversion, and very genuine. It had to have been a huge leap for her. She was immediately an outcast, disavowed by her family and society. Indeed, everything in her life was turned upside down. There was no home to go back to, no parent to find her a husband, and no one who would want her as a wife. I wish I knew the whole story because, from that point on, my heritage was going to change in dramatic turns. My life, which could well have been spent in the temples of Kerala, is now spent in a different world and with a different worldview.

So the missionaries became my great-great-great-grandmother's family and cared for her needs. They even arranged for her to marry a fine Christian man. The only downside of it in that context was that he happened to be originally from a lower caste, a boatman. This twin step of a marriage to a man from a lower caste who was also a Christian sealed her eviction from her blood relatives. (Contrary to what is popularly believed, deep in the heart of India, especially with the Nambudiris, society is quite matriarchal. Her step of faith in Christ, therefore, was a bigger blow to the family than one might expect.) Despite these things, she had no doubt that this was the answer to the struggle of her soul. Jesus Christ was now the shepherd of her life, and her new beginnings were profoundly altering to her and to future generations.

No one knows how the name Zacharias was decided upon. It may be that the missionaries suggested the name because of the fact that Zacharias, the father of John the Baptist, was a priest in the New Testament. It is also true that German Christians have used the name often; and if you go to Mennonite territory anywhere in the world, you see the name Zacharias quite frequently.

The Basel Mission churches in India still have quite a presence, especially around Mumbai, the teeming city formerly known as Bombay. In fact, I had the privilege of preaching in one during a trip years ago. At the time, I did not know of the connection between my Christian roots and the Mission, which has had a significant impact in India, as it has in my own history. There is only one other fact I know about this important tributary of my family's heritage, and it is that one of my ancestors (from my paternal grandmother's side) was an ordained minister under the Basel Mission, having married another high-caste convert.

As I consider these wonderful things, I greatly regret not talking more to my dad and his relatives about their story. Only now, as I see the Lord's hand at work so clearly in my family's tapestry, do I regret not seeking to know more about the pattern He has woven. You can become interested too late to realize how important your family tree is.

The grandaunt I mentioned was my best source of information. So I asked her, "If we came to know the Lord through German-Swiss missionaries, how did we end up in the Anglican Church?"

She smiled. "You're the first one to ever ask me that question," she noted. "I can give you the exact reason."

You would have to know my grandaunt to know the precision with which she handled questions. In her professional days, she was a high school principal, and even when she was well past her hundredth birthday she read one book a week. A fascinating woman indeed—her silvery-gray hair, her face wrinkled and blotched with age, dark rings around her eyes, her sari all crumpled as she sat up in bed in the lotus position to talk to us in her soft but articulate voice—she constantly moistened her thick lips as she told us the story with a touch of nostalgia.

The German-Swiss missionaries who were involved in leading my ancestors, as well as many other Indians, to the Lord had a strange custom of cultural distance: they refused to allow Indians to participate with them in Holy Communion. Indians had to celebrate the Lord's Supper separately. Sadly, this belief placed the German-Swiss in a superior posture to the Indian churchman and woman in what is the consummate act of devotion to Christ.

At the time, my great-grandfather Tobias Zacharias was a very prominent attorney. This discriminatory act troubled him greatly, and he took issue with the missionaries' stance, declaring, "This is not right. We are now one in Christ. There should be no separation at the Lord's Table." But the missionaries, whether from higher authority or on their own, continued their policy. So, with much heartbreak, the family left that denomination of believers and joined the Anglican Church, where Indians were allowed to celebrate joint Communion with English Christians.

In the meantime, my great-grandfather was encouraged to take the issue to court for the sake of posterity and for the sake of the true gospel. He was told that this was the only way it would be resolved. So he battled it out legally until the English government passed a law stating that Indians had to be treated with equality. This meant allowing them into the fellowship of Communion within the church.

By this time, however, there must have been some hard feelings involved, because my family's decision about a church was not reversed, and we began our journey into Anglicanism. Until the day we left India, the Anglican cathedral in Delhi was our home church.

As dramatic as my ancestors' conversions had been, over a period of time in the succeeding generations, true belief in Christ dwindled into nothing more than a nominal adherence. There was no true personal faith and trust. Somewhere down the line, that first conversion in the Basel Mission compound was watered down, and the weeds of culture choked out the new life in the heart. Christianity became less a matter of faith than the fact that my family simply wasn't Hindu or Muslim. We were all part of a great mix. There was intermarriage in terms of faith, and virtually every faith played into that mix.

Even as I say this, I cannot shake a certain feeling about Agnes Manickam, my grandmother on my mother's side. She was a sweet, lovely lady. I don't think I ever heard anything harsh or rude from her mouth, and she always brought a warm, caring, loving presence when she came to visit our home. We all loved it when she came, especially me, because it meant a break from the tension I felt from my father.

At that point, we were living in Delhi, and my grandmother made the trip northward by train from Madras. The journey took over two days, and our whole family went to the railway station to meet the train and bring her home. She was always such a glorious sight when she arrived. She would descend from the car with a simple magnificence, a porter carrying her old trunk and other bundles crudely tied up with sheets or saris. She unfailingly brought loads of sweets and goodies and mangoes for us, and she had a habit of affectionately biting our noses when she gave us our first hug, making us squeal, "No, Ammah, no!" Did that ever make some "after the pleasantries" conversation for us kids!

She was also a very reverent and ritualistic woman. She was very High Church, always making the sign of the cross on our foreheads after kissing us. I don't remember that she ever talked about her faith or that anyone in our family engaged her on the topic. But the fact is, when it's not an important issue to you, you tend to overlook the deep faith that may be in someone else. The subliminal impact of her life and the seeds that were planted by just being near her would be revealed years later.

There is a beautiful story by F. W. Boreham that reflects this. He tells of a woman who was sitting beside him on a bus. As the journey progressed and the conductor came around to check the tickets, the woman was dismayed to realize that somewhere during the ride someone must have dipped into her purse and stolen two gold coins, along with her ticket. Boreham reacts by saying how embarrassed he was because he happened to be sitting next to her and she kept giving him a look of suspicion. But thankfully, he said, the problem was resolved quickly when, digging her hands deeper into the purse, she found the coins. Promptly and with a red face she apologized, saying that it was her birthday and this was a new purse her daughter had given her. "The compartments of the purse were more elaborate and ingenious than she had noticed," he said.

Boreham, in his inimitable way, titled his essay "Hidden Gold," reminding the reader in the following words: "Now this sort of thing is very common. We are continually fancying that we have been robbed of the precious things we still possess. The old lady who searches everywhere for the spectacles that adorn her temples; the clerk who ransacks the office for the pen behind his ear; and the boy who charges his brother with the theft of his penknife that lurks in the mysterious depths of his own fearful and wonderful pocket."[*] Often we are not aware of how close we are to that which we need but we think we do not have. In His grace, God has placed some hidden gold somewhere in all of us that meets our need at a desperate moment.

For some, faith is something like that. We find we have it at a time when all seems lost. The gold I had was of just such a hidden nature, and it would come to light only later. My grandmother's faith, though not often spoken, came back to speak to me in a most profound way. Suffice it to say that somewhere in my ancestry God placed an investment in my very soul. It would shine in the years to come in a manner I never could have imagined.

There is another important line laid in my spiritual DNA. To me, this line has had as profound an effect on my life as my lineage that goes back to the Nambudiris. It was laid for me by the apostle Thomas.

---

[*]F.W. Boreham, *Mushrooms on the Moor* (London: Epworth, 1915), 34.

Yes, the "Doubting Apostle." I have always felt a special affinity with the one whom the church has seen for centuries as the disciple who had difficulty believing. I think of Thomas not as a doubter but as the "Questioning Apostle."

Tradition holds that Thomas brought the Christian presence to India. Several notations in early church history refer to his coming here. Indian tradition has held tenaciously to this. We know that Barnabas went to Cyprus, and Paul to Greece and Rome. The one known as "the great doubter" was evidently commissioned to the second most populous nation on the earth and established the church here that remains to this day.

The oldest denomination in India is the Mar Thoma Church, named after the apostle. There are commemorative stones and inscriptions in Kerala marking his arrival. And there is a church in Chennai, high atop a hill overlooking the city, called St. Thomas Mount, a spot venerated by Christians and maintained in honor of the apostle. Church tradition in India holds that under Thomas's ministry the queen of the area converted to Christianity. Her husband, the king, was enraged over this fact and had Thomas murdered while the apostle was on his knees in prayer. His body was brought to this spot for burial and later removed to Rome out of fear that his grave would be vandalized.

Several notable early church fathers, such as Ambrose of Milan and Gregory of Nazianzus, and other distinguished historians have made reference to Thomas going to India. There is also no compelling contrary evidence to Thomas's being anywhere else, and every time I come to Chennai I visit St. Thomas Mount, a quiet, serene spot overlooking the massive city below. Inside the church, the wall is sequentially painted with two scenes from each of the twelve apostles' lives: first, as the artist pictured them, and second, their martyrdom, with the killing of Thomas as the centerpiece. The devout who come here also believe miracles have taken place in that location. A sign outside the shrine reads, "If anyone has ever experienced healing or received graces, come and report it to this office."

This shows the Indian culture's propensity for the dramatic and the spectacular, yet these sentiments also reveal the culture's desperate longing for healing. The people of India yearn for the physical touch of God, for the miraculous, because their need is so great with the deprivation all around. And of all the disciples, Thomas was the man for this cause. He was the one who declared, "I will not believe under any circumstances unless I see and feel the wounds of the Lord in his body." In His loving grace, Christ offered Thomas that evidence.

Today, when faith healers come to India, they often prey upon a deep hunger that is connected to the physical. This ministry can easily become an exploitation of the masses. Yet I believe there are times when God *does* meet the hungers of a people. And it seems to be that, in a land where the physical needs are so pronounced, God often chooses to reach many by meeting their physical needs. It is significant to me, therefore, that the church in India was founded by one for whom the physical evidence of the risen Christ was indispensable.

There is another reason Thomas was the right man for India. Here was a man who needed a solid apologetic, some kind of hard evidence. He wasn't just going to take somebody's else's word for it. When his closest friends spoke of seeing Jesus alive after the crucifixion, Thomas responded, "Show me." He questioned them because he had to be sure for himself. And in his postresurrection encounter with Jesus, he made his memorable declaration: "My Lord and my God!" After that, nothing could stop him.

Think of it: Thomas came into a land that had more gods than any other nation. Hinduism alone has 330 million deities. India has an ancient religious culture whose origins date to history's beginnings. There were the dark-skinned Dravidians in the South, India's original inhabitants; into this realm came the lighter-skinned Aryans with their own mixture of paganism. That complex amalgam of the Dravidians' and the Aryans' beliefs gave birth to Hinduism. All of this is why it is impossible to write a systematic theology of Hinduism. It is just not monolithic; more often, it must be grappled with by studying its exponents. When you add to India's religious history from ancient times to the present, you see the arrival of Islam, followed by the founding of Sikhism in an attempt to find middle ground. Today, India boasts of being the most religious country in the world. Eighty percent of India is Hindu, and if India and Pakistan had not separated, it would also be the largest Muslim country in the world.

But long before the incursions made by Islam into this complexity of 330 million deities came the apostle to whom Jesus said, "I am the way and the truth and the life. No one comes to the Father except through me." The once-questioning Thomas—who was now the convinced Thomas—came to my homeland and dialogued with the skeptics and the religious, pointing them all to Jesus. He paid with his life. But the church he founded here remains one of the oldest in the world.

I was born in Thomas's shadow, here in Chennai, six miles from where he was buried. Many times I have said to my wife, Margie, "If I were one of the Twelve, I could see myself saying exactly what Thomas did." I can hear myself telling the others, "I can't take your word for it. I have to see it for myself." When I went into my studies in Christian apologetics, my mother often asked me how I thought up all the questions I had.

As I picture Thomas in his questioning of Jesus, and imagine the future that the Lord had planned for him, I think Jesus must have wanted to add, "Thomas, I am going to send you to a doubting and questioning people. The spear-thrusted side of mine will one day be yours for telling the world what you have seen, felt, and believed."

Like the apostle, I have found myself in places of heated questioning, where I've had to present a witness—sometimes at the risk of my life. There are realities in the Eastern world today that I have to consider every time I go there. I've been to numerous Middle Eastern countries—some that are not open to a Christian witness—and have had to go in under the most highly sensitive security measures. The Lord has marvelously opened up these places for me, giving me the opportunity to present the love of Christ. Yet, to do this I have had to conclude that, though I don't know what the Lord has ahead for me, I am committed to Him and to the calling He has placed on my life. I believe Thomas counted the cost the moment he made up his mind. I must do likewise.

There is a story in 1 Samuel 16 about the prophet Samuel coming to Jesse's home and asking to meet his children, for God had an anointing in mind for one of them. Both Samuel and Jesse had their eyes on outward appearances, however, and were missing what God had in mind.

I chuckle, thinking how Eastern this story is. I can picture it. Indeed, years ago, if someone had given my father a written description of my life, and my dad had lined up his five children and been asked to guess whose life this would be, he would have pointed to any of the other four. He would never, by his own admission, have pointed to me; for that matter, neither would I have considered myself. Everyone, but especially my father, would say that my life has been the biggest shock of the family. Timidity and repeated failure do not provide a good mix for the kind of calling I have. Yet God made it possible.

In Psalm 16, King David writes this:

> LORD, *you have assigned me my portion and my cup;*
>   *you have made my lot secure.*
> *The boundary lines have fallen for me in pleasant places;*
>   *surely I have a delightful inheritance.*

As I look back to the lines laid down by others in my heritage, I see Thomas's impact in this country, in this culture, and in my own family, dating back to the Basel Mission in Kerala. Thomas's conversation with Jesus would also figure very specifically in the origin of my own faith, which would come at the point of deepest crisis in my life. Like the questioning apostle, I had questions that were central to whether I even had meaning enough to live. And with meager similarity to my dear Nambudiri ancestor—my great-great-great-grandmother, whose life was ultimately turned upside down by her questioning—mine would be turned right side up in a circumstance that to this day brings me the mixed emotions of a somewhat aching, yet jubilant heart.

The lines were to fall in a strange way, but in a clear pattern.

CHAPTER 4

MY FATHER'S HOUSE

WHEN MY FATHER FIRST MOVED US FROM CHENNAI TO DELHI, EVERYTHING began to change for me. We still had to live in close quarters, but soon afterward we moved to a larger home. Our new home was in a government housing complex, built in what is called the "D2 style," which was reserved for a certain level of officials.

There were four flats to each building, two upstairs and two down. Ours was a ground-floor flat, and my siblings and I couldn't believe our great fortune. No longer were we confined to two rooms. Inside this home was a living room, a kitchen, and two bedrooms. There were also a front veranda and back veranda. Best of all, we had our own yard in both front and back. That meant makeshift cricket games or playing with marbles in our yard at any time of day. We really thought we had made it big. Actually, it all sounds bigger than it really was. When I go back and visit now, I wonder how we kept sane in those small rooms. But that is reality, and that is recall.

To celebrate, I planted two mango trees, one in seed form after I had just enjoyed its juicy morsels, and the other a small sapling I picked up that was growing on the side of the road. I was bicycling home when I saw this little mango plant. I came back with a little spade, dug it up, carried it home, and planted it several feet away from the seed I had planted. Forty years later, when I visited, they would greet me at towering new heights of thirty or so feet, with the present residents telling me they harvest a huge crop of mangoes each year from those two trees. They now shade the back lawn with the rich aroma of mangoes in season.

Just around the corner from our home was a little park where we gathered with the other children from our neighborhood. There

51

was always a game of cricket to be joined there or a game of field hockey to be played in the street off the main road. And I particularly remember the Muslim grave nearby, where a man came at sunset every evening to pay homage to his departed loved one, bowing down and kissing the headstone while we quietly watched. Down the block was the milk stand, where I or one of my siblings often went on errands for my mother, standing in line to get the allocated ration for our family.

Best of all, I was surrounded by friends. I had them in virtually every home in the neighborhood, and there was always someone ready to play. In that culture, you build a relationship with everyone around you. You don't operate too much as a loner or stranger. Your friends come into your house with the same ease as any family member would, and the adult neighbors know you as well as they know their own sons and daughters. The doors are literally always open. Everybody goes to the same grocery store and shops, and the shopkeepers know your family's order before you even walk in.

Our favorite shop was called Sweets Corner, a little café with a handful of tables and two long, refrigerated glassed displays holding dozens and dozens of handmade sweets and savories. It's still there, in fact, with the same delicacies I loved back then. A typical Indian sweet is made purely from milk and sugar that's repeatedly reduced until it's thickened and then loaded with pistachios or coconut or almonds or other genuine flavors. In its preparation, as the mixture is boiled down to fudgelike consistency, it is then emptied into a thin baking sheet about an inch deep. While it is still hot, the thinnest shining sheet of pressed silver (pounded so thin that you can barely hold it without damaging it, but now made edible) is draped over it to give it that glistening, eye-catching, mouthwatering look. The silver just sinks into the surface of the delicacy as it hardens and becomes part of it, giving it a glimmering surface. A mouthful of that sweet, and you'd think you had died and gone to heaven. In those days, since I had no pocket money, I stared at the displays and wished somebody would just buy me one. Today, as I look at it and can afford it so easily, I have to hold back (not without an inner struggle), thinking of the hours on a treadmill a moment of such pleasure would demand. Life just isn't fair, is it?

Every Saturday evening or Sunday afternoon, my father would order a pound of treats from Sweets Corner, with a sampling of various things. Being part of a large family, each would only get a piece or two, but it was worth the week's wait. Every evening, my mother would have the household help make some kind of treat for us at tea-time. We didn't eat dinner until late, around 8:30 p.m. or so, so she tided us over with sweet puff pastries and other treats.

Our marvelous new home was located on Cornwallis Road, a major boulevard now called (thanks to new nationalistic impulses) Subramania Bharti Marg, after an Indian political leader. It was on this street that I met my three closest friends — Baby (his actual name was Vinod, but parents in India do not hesitate to give embarrassing nicknames), who went into business; Ashok, also today a business-man in Mumbai; and Sunder, who would become a mechanical engi-neer and a nuclear physicist, marry my sister Sham, and thus become my brother-in-law. Maybe it was the warm, neighborly spirit of our block, but it seems we all knew, even then, that we would be buddies for life. Friendships go deep and are treasured.

We were cricket buddies, hockey buddies, tennis buddies, table tennis buddies. My friends also were the reason I became fluent in Hindi, because that is what they all spoke. And their friendship pro-vided me with a wonderful respite from school, where things were always tough for me. I barely squeaked through each level or grade, and at times I was punished severely both at school and at home.

All through school, from lower kindergarten to high school, our classes were held in open-air tents. Therefore, you were very vulner-able to the seasons. In April and May, the heat was always fierce, consistently over a hundred degrees, with a hot crosswind blowing through our classes. When the dust storms came in July, everything was covered in grit. You could actually see the dust grains swirling in the air around you. And as the monsoon season approached, if you sat near the tent's edge you would go home soaked. Every desk was weather-beaten and at the mercy of the elements. You couldn't leave your books there overnight, for fear that they would be soiled or dam-aged the next day. Needless to say, my favorite time of the year was when the schools closed because of the intense heat during summer vacation, even though we were saddled with about three hours of homework a day.

My brothers and sisters and I walked the mile and a half to school each day. In the hot months, classes started around 8:00 a.m. and ended by 1:00 p.m. or so, because beyond that the heat became so unbearable. Then, in the winter, classes started at 9:00 a.m. and ended around 3:30 p.m. My mother used to put coconut oil in our hair to keep it soft and shiny. That was as far as its benefit went. The problem was that in the winter you would leave home with the oil caked and hardened in your hair, but by afternoon, when the temperature had risen, the oil began to melt and would run down the back of your neck. It did not make for a feeling of pride as you tried to covertly dry it off with a handkerchief.

The school I attended, Delhi Public School ("public" actually meaning "private" in the British system), had about two thousand students then. Today, the enrollment is closer to five thousand, and it is one of the city's top schools. In fact, it now has several branches across the country. Its standards have always been high, as they were when I attended, and we studied in a British system called the "Senior Cambridge."

Yet, from my earliest days, there were signs in my life that I just lacked the disciplines of study. I never adapted to a routine, and, of course, that was not a good thing in a highly competitive culture like India's. I know if I had worked hard, I would not have suffered as much as I did. I continually pushed the lines, although never in the realm of immorality. Instead, I was just irresponsible.

In Delhi Public School, corporal punishment was very severe. When I was nine or so, my teacher in the third standard, Mrs. Nelson, was as tough as they came. The school's worst students were always placed in her class, because she had a reputation for straightening them out. I was one of her students.

One day, when I came to class I hadn't done my homework—as usual. She decided to make me sit on the bare dirt outside the tent during class. Then, during lunch hour, I had to stay there on the ground, humiliated, doing my homework as my classmates walked by me enjoying their lunch.

The next day, I hadn't done my homework again. This time, Mrs. Nelson called me to the front of the class. When she asked me where my homework was, I told her I'd forgotten it. I suddenly remembered that Mrs. Nelson had a reputation for slapping a student's face until his ears rang. And at that moment, I thought I saw her rearing back to do just that.

I braced myself, tilting my head to the right. But, unknown to me, my teacher was left-handed. Her palm came up with lightning speed and a thunderous force against the side of my face. She slapped me a couple of times so hard that my head rang and my body trembled. It was punishing in force and embarrassment.

"The next time that happens," she warned, "you'll be in the principal's office. And you'll get the cane." Thankfully, I never let it go that far, but Mrs. Nelson's name and ferocity remain ever in my memory. A few months ago, I was sitting in a plane heading to Dallas, when an Indian gentleman sat down next to me. We got talking, and to our utter surprise we found out we both had gone to Delhi Public School in our school days. "Were you ever in Mrs. Nelson's class?" he asked.

Somewhat embarrassed, I said, "I'm afraid so."

"So was I," he said. He reached out his hand, shook mine, and said, "Congrats! We both made it!"

I think now of the wisdom of a statement by the famed writer Professor E. M. Blaiklock from New Zealand, who said, "God alone knows how to humble us without humiliating us, and how to lift us up without flattering us."

Unfortunately, in those days, the Indian culture was plagued with the methodology of humiliation, and that plague has wrought many suicides throughout the years. It was also a culture plagued by flattery —"Yes, sir"; "No, sir"; "Very well, sir"—people always saluting the high-placed to make them feel honored, but there is a thin line between respect and undue exaltation.

The move to Delhi had been a significant promotion for my dad. Industrial relations was his field, and he was involved in negotiating settlements in government-owned corporations. At first, he was mainly doing that in the hotel industry across the country. Later, he became the government's chief industrial relations officer in the Indian Airlines Corporation, bringing his skill in mediating to that strike-prone corporation.

All the high-powered union men would come to our home to see my father. These were men you wouldn't want to see within a country mile as acquaintances. They were known as thugs and shysters, people who would have no trouble putting you away if you stood in their path. Seeing them come into our home always made me feel a little uneasy.

How my father developed the skill to deal with those men, I'll never know. But they always respected him—which was remarkable, given that he represented the government. They weren't embittered toward him, so there was never any trouble. On the contrary, we would peek into the room where he was meeting with them and hear these thugs saying, "Yes, sir. No, sir. Thank you very much, sir. See you tomorrow then, sir."

He was tough, yes, yet he obviously had the ability to be fair. One thing I remember about my dad was that he was very honest. Because of the power of his position, he was given all kinds of gifts—which were actually baits and bribes—from people who wanted to corrupt him. But he never brought those items home. If someone gave him a beautiful gift, he would leave it in a cabinet in his office. That also was remarkable about him. In a culture given to corruption among officials, my dad stayed above reproach. He was undoubtedly threatened at times, but nothing ever happened that caused us to worry.

He was very influential and could help many a person make a living. Every morning, there would be a line of people outside our front door, waiting for my father to emerge on his way to work. They were there to get just a few seconds with him to ask for a job. Invariably, he would walk straight to his car without looking at the person and say, "Come and see me at my office." Sometimes he acted as if he were going to bypass them, but my mother would plead, "Please, see this man. He has been here since six o'clock this morning." All sorts of people attained key positions because my father made a single phone call for them. He had those kinds of connections. That was the philanthropic side of him.

Twenty years after his death, I still encountered my father's reputation in surprising places. Up to seven or eight years ago, whenever I flew Indian Airlines, at least one person would see my name on the ticket and ask, "Are you the son of Oscar Zacharias?" He was widely admired for being a great mediator, a man with a skill for reconciling sides. I sadly used to think how wonderful it would have been if he had directed those efforts toward me, his middle son.

He moved up the career ladder quickly, shifting from the Department of Labor to the Department of Defense. Eventually, he went into the Home Ministry (which, as I mentioned, in the United States would be the State Department), where he served as deputy secretary. At that point, he became very much the State Department man, always present at important functions.

Though my father held these coveted government positions we were not wealthy, even in Indian terms. Comfortable, yes — money to spare, no. The simple fact was, my father was helping to pay off a lot of family debts he had inherited. Only on special occasions would I ask my parents for something—say, if I wanted to go to the movies. But they rarely were able to meet my request.

Some of my buddies were from wealthy, well-to-do homes, and they often paid my way. Whatever they were doing, they always wanted me to go with them. They were always good to me. That made for some pretty close friendships, because India is quite the moviegoing culture and I would be at the movies at least once a week—courtesy of a friend.

My buddies were also brilliant, always at the top of the class. I was never up there with them when it came to school. Yet, as it turned out, this was the only area in which my father ever interacted with me. He never asked about my sports activities, at which I excelled. He only asked about my studies, at which I faltered. The worst time in every semester was the day report cards came. I feared his arrival at home those nights. There was a lot of red on the report card—and now I quip in good humor—"as well as on my face when he was finished with me."

My father's violent temper took its toll very heavily on me. When his rage would peak, he would become quite irrational, both in what he would say and in what he would do. It made for some heartbreaking moments in the home. One afternoon, a buddy and I were talking while, in the next room, my father was trying to take an afternoon nap. I guess he thought we were a bit too noisy, because he stormed out of that room and toward us. I took off, but my buddy wasn't so fortunate. My friend came out shaking with shock after getting the brunt of my father's fist in his back. To this day, my buddies remember, whenever they heard the horn on my father's car, signaling that he was in the driveway, taking off as fast as they could if it were past my curfew.

To some extent, we can joke about that a bit now, and in our adult years we would remember those incidents with some lightheartedness, even in my dad's presence. But there was a serious side and a traumatic side to it that was solely mine. He had his own way of trying to make up after a night of severe reprimand or thrashing. Two or three days after an episode, he would obviously feel some sense of remorse. He would never tell me that he was sorry or that he hadn't meant to do it; he would just call me to the bedside, where he was sitting, and ask, "You OK, son?"

"Yes, Dad," I'd say.

Then he would sort of pat my face or stroke my chin to say, I think, "Let's get over it and move on." All it meant to me was that I had a few days of reprieve. I would breathe a sigh to myself and think, "I'll have a respite now." But I was never convinced it wouldn't happen again. I would replay the scenes, still wondering why it had happened.

Having said all this, I must honestly add that I have never felt any bitterness toward my father. That is the absolute truth. I have never resented him or thought hatefully of him. I loved my dad, warts and all. I truly believe that he always wanted me to succeed, and that he thought this was the way to whip me into shape and make it happen. Also, he was a victim of his own time and temperament. I must say more about this later, because it took me to ends I myself hadn't envisioned.

The one escape I had other than sports was the movies. I enjoyed the Westerns, where the bad guy was caught because the good guy had tracked him down. I liked some of the old classics, such as *South Pacific*, and I thought the World War II movies were great—films such as *The Guns of Navarone*. I was never quite a fan of Hitchcock; I liked a strong story line more than a film that tried to scare you. And I really liked historical movies. For me, good entertainment fell back on history.

That's why my favorites were Indian movies. I loved the romance stories, which were portrayed with such innocence. There was never any kissing on-screen, just a chase around a tree to preserve Indian modesty. That was funny to us, but it was intended to be very romantic. When an Indian comedian was asked to give the difference between love on the Western screen and love on the Indian screen, he answered in one word: "Trees."

Mostly, I loved every movie that applauded the human spirit, which is at the core of most Indian movies. The very best of them was *Mother India*, which I saw in the 1960s. The story focuses on a family from a small village that was struggling to make it in their world wracked by tragedy, deprivation, and conflict. It is reflective of the larger picture of India's struggle for survival as a people. It is truly a masterpiece, and I do not believe it has been surpassed, even forty years later. Its story of the indomitable human spirit had such great appeal to me, and I saw it again and again. *Mother India* starred an actress named Nargis, who became famous after that role, and her son in the film was played by the actor Sunil Dutt, who also became a famous matinee figure in India. The movie portrayed a significant age difference between the pair, but in real life they later married. I was in my young teens when the movie was released.

Another one of our favorite escapes was to a centuries-old place called the "Old Fort." It had been an actual fort built by the Persians in the 1500s, and it was only a short bicycle ride from our neighborhood. It provided a great place to wander around, scale walls, and spy out from the minarets at the top. It was also a great place to find some delicious food on Saturdays, when vendors and hawkers set up their food stalls along the inner wall.

Even as I nibbled on snacks of bread, potatoes, and chickpeas, history again made all the difference for me. I loved knowing that the Old Fort had been built by the Persians after they attacked India. The Mughals also invaded and established India as a major center for themselves. I actually had to study all that in history class. But I associated it with the great food we got to eat, because it was during the Mughal period that Indian food became essentially what it is today. The Mughals used almonds, cashews, and crèmes to marinate their foods, while India supplied the spices. Combined, it became known as Mughlai food.

I also used to love riding my bike up a steep hill into the fort and then come tearing down at a furious pace. This was actually quite foolish, because most of the time my bike didn't have brakes that worked and it put both me and the motorized rickshaws and masses of people cluttering the road at risk. That was youth in the name of bravado—in reality, being foolish.

There is a memory, though, from that steep slope that I remember only too well. One Saturday, I was on my way into the Old Fort when an older man came riding his bike out through the front gate at a good speed. As he came down the slope, his bike hit a stone, flipped over, and threw him to the pavement, cracking his head severely. I quickly dismounted because, in an instant, the man was lying, totally unconscious, in a widening pool of blood.

I stood frozen, not knowing what to do, while people casually passed him by. Some stared and tittered with embarrassment, while others turned around as they walked by. But nobody stopped to help. No one called for the police or for medical help — no one did anything. Not knowing what to do, I slowly remounted my bike and moved on. Several minutes later, I came back, and the man was still lying there. By this time, the blood had congealed, and those in the area were just muttering, "He's dead. They'll come and pick him up." I was horrified. I had thought that an adult, someone who could rise to the task of confronting this tragedy, would have stopped to help. But they hadn't. It was an early taste of life in the raw for me. I remember the thought registering with me that life was cheap.

Finally, in a daze I rode home and frantically told the servants in the house what had happened. They told me that sooner or later the police would be there, not to worry. Years later, when I read the story of the Good Samaritan for the first time, I remembered that old man and his horrendous accident, and I thought how real such imagery from the mind of the Lord was — people walking by and leaving a dying man even more destitute.

One of the memories from those days well sums up what was going on inside me and who I was really leaning on. I had a daily practice that I wouldn't have been able to explain if anyone had asked me. But my mom often commented, even in my young adult years, that she remembered this too.

There was a bus stop at one of the main intersections near our home. As I visit that spot today, I see it is such a brief walk from our home, really just a couple of blocks away. But back then, it seemed like such a long way off.

My mother used to teach at a school a short bus ride away, to help earn income for our family. She used to come home every day at about 3:45 in the afternoon. For some reason, out of all five kids, I was the one who would always wait outside the front of our home until I saw her get off the bus. I wouldn't let myself go into the backyard to play or head off to meet my friends at the park until I was completely certain that Mom was coming home. She arrived almost spot-on-the-button every day at 3:45, so I knew I was safe in predicting when I would see the bus rolling around. I could see it coming in the distance. And that's when I told myself, "It's OK. I'll be able to go now."

She was a very small woman and very slightly built, barely five feet tall, not able with only for me to recognize from that distance. And only when I saw her step down from the bus, clutch her purse close to her, and start walking toward home did I feel everything was OK. It is so ineradicably etched in my memory that I can relive that scene vividly. She later told me she always wondered why I was the one who would wait there. But she must have known.

I did that until I was fourteen or fifteen. Although the reasons may be apparent now, I still don't think I could explain exactly why I did it. At the time, I might have felt I wanted to make sure she was OK. I suppose I was afraid of losing her, as she was my only hope in a young life stalked by failure and haunted by shame.

CHAPTER 5

THE CRICKET FIELD

MY MOTHER ONCE BROUGHT AN ASTROLOGER TO OUR HOUSE TO READ OUR palms and tell us our future. Actually, he was a sari seller who came once every few months, with a big trunk saddled on the back of his bicycle. He would customarily spread out a sheet on the floor, unload the trunk, and display his beautiful saris for sale. Often it became a neighborhood Tupperware-style gathering, only with saris instead of containers. Life in India is delivered at the door daily.

This man also claimed to be a palmist. He put on his old-fashioned, thick glasses, which dropped down halfway over a nose that was constantly sniffling, and in turn held our palms in his hand with total concentration. The "hmm's" and "oh's" and "ah's" that issued from him kept each of us riveted on what he was doing as we awaited his final pronouncement. One after the other, we took our turn, and the futures he read for each of the others were all positive. But then he came to me, and the first note of uncertainty was sounded as he kept shaking his head with bad news about to spill out. "Looking at your future, Ravi Baba (Ravi, little boy), you will not travel far or very much in your life," he declared. "That's what the lines on your hand tell me. There is no future for you abroad."

To say that I was deeply disappointed is putting it mildly. The one goal everybody had at that time in India's fledgling economy since Independence was to go abroad. Of course, I had no reason to disbelieve this man, or for that matter to believe him. But it did plant another seed of uncertainty, however small.

Why an astrologer? It was just the done thing. As far as this one was concerned, I sincerely hope his sari sales did better than his astrological avocation. Today, travel is the hazard of my existence; I would love to cut it short a little. But the very fact that our family had such a reading reveals the cultural mix of religion, superstition, and "cover all bases" mentality with regard to the supernatural. From palmists, to Saint Philomena, to the Jehovah's Witnesses, to attending festive celebrations at the local temple, to Anglicanism—ours was an eclectic faith and typical of an Indian Christian family, nominally Christian and nothing more than that. It never bothered my parents that I went to temple ceremonies with my buddies' families. I thrived on going to all those annual festivals, and I did it unabashedly for the food. I couldn't wait for festival times to come around so I could feast on all the goodies in the name of religion. I can't tell you the number of times I ate food that I am sure had been offered to temple idols. Whether I knew it or not would not have made any difference to me.

And I never took any of my friends' religions seriously. I respected them, yes. But believed what they did? No. It strained credulity to think some of my friends actually believed all that. Sometimes I wonder if they even gave it any critical thought. To me, their religion was nothing more than a combination of fear and culture. Gods who were half animal and half human, posing with their consorts in rather sensual poses; castes that doomed one to certain stations in life; priests who chanted all kinds of mantras at weddings to ward off the evil eye—I never bought into that worldview. Not because I was a Christian, but because I was a true skeptic. So nothing about it ever affected my life with any degree of persuasion. Its value lay in that it was their belief, and so I must at least respect it. You just accepted it as part of the culture, a historical legacy you were cloned into. And my parents never asked me a thing about it.

Once we moved to Delhi, my family became involved in the Cathedral Church of the Redemption. If I'm not mistaken, my brother Ramesh was christened there. But I can tell you almost certainly that my family never once heard the gospel message there, at least not to the recollection of any of us. The rector for years was a very ostentatious man, sprinkling ceremonial fear as he walked and, with his glares, frightening you into listening. His affected reading of the Prayer Book was always in the tones and inflections of which comedic representations are made. In a mixture of a "wannabe" English accent and Indian pronunciation he would deliver his sermons from a pulpit high over the congregation. For me it was the best time of the week to mentally check out of everything and just think cricket in the midst of sacred surroundings.

The Cathedral Church was not only very High Church in its liturgy; it also held a very prominent profile in the city. Father John made sure everyone knew this. He had a stern demeanor, including a nasty practice of humiliating anyone who came into the service late. He would simply stop his sermon and stare at the offender until he or she was seated. In that high-domed cathedral, to hear someone tiptoeing into the full congregation did make for some smothered chuckles and embarrassed looks. He also possessed a penchant for reprimanding people on the spot, no matter what the offense, because they weren't measuring up to what he expected of them. He was revered not because he was a minister but because of his power. Not surprisingly, all kinds of unkind nicknames for him floated around.

Because my father held such a prestigious position in government, he was a prominent member of the congregation. Nothing ever came of that role insofar as it affected our family, although the rector did come to our home a few times to visit my dad. No matter what the occasion, Father John's countenance was invariably stern and forbidding. In the words of the famous popular writer P. G. Wodehouse about one of his characters, "While not exactly disgruntled he was very far from being gruntled."

He did receive a kind of comeuppance once when a particular visitor walked into a church service late. The visitor was a friend of my father's and a very powerful man in government. As the man strolled in casually during the sermon, Father John stopped preaching to glare at him, as was his custom. The visitor stopped and stared back until he continued his sermon. Father John had clearly picked the wrong man. I'm not sure of the exact exchange that followed the service that day, but according to my dad's version of the conversation, which he gave us much later, this man went to the vestry in the back following the service and promised the rector that if he ever did that to him again, there would be serious consequences for the rector himself. I'm not sure what that meant, and I didn't care to find out, as the church didn't seem an appropriate place for such altercations. But, as the old adage goes, he who throws the first punch loses the right to determine when the fight is over.

I couldn't help detecting a barely discernible grin in my dad's expression as he told us about this. And, as I recall, for a while we did not see an instance such as that repeated.

THERE WAS A CERTAIN COUPLE AT THE CATHEDRAL CHURCH WHO WERE very special friends of ours. Arthur Mahinder was the organist, a great musician, and his wife's name was Blossom. Yes, these names we owe to the British Raj and to our propensity for clinging to the English touch in our Christian distinctive to the Hindu mainstream. That is why in India you can often tell a person's religious background just by their name. The Mahinders invited us over for dinner every Christmas Eve, and they really laid out the goodies for us. That was one of the highlights of the year for me. I remember the cold winter nights as we would huddle in our small car and head over to their home just after what was called "Midnight Mass." In their home there would be music in the background, beautiful decorations, and food decoratively presented all over the room, which, with nobody watching me too closely, I could enjoy until it was time to leave.

There was always something wonderfully warm to me about the couple. I realize only in retrospect that they were just lovely people without their own children, who loved having us in their home. In spite of the atmosphere established by Father John at the church, Mr. Mahinder was a jovial man and a master organist. He could make those pipes bellow the great hymns and fill that cathedral. I was so surprised on a recent visit to see a stone in the wall memorializing Arthur Mahinder's contribution to the church through his gifted music.

In fact, that may have been one of the reasons for the Mahinders' relationship with my family. You see, my father had a wonderful singing voice, one of the most striking baritone voices I can ever recall hearing. It had such a timbre that when people in the next flat heard him singing, they stopped what they were doing and listened.

I always loved to hear my father sing, and eventually he helped to organize the Delhi Choral Society. When his brother-in-law, our uncle, Percy Shastri, came to visit our home, he joined his dramatic tenor to my dad's baritone. The two would sit on the front veranda and sing arias, including some of the great pieces from Handel's *Messiah*. I came to know every one of the songs they sang, from "Comfort ye, my people" to "Thus saith the Lord"; from "But who may abide the day of His coming" to "The people that walked in darkness." Or they would sing the works of Mendelssohn and Bach that were often performed in the church, or Maunder's *Bethlehem* or Stainer's *The Crucifixion*. What magnificent pieces they were!

Once a year, during a choral celebration, my father would sing, "Lead me, Lord, lead me in Thy righteousness; make Thy way plain before my face. For it is Thou, Lord, Thou, Lord only, that makest me dwell in safety." This song, based on Psalm 4, has such a beautiful melody, and I would think as I heard it, "This is so foreign to me, yet it seems like home should be." Although I knew nothing of the meaning of the lyrics, I recognized in the music and in the words an exquisite beauty that lifted me to an unfamiliar realm I wished would linger. It was very different from Indian worship music, which is very nasal, tinny, and repetitive, like a form of chanting. With this music, however, I became lost in the song. And the words became indelibly imprinted on my memory. There was clearly a plea within me rising to the surface when I heard that. Even now when I sing these words to myself, the floodgates of the past are opened with a fond memory for hearing my father sing.

I have to say that I never had any contrition over sin as I sat in church. The closest I came was whenever my father sang some lines from a hymn that portrayed grief over wrong. I was stirred as well every year at Christmastime, when my dad took the part of the third king in the annual cantata. He sang his part with such poignancy: "Myrrh is mine, its bitter perfume breathes a life of gathering gloom: sorrowing, sighing, bleeding, dying, sealed in the stone-cold tomb" (from "We Three Kings of Orient Are").

My siblings and I attended Sunday school classes, but it was never to my liking. For the life of me, I can't remember a single one of the lessons. Even so, when it was time for the nativity play, I was tapped to play Joseph. Naturally, I resisted—until I saw the girl who was going to play Mary. She was lovely, and instantly I decided I would be Joseph after all.

One afternoon, I arrived early for practice. As I waited for the rest of the cast to show up, I satisfied my curiosity, wandering around the vast church sanctuary. Suddenly, I came upon a bowl of what I thought were biscuits (or cookies, in American parlance). They were actually Communion wafers, but because I'd never taken the Lord's Supper, I had no idea what they were. I thought some kind person had left them there for a treat.

I dipped my hand into the bowl, pulled out a few wafers, and began munching on them. They were tasteless, but since they seemed to be there for the taking, I placed a few in my pocket and continued wandering around the church, looking at the paintings and statues, enjoying those snacks as well as the sound of my echoing steps.

Then Father John appeared out of the vestry, straight into my path.

I'm sure I had crumbs all over my face. He stopped me on the spot and angrily demanded, "What are you doing?"

"I'm Joseph in the nativity play, Father."

He pointed to my hand and asked, "What are those?"

"Biscuits."

He stared at me for a moment. Then abruptly he turned heel and commanded, "Come with me."

He led me to the vestry in the back of the church, where he let me have it. It was one of the worst tongue-lashings I had ever experienced. Yet, I still had no idea what I had done wrong. He kept using the word "sacrilege" again and again, but I didn't know what it meant. The torrent of words was so vehement I was convinced he was going to call the police.

Finally he sent me home trembling, frightened by that word "sacrilege." I desperately wanted to ask my mother what it meant, so I could better know my offense and the retribution that was surely in store for me. But I was afraid to ask her, because she would want to know why.

Years later, as I was preparing a sermon, I was reading G. Campbell Morgan, the famed preacher. He made an observation that took me back to that day. He said, in essence, "Sacrilege is often defined as taking something that belongs to God and using it profanely. But there is a bigger sacrilege we commit all the time. That is to take something and give it to God when it means absolutely nothing to us."

I believe both of these definitions describe what happened in the vestry that day. I know the episode typified my attitude toward Christianity: it was a grim rap on the knuckles for me. I gave God nothing and took what He intended for honor and treated it tritely. I just didn't know any better. With a life full in many different family pursuits, I drew my fulfillment from knowing my friends, feasting every now and then on some treats somewhere, and, most of all, enjoying sports.

AS MY CHUMS AND I GREW IN OUR FRIENDSHIP, WE VENTURED FARTHER FROM our neighborhood and its nearby environs. We grew to love the taste of roasted corn ears offered by the street vendors. Those vendors gave their wares an incredible flavor by taking half a lime, dipping it into a mixture of dry spices, then rubbing the lime on the roasted corn.

We learned to jump onto buses on the fly, catching them at mid-speed, and to jump off just as intrepidly. This sounds dangerous, but it was no more so than the daring feats we performed on our bicycles. If I was running late, I would pedal up to a slow-moving bus before it picked up speed and, with one hand clinging to the bar at the door-way and a life-risking negligence, get the benefit of the bus's speed as it went from stop to stop. These kinds of foolish antics we would do on a dare, sometimes taking nasty spills, with our limbs and at times our heads banging against the concrete or into the gutter. But we learned to just get up and keep going. I remember my head often being in a daze as I would struggle to my feet. Medical care was not exactly given priority, and you only went to the doctor if you couldn't get up. I took my fair share of spills, as did my friends. Of course, having no brakes on my bike made every biking trip a hazard.

I had my first real bout with guilt on those streets. My mother had given me a five-rupee note with which to buy ice cream when I was at school, and I was to bring back the change. When I bought the ice cream and proudly paid with my five-rupee note, the vendor handed me the change, and I noticed he'd given me change for ten rupees, not five. As I gazed down at my palm, I couldn't believe my good fortune. I thought, "Wow! I just made five rupees."

That felt good the first day. But every day thereafter, when I had to pass this ice cream vendor at school, there was a strange feeling of wrongdoing inside me. He was a big, rather rotund Sikh man, with a somewhat scraggly beard and a cheerful countenance, and he was friendly to all who walked by. Each time I saw him, I struggled inside, saying to myself, "I cheated that man." Then I began to see him in other places, happily pedaling along on his bike with his ice cream cart in front of him.

Finally, I could take no more. I saved up every coin I could, from here and there, for several months, and I finally went back to the man. Very respectfully, I said, "Sir, I have to ask you to forgive me for something. I made a big mistake. You gave me more change for an ice cream some time ago than you should have."

He eyed me for a moment, as if trying to remember the previous exchange. As he did, I stood there quaking. I thought he was going to clobber me or, at the very least, soundly berate me. I waited to hear him say, "You scoundrel. You stole from me, and here you've passed by me every day!"

As he continued to say nothing, I swallowed hard and offered, "I would be willing to give you more than what you gave me back because," I stammered, "I've had your money all this while."

When I raised my eyes, I saw that he didn't know what to do. He was profoundly moved, and, almost in a state of shock, he took the money that I held out to him. He may have offered me a free ice cream in return; I don't remember. All I know is, as I turned to go home, a huge burden had rolled off my shoulders.

THE SAD DAY CAME IN OUR LIVES WHEN MY GRANDMOTHER, AGNES Manickam, passed away. It is fitting that she was at our home, because she particularly loved my mom. I remember the day with a beclouded memory, for I was only nine at the time. It was a sunny day for the funeral, and Father John presided. The most riveting memory was the hymn they sang at the service: "Abide with me—fast falls the even-tide; the darkness deepens—Lord, with me abide." I remember those words so well. They spelled death and farewell.

Years later, I would study the words of that hymn in church. That second verse is powerful: "Swift to its close ebbs out life's little day; earth's joys grow dim, its glories pass away; change and decay in all around I see; O Thou who changest not, abide with me." Even today, whenever I hear that hymn, the memory of my family standing at the gravesite comes flooding back.

As we drove home afterward, my brothers and sisters all talked about the fact that our dear Ammah was gone. None of us knew what her death meant, exactly. I just knew that I had lost someone who had been very good to me and whose memory was dear to me for that reason. That awakened me to the stark realization of life's end that awaited each one. I thought of it often and wished I could push back the veil of death.

Sports again provided the escape. Every once in a while, my father brought home a warped or broken tennis racquet or some other piece of sports equipment that had been thrown out at the YMCA, of which he was president. There are buildings standing there today that he was instrumental in having built, and he often hosted well-known dignitaries there. It was at the Y where I met the famed Jesse Owens and heard E. Stanley Jones, one of the most notable missionaries India has known. He was in his eighties at that time. I had no clue of the greatness of the man I was listening to, unaware, for example, that Mahatma Gandhi held him in the highest esteem.

Occasionally, I approached the sports coach at the Y to see if he had any old cricket bats, tennis nets, or other equipment he might be ready to throw into the garbage. Even though the stuff he gave us was well-worn, it made all the difference to us in our street games, and the Y became a sort of reliable supplier for us in that regard.

Even as we buddies grew closer in friendship, however, something was beginning to happen in me. There were nights I lay in bed wondering if I was going to make it. I began to feel a loneliness I couldn't explain. If you had asked any of my friends, they wouldn't have been able to explain it either. We were together for everything, going in and out of each other's homes regularly, having lunch or dinner with one another's families. It was as if we were all one big family.

But over time, I began to suffer from a sense of purposelessness and inferiority. My loneliness stemmed from the fact that all my friends were either rich or brilliant, and I was neither. While they were always at the top of the class, I never did well in studies. And because I never had any pocket money, I couldn't go anywhere unless I was with them and benefiting from their generosity. Of course, they always wanted me to be with them, no matter what we were doing. That's why they always paid my way, even to the point of buying me things.

Still, I knew I wasn't in their ranks on either level. So it helped that in sports, I was the best of the group. Whatever sport I played, I generally came out near the top. And because I excelled there, sports became my escape from the loneliness I otherwise faced. In fact, it became my primary motivation.

I used to be in the sporting field for over four hours every evening, from four o'clock or so till around eight thirty, when my mother served dinner. I loved tennis especially, because I could get out into the open air for match after match. And I did very well in the sport, playing in clubs and competing at a high level. In table tennis I eventually reached the city semifinals, the top four, which wasn't a small thing in Delhi, a city of millions.

Yet, I had no encouragement and no equipment. I never owned a new or even a decent racquet. I always had to play with borrowed or half-broken ones. My buddies usually came to my aid, loaning me theirs. And I never owned a set of pads for cricket, which became my favorite sport. I always had to borrow those too, because you can't play without pads (a little similar to a baseball catcher's wearing shin guards)—not at the level we were playing. My buddies' fathers were very fond of me, and occasionally one of them would step in on my behalf, encouraging me or giving me a piece of equipment. To some of my friends, it must have looked as though I had everything going for me. I was very outgoing, with an abundance of athletic talent, humor, and a great social life. Any one of them would have told you I was the most popular guy in the group; even my closest friends, Sunder and Ashok, never guessed how desperately lonely I was. Indeed, they were stunned once the depth of that desperation was revealed.

I was a sportsman, made for the field, and I loved cricket especially, so that excelling in the sport became my life's dream, my one goal. I ended up playing competitively at a community level and later at the university level, which was no small feat. To this day, when I lay my head down on my pillow, I daydream of cricket. I'm coming to bat or winding up to bowl, when I finally begin to drift off—

There was something else about cricket's appeal to which I gravitated: it is known as the gentleman's game. You play it fair, and you play it for the thrill of the game. There is style, brilliance, strategy—all of which makes for a young man's hard-fought efforts. I used to watch great matches between the world's best; these lasted five days, and what a thrill! Even now, I light up when anybody asks me to explain the game. To an American, I must concede explaining it is an almost impossible task without watching the game at the same time, and even at that, it would take a few games. They marvel that a match could take five days, and when I respond by mentioning the length of golf tournaments, there is a fanciful linguistic footwork that takes place. A great thrill to me is that my son, Nathan, has taken so well to the sport.

It did bother me a bit at the time that my father never came to watch a single game in which I competed. I know that in his later years my dad came to deeply regret his indifference of those days. I have no doubt whatsoever now that if he could do it all over again, he would do it differently.

And so as dismal as things seemed at times, cricket became the love of my life and kept me from losing all heart. The struggle of my soul was building, but God in the shadows gave me this success to remind me that all was not lost and that there were gifts and skills not to be taken lightly. But life could not be lived on the cricket pitch. There was a home to return to and an inner life to be faced. If only I could play it professionally, maybe the game would change the home. That was my dream. Toward that I labored.

CHAPTER 6

WEDDING CRASHERS
AND ASHES

THERE IS A HINDI WORD, *BAYSHARAM*, THAT LITERALLY MEANS "DEVOID OF shame." To call a person "baysharam" is a strong insult; here in the West, it would be like calling a person a pathological liar.

This is part of the reason Eastern culture is not a culture in which we emotionally undress or, to use the Western metaphor, wash our dirty linen in public. In many ways this makes sense. Why and to what purpose does one need to bare all heartaches and inner struggles? Even if you do share some of yourself, you certainly don't betray the inner workings of your home or relationships among your loved ones. It is one thing for you to bare your own personal shame; it is another thing to bring shame on another.

For that reason, I guarded my own inner agonies. One way or another, to let anyone else know what was going on inside me would reflect on my family. I successfully bottled up all my hurts and struggles, and no one had a clue about what was going on inside—except, perhaps, my mother.

I have said that my brother Ajit is like my father. Everyone who has known my mother says that I'm very much like her, both in personality and habits and in my features. If a mere morsel or two of food was left after a meal, she would save it. "You never know when you're going to need it" was her approach. With a family of seven, she no doubt did that out of necessity. But to this day, those same traits show up in me. If even the tiniest slice of cake remains, I'll wrap it up in a napkin and store it away. Or if I'm in a hotel and I'm about to toss a half-used miniature bottle of shampoo, I'll instinctively stop myself, thinking, "Why am I throwing this away? I should take it home. I might need it." That has its benefits, like hidden gold at a time you need it. But it has also brought me moments of red-faced discomfort when Margie is cleaning out my suitcase and says, "What on earth did you bring *this* back for?" Yes, I am the proverbial pack rat.

My mom was also very much a people-person. She was attuned to meeting others' needs and had her own network that touched people's lives. If she was ever given a position of authority, whether at the school where she taught or elsewhere, she always used her position to help people. Whatever she could do to meet another's need, she did it.

She was a very gentle person, and she was also more of a story-thinker, never short of a proverb or a parable, in contrast to my dad. Whereas my father was skilled at making complex decisions in the moment, my mother never rushed to any conclusion on a matter of importance. She was very reflective, not so much in terms of philosophy, but in regard to people's emotions and needs. I never heard her utter an ill word about anyone, and if she ever came close to it, it was almost humorous to hear. We would chuckle along with her whenever that happened. People connected with her readily, and our house always had a stream of walk-in visitors to see my mom.

There is one particular trait I continue to share with her. My mother was always aware of her roots, her small beginnings, and she never grew out of that. No matter how "big city" my dad's life became, my mom's heart was always "small town." She was kind and generous to the poor and the needy. Many times I saw her give something extra or do something special for the people who cleaned the houses in our area. These people were called *jemadars*, meaning "the sweepers." Sweeping and mopping floors was their trade and the entire source of their income. Some of them cleaned up to twenty houses a day, sweeping, mopping, and scrubbing the bathrooms of each home in the neighborhood every morning and evening. They are on the lowest rung of this highly stratified society—the "untouchables."

The *jemadars* who worked in our area were a family who lived in two little huts behind our home. The huts, with thatched roofs, were made of cow dung and straw. About ten people lived in those two huts, really at the mercy of the elements and an ever-increasing family. Living so closely to such poverty, life and death takes place before your eyes. On a given morning you might hear some weeping and find out that there was a death that night—the death of a son or daughter or parent. But life went on, with an accepting of all this fatalistically. Their whole world was drudgery and minimal survival. My mother regularly saved up things to give to them—from our outgrown clothes, to old watches, to jewelry of various kinds.

Years later, after we had moved overseas, the *jemadars* were the ones for whom my mother loaded me down with things—food, clothes, and money—each time I went back to Delhi. They would hover around me and ask to see pictures as they oohed and aahed, watching the way our family had grown. They were always grateful for whatever I brought them, and they remembered my mother fondly. They called her *Memsahib*, a very fond and respectful term that means "the lady of the house." On one occasion, when I went back and looked for them, I saw that the huts were broken-down and that nobody was there. On asking around, I was told that the parents had died, and so the family had moved back to a village, but no one knew where. I miss staying connected with them. I often wish I could find out which village they live in and go to visit them.

My relational skills also must have come from my mother, and I didn't lack in them as I entered my teenage years. My friends and I had formed very close relationships, from being cricketmates to just hanging out together. There were ten or eleven of us, all from the neighborhood, and once a month we held a big lunch at one of our homes, during which our mothers cooked for us. But we cooked, too. We used to look forward to that monthly Saturday. My mother always put on a big spread when the time came for us to hold it in our home.

Ajit and I each had our own set of friends. But as he moved on to college in Madras and I remained in Delhi, there was also a growing sense of different values between us. "You and your friends," he would often remark then—a typical older brother—"you're all such innocents, so naive." He knew that the mischief we got into was innocent, contrary to some of his new experiences at college. And today he would admit that his college friends had a different way of looking at life from the way we had been raised. I always admired him and loved to listen to his stories; he could really tell them. But we were on somewhat different paths.

I was seen in my family as very much a pragmatist when it came to humor. I knew how to joke my way through various situations.

It never worked with my father, of course, but my buddies knew to beware around me. I was a practical jokester, ever on the lookout for mischievous pranks to pull. None of the stuff was ever intended to hurt anyone, but I didn't pass up an opportunity to take advantage of a potentially humorous situation.

Before cricket matches I would limp a little, feigning injury so that our opponents would think, "Ah, here's a hurt one. This should be an easy out." I would step up slowly to the wicket, only to let loose with a fluent, powerful stroke to score the runs we needed.

My buddies were usually involved in my pranks. At times, Sunder was reluctant, being more serious-minded, but Ashok was always a willing participant. We might swipe a guy's books before an exam to watch him begin to panic when he couldn't find them. Or we would work in tandem to play some trick on a shopkeeper.

Once at summer camp we met a guy named Eugene, whose nickname was Turkey. (The reason isn't important!) Turkey foolishly admitted to the rest of us that he was scared of the dark. As soon as he said this, I saw a look register on my friends' faces that seemed to say, "Uh-oh. Turkey made a mistake by saying that. He never should have admitted it in front of Ravi."

I asked Turkey, "Why do you get afraid?"

"Unexplained noises," he said. That was another bad confession.

Somehow that afternoon, I found time to sneak away and implement my scheme. I tied some tin cans together onto a long string, then draped the string through the ventilation opening that ran from Turkey's room to ours.

That night, well after lights were out, I tugged at the string gently at periodic intervals. We all heard Turkey climb out of bed and start pacing the floor. Every ten minutes or so, I gave another yank, and Turkey would get up again. We could tell he was looking around, trying to find out where the noise was coming from, but with no success. The next morning, one look at Turkey's face told us he hadn't slept a wink. That was mean, but, for my youthful sense of identity, successful. Today it troubles me a bit to think that such things gave me a laugh.

I found one prank to be particularly advantageous. I must confess this was not a good one. I pretended to be a go-between for any fellow and girl who were trying to establish a friendship. I loved pastries, so I would tell the guy, "You know, she really loves cakes." He would bring cakes to me to pass on to the girl but, of course, half of them never made it to her.

Or I would pretend to one of them that the other was in the next room. I would say to the girl, "What do you want him to know? I'll give him your message." I would step into the next room, which, of course, was totally empty, and come back with a fake message from him. Then I'd pull the charade on the fellow. My sisters still talk about what a dirty trick this was. To understand this, you really need to understand how our culture separated the genders so as to limit any romantic involvements. So time spent with a member of the opposite gender, alone, was almost nonexistent. We had to find ways and means of something to entertain the fancy, even if it meant just sending a pastry to the other. When the day came that I had to disclose this whole thing as a farce, the two didn't know whether to choke me or to say, "How did we really get taken in?" Again, I must say I feel pretty bad about this now because it exploited people, but at the time, I thought of it as merely a short-term prank that would not hurt anyone too much.

One of the benefits resulting from another of our pranks — and on this my friends and I all agreed — was that no one in India attended more wedding dinners than we did. In northern India, weddings begin with the bridegroom riding on horseback to the bride's house. He is followed by what is called the "bridegroom's party" — a company of up to three or four hundred people, with musicians playing, women waving lanterns, and others happily taking part in the celebration. When the bridegroom's party arrives at the bride's house, they are welcomed in a brief ceremony. Then all of the bridegroom's guests are seated and served a royal dinner; the bride's guests are served in the second round. As for the menu, it consists of the best chicken, rice, and curry dishes you've ever tasted. India's delicacy is tandoori chicken — chicken that has been marinated overnight in spices and saffron in a yogurt base, then put on a skewer and barbecued in a clay oven. You talk about succulent, mouthwatering food! We couldn't afford it very often, but it was served at every wedding if the menu was nonvegetarian.

Now, because these weddings can be so large — sometimes up to 1,500 or 2,000 people — it's easy to get lost in the crowd. My cricket-mates and I found this to be a very advantageous situation. In fact, we relied on it to secure probably a significant number of the best wedding dinners in Delhi over the course of any given summer.

Sometime around late April or May, the wedding season begins. About six thirty every evening, you'd hear a band playing in the distance and see a procession coming down the road. Calling it a band is very generous. The instruments were probably left over from some prehistoric collection, and the out-of-tune sounds made for grimaces as we listened. Oh, but what an omen it was to hear a band playing in the distance, getting closer by the minute! That was the signal for us to drop our cricket bats, rush to our buddy's house—where we'd made sure to bring our dress shoes beforehand—change out of our cricket shoes (maybe change our shirts as well), and casually join in the procession.

If you're going to be part of the bridegroom's party, it's important to congratulate him heartily and cheer him on. With this rule we gladly complied, waving happily and calling out the lucky fellow's name—once we learned it!

However, there were some risks. Since we were never dressed in typical wedding attire, we needed a plan in case a waiter became suspicious and started giving us the eye. When that happened, one of us would say to another, purposely within earshot of the waiter, "What time is your father coming?"

This usually gave the waiter reason to pause, because he would not want to offend a legitimate guest whose father was about to appear. It was also the signal for one of us to look at the waiter and order with great confidence, "What are you standing there for? Get us some cashews!" This would cause the waiter further hesitancy, we thought, as he would reason that we must belong there—otherwise we wouldn't be ordering him around.

After these wedding-dinner outings, we'd usually get home around eight o'clock, just as my mother was serving dinner. I would walk in and say that I really wasn't hungry that night. That in itself would be a shock to the servants. My mother would ask, "You're not having dinner?"

"No, Mom, I'm not that hungry."

"Have you eaten at a wedding again?" In utter frustration she would ask me, "Ravi, why do you keep doing this?"

"Mom," I would assure her calmly, "all wedding invitations say, 'We invite you along with your family and friends.' There's always a distinct possibility I might have had a friend there." I'd pause and then say to my brothers and sisters, "You really should have tasted that tandoori chicken."

Only once did a prank actually come close to risking someone's life, including my own. A group of us, about half guys and half girls, were taking a train to a summer camp, when we made a stop at a certain station. A huge, burly Sikh wearing a turban was standing on the platform, waiting to get into our compartment. I could tell there would be trouble if I crossed this guy, but the opportunity was irresistible.

As the train began to move, he stepped onto the footboard to enter our compartment, which he was not supposed to do because it was reserved for our group. I was parked at the door and given the terrible assignment of blocking his way. "I'm sorry, sir," I began, "but this compartment is reserved and full."

He started to push and shove.

Now, I was just a skinny teenager then, and this guy was twice my size. But that was where the fun was.

"Let me on," he demanded.

"You look like a nice man," I noted, peeking back into the compartment, pretending to survey a full coach. I assured him, "We might try and find a spot, but just wait here."

"Step aside," he threatened.

"Please, sir, just give us a few moments to move some things to make room for you."

I don't know how I held him off for so long, but I succeeded. The train was moving slowly. He was standing on the step, holding on to the bars, and he began shouting at me that either I let him on or else—

That's when I did the unthinkable. I furiously started to tickle him under his arms.

By this time, a horde of my buddies stood behind me, watching the scene. Panic set into the group. But my prankish mind was fast at work. As I kept tickling him under the arms—his arms shooting like pistons, holding on only one at a time—I wondered if this was going to be my last day on earth.

By this time, the train had picked up some speed. My tiring attempts to throw him off and his determination to hold on were growing old. One of us was going to have to give way. So I did the only thing I could think of: I went for his midsection.

In his attempt to push me off, he unwittingly let go of the bars and had to jump down, stumbling along the side of the train to keep from biting the dust. I really did not intend for it to get this risky, but I have also no doubt that, had he gotten on, we could have had a very fearsome situation. The Sikh shook his fist at me as we pulled away, and I returned to my seat drained, my heart pounding. I was applauded as a hero but would gladly have given somebody else that privilege.

A lot of these things I did to hide the inner struggle of my soul and to feed my need to act like I really was somebody. None of those friends, nor anyone in my family—not even my mom—would ever have guessed the depths of the loneliness that stalked me. Though I was close to my buddies, I still felt a sense of inferiority when I was with them. Maybe I even did some of these things to prove some sense of identity. It was during this time in my life that my dad, probably trying to shame me into facing reality, started saying things to me that cut deeply into my soul and seemed never to exit my thoughts. It culminated in one brief torrent when I found myself standing before him.

"You're a complete failure," he said. "You're an embarrassment to the family. You'll never make anything of your life."

He could not have known my shame at those words, or my despair at his final summation of me.

To be honest, at that time I thought this was my loneliest moment. But there was worse to come. And then the wheels began to turn to make my plans.

In that culture, you were supposed to bear responsibility early on. At fifteen years of age, I was considered an adult, yet I knew I wasn't doing what I needed to do with my life. And it weighed me down, burdening my every thought. I sat in my classroom at school thinking, "What is going to become of me?" That thought constantly haunted me. And so I found myself asking, "Am I a complete failure? Can I get out of life some way, painlessly?"

I didn't talk to any of my siblings about it—I couldn't. It just wasn't done. Nor did I talk to my friends. I was aware that something deep and downward had begun in me, but I didn't know what to do about it.

My mother must have known something was going on inside me. She knew that I felt I was the loser in the family. For that reason, I know, she always had a special place in her heart for me. She was a saint and watched me closely because she knew I was hurting. Margie continually reminds me of this. "Your mom had your heart in hers," she says.

But my mom couldn't have known what I was planning.

There is a certain story in my family that none of us want to dwell on today. Whenever we are together and one of us begins to reflect on this incident, the story never gets finished, or it's somehow abridged. Even now, I can only relate it in its mildest form.

One night, my father kicked us out of the house—all of us, mother and children. It had begun with his verbal abuse of my mom, such as none of us had seen before. Then he turned his abuse on us, and we were taking some hits. It was a cold night in Delhi, and he told us all to get out. None of us can recall what caused such rage. We were all in our nightclothes, outside the house and shivering. My mother quickly led us to a stairwell between the flats in our complex. There, under the stairs, she gathered us together and, unwrapping her sari, covered us with its flimsy warmth. She protected us as best she could, while we trembled in the cold.

I said to my mother, "Why don't we go to one of my friends' places? They'll let us in for the night."

"No, no," she answered. "Your father will get a bad name in the community. We can't do that."

So we sat there underneath the stairwell, wrapped in our mother's sari, the only shelter we knew.

I cannot remember if Ajit was there with us or had already gone away to his university studies in Madras. We just don't talk about it. That's what actually makes writing all this quite hard. Yet, I should add, even if Ajit had been with us that night, I don't know whether things would have turned out any differently.

I cried a lot that night, sitting in the cold under that stairwell. I was already aware of my despair. But I had become more aware of its great degree. All I could think of were my failures in life. "I'm not doing well in my studies. I'm not getting anywhere. I'm empty and lonely. And now this."

I thought of what my father had done. And I decided, "This isn't right. I have to find out how we're going to survive. I have to find out what life is about. I have to do something."

I decided I would deal with it in a serious way. I was determined to seek some answer. And if I couldn't find one, I would let everything go.

"If this is what life is, then I have no hope."

I turned my thoughts to the only remaining place there was to go.

"If there is a God, I want You to reveal Yourself to me. Otherwise, I am no more."

Sometime that year, I faced another deeply unnerving moment. A very good friend of mine died in a botched operation, and I was quite shaken by it. I simply couldn't come to terms with her death.

I decided to ride my bike to the site where our friend had been cremated, and just as I arrived, her ashes were being shoveled away. There was an old, bald man at the site, whom I recognized to be a Hindu priest.

"Sir?" I said, "may I ask you something?"

"Yes."

I gestured to the ashes. "This was my friend."

"I'm sorry for you."

"Sir, please," I stammered, "can you tell me where she is now?"

The old man looked at me very soberly. "Young man," he began, "that is a question you'll be asking all your life. And you will never find an answer."

His words shook me. If even he, a man of such devotion and dedication, could not answer with any certainty what happens after death, what hope did *I* have to find the answer?

I could not accept it.

I got back on my bike and rode away. The search was building, the answers seemed nonexistent, the fears were mounting, and my heart was scheming toward something else. Neutrality to reality was no longer an option for me. I began my search in earnest.

CHAPTER 7

THE RAJ PATH
AND THE ASSIGNED WAY

WHEN MY FATHER WAS APPOINTED TO THE HOME MINISTRY, HE MOVED into an even more powerful sphere of influence. His office was now in one of the wings that was proximate to the presidential residence, the magnificent palatial home built at the turn of the last century for the British viceroy. At the time of India's independence in 1947, the home was turned over to the new Indian government, and it became known as the Rashtrapati Bhavan. The first word means, literally, "father of the nation"; the second means "house."

It seemed a fitting environment for my dad. His appointment was the result not only of his brilliance and successes but also of his loyalty to his superiors. My father was very much the foreign-service man. He always stood when he talked to his boss, even on the telephone: "Yes, sir"; "no, sir"; "thank you, sir"; "I'll be there, sir." His tone of respect for authority was very much a part of his makeup. It was also a reflection of his own determined, forward-thrust approach to India's hierarchical culture.

We occasionally visited my dad in his office near the Rashtrapati Bhavan, on the west end of the impressive Raj Path. Translated "the way of the king," the Raj Path is a long, scenic mall of green stretches, floral gardens, and walking paths at the heart of Delhi's capital district. If you drive westward along the Raj Path leading up to the president's home, you pass between what are called the East and West Block buildings. That's where his office was. These red-stone structures, facing each other in an arc, house the offices of India's highest government. To pass between them inspires awe in any visitor, even as troops of monkeys make themselves at home everywhere on the grounds.

Even more impressive is the Raj Path itself. Stretching almost two miles, the monumental mall is adorned with beautiful gardens and long, shallow pools filled with colorful boats. The Raj Path ends its eastern point at the massive India Gate, a sandstone arch (reminiscent of the Arc de Triomphe in Paris) that serves as the symbol of India's freedom. It is the nation's war memorial, with the names of the fallen from World War I inscribed on it. If you stand on the east side of the gate, you can see the Rashtrapati Bhavan at the other end through the arch. In the film *Gandhi*, this magnificent stretch is shown teeming with millions of people following the slain leader's funeral cortege.

This historic part of town was close to where we lived, and we often walked to it on the weekend to buy some hawker's food sold on the lawns or to enjoy a boat ride. The setting made for bragging rights to a young man whose father's office was so prestigiously positioned. I remember the other impressive edifices along the Raj Path, including a black stone statue of Edward VII riding a black horse and, in proximity to India Gate, a white marble statue of King George V. My teenage years, the 1960s, saw the rise of Indian nationalism and with it the removal of many of those British symbols, including the magnificent statues, which were packed up and sent back to England.

None of this sat well with my father, who was very respectful of the British. He always believed they did India more favors than people were willing to admit. Indeed, when England began to withdraw its presence after Independence, he felt the ominous approach of events to come.

"The British shouldn't have left then," he said. "We were not ready."

His sentiments reflected those of many Indian civil service workers at that time, and they were right. The partition of India occurred (creating two countries—India and Pakistan), and there followed a bloodbath between Hindus and Muslims in which a half million Indians were killed. My dad recounted horror stories of what he saw taking place. Those were deadly times to be traveling, as mobs would sometimes attack trains or buses. I was too young at the time to remember any of it.

Every January 26, along with millions of other Indians, my family would attend the Republic Day parade down the Raj Path. Bleachers were set up on either side of the mall near the East and West Block buildings, and my father always secured VIP seats for us within eyeshot of the president's and the prime minister's platforms. Our family arrived at six in the morning, shivering, our teeth chattering and our breath forming vapor as we huddled under blankets to warm ourselves from the January cold. There we waited for three to four hours alongside other officers' families to watch the great dignitaries pass before us in the parade.

India is such a multicultural country that those parades were filled with costumes, bands, and styles of dancing that reflected a multitude of peoples. Sometimes schools would be asked to take part, and on one occasion I had the privilege of marching in the parade. Three days following the parade, on the 29th of January, the ceremonial "Beating Retreat" was held. Bands from the armed forces performed, and as a finale two buglers stood atop the minarets of the East and West Block buildings to mark the end of the celebration. Each year on this occasion, as the sun set, the bands played two hymns that Gandhi loved — "Abide with Me" and "Lead, Kindly Light." "Abide with Me" always brought back memories of my grandmother's funeral.

The "Last Post" sounded the finale, bringing to an end the days of celebrating the Republic. As a historic footnote, the very tune of the Last Post was composed during the days of the Raj and was the signal on military bases to end the day's activities, return to the barracks, and rest. It is interesting that now, when it is played at funerals, people do not realize the symbolism of the Creator calling a life to its eternal rest.

At this point in his career, my father began to have contact with ambassadors and heads of state from other countries. Our family got used to seeing world leaders at various receptions, which were held at the president's palace and at Prime Minister Nehru's home. My siblings and I visited the prime minister's home on a few occasions and were even privileged to shake his hand, experiencing up close the combination of immense charisma and great humility that won the hearts of the Indian people. I remember his booming voice when he spoke to the nation. Little did we know then the legacy he would leave — at least two further prime ministers, Indira Gandhi, his daughter, and Rajiv Gandhi, his grandson, both of whom would be assassinated by extremists.

To us, the whole world seemed to pass through the portal of our father's life. Our dad was part of the host committee for a reception to welcome Nikolai Bulganin, the president of the Soviet Union at that time, and his associate, Nikita Khrushchev. On other occasions, he was with the president of Laos and Marshal Tito of Yugoslavia. Even little Ramesh, my younger brother, got to meet Queen Elizabeth and Prince Philip, who attended the service at our church one Sunday. Ramesh had been chosen to be presented to them because he was the youngest member of the choir. (To this day he gets a lot of mileage out of that introduction!) When the event was telecast in England, many people wrote to India's broadcasting station, asking if there was any possibility of adopting that little boy. As the years went by, any time he misbehaved one of us would quip, "We should have taken the British up on their offer!"

It was around this time, when I was an adolescent, that I began going to the Cathedral Church of the Redemption with a greater purpose, sometimes just to kneel. I didn't know why I was compelled to do this, but I did it. There were times I knelt there, leaning against the rail as if I had thrown myself at the mercy of whomever was in control of the universe. The quietness of the cathedral made honest reflection possible, especially as I came away from the din and noise of everyday life.

In many ways, Indian culture is a melodramatic one. Life is snuffed out so easily by so many things, and that reality itself becomes a part of the cultural consciousness. This may be the result of the severe extremes of life in India. At one end is the escapist dream portrayed in the cinema, with its grand endings of wishes fulfilled. At the other end is a deep inner sense that there is nothing beyond the grave and that life itself is protracted grief. Many of India's movie songs capture this angst of extremes.

I found myself caught between these two poles. Whenever I saw movies with a happy ending, I longed for that; and when I saw one with a tragic ending, I placed myself in *those* scenes. The latter was more of a constant fear, however, and, as far as I could discern, my life was without any purpose and going nowhere. I had nothing ultimate to hope for and no one to counsel me either—nobody to put an arm around me and offer, "Can I help you through this? Can I walk with you through it?" There simply were no glimmers of truth or optimism for me in anything.

None, that is, except in *escape*.

Beyond my friendships, I continued to find my greatest fulfillment in sports. I loved them deeply, and by my midteens I had begun to excel in them at a serious level. I had blossomed as a tennis player and at sixteen was playing competitively in clubs. But as I have said, cricket remained the game for me. It was always my greatest love, and I poured all my aspirations into it.

I was known to my teammates as an all-rounder, someone who could do several things well on the cricket field. I bowled some and was also a good fielder, but batting was my greatest strength, for which I was always selected. We played our matches all day long on Saturday and Sunday, from nine in the morning until well into the evening. Even though these matches often took place at the very height of the summer heat, we never seemed to tire. My mother would ask me, "How can you play for hour after hour in such heat?" But I was hardly aware of it.

I recall one year when our team had a flawless record going into one of our toughest matches against a strong team from the other side of the city. Something happened at the time that revealed to me, at least subconsciously, how important cricket had become to me. Sunder was our captain, but he fell ill as the match approached, and I was asked to step in and lead in his place.

The anticipated match ended up being very close. Sunder was a great bowler, the equivalent of an ace pitcher in baseball, and during the match we missed him badly. He was our opener—a speedster who could be counted on to knock off the top opposing batters at the beginning. That's a crucial strategy in cricket. But in this match, we weren't able to do it. Their batters scored against us almost at will.

As the match wore on, we began to realize that we were likely facing our first defeat. It all came down to this: we could salvage a win, but we needed to get one more opposing player out. As captain, I wasn't sure what to do, what call to make. Finally, I decided to put myself in as bowler.

This was not a rash or panicked decision, as I was confident in my abilities. Yet with each step I took to bowl, the possibility grew in my mind that I was on the verge of blowing the match for my whole team. I wondered, "Would we have been able to win if Sunder were here?" This match no doubt meant more to me than to any of my teammates, as I thought of sports as my only strength. And now, once again, I was facing failure.

At my first bowl, the batter skied the ball overhead, and my heart fluttered. Unlike baseball players, cricket players don't use mitts; they use their bare hands. In sheer desperation, before I could even think what to do, I leaped skyward, hoping somehow to alter the ball's flight. While in midair, I felt a sting against my palm. And as I came down, I looked into my hand. I'd caught it—we had rescued our streak!

In cricket parlance, the batsman is out—caught and bowled. In this instance, he was caught and bowled by me. The ball was in my hands—and the ecstasy I felt was both from delight and relief.

Sunder's father had come to cheer us on that day, even though his own son wasn't playing. It was a wonderful gesture from an extraordinary man. In fact, he had led the cheering from the sidelines throughout the entire match. This was not out of character for Mr. Krishnan, a roundly respected man who was also an incredibly devoted Hindu. His character was his most striking feature, as he was not blessed with the finest of physical features and had a very high, shrill voice. We used to unthinkingly chuckle about it, because at times it could sound almost freakish.

Sunder's dad's story is a textbook example of how things go in the Indian culture. He never met his wife until the day they were married, which was the Hindu cultural way, at least at that time. After the wedding ceremony, the couple went to the home where they would now live out their years together, and it was then his wife saw him for the first time. She was deeply disappointed by his awkward physical appearance.

When he saw the look on her face, he was silent. "I'm sorry" was all he could bring himself to say. After he gathered his thoughts, he told her, "I can see why you have reacted as you have. I want you to know, you don't owe me anything. We have one bedroom, and that will be yours. I will sleep in the verandah."

Then he made her a promise. "I will treat you with dignity and respect," he said, "and do all for you that you ask of me."

One thing everyone knew about Sunder's father was that, despite his status in the community, he never put on airs. This man held as high and influential a position as my own father. Yet, each day, as Sunder's dad went to work, he never went by car. He always took the bus, which was the way of the common people. It was something he didn't have to do but chose to do.

Day after day, his wife watched this man conduct himself honorably, and over time his character won her over. She began to see him for the extraordinary human being he was—and ultimately the marriage worked.

Honor—it was the way Mr. Krishnan carried his life, and I responded to that. Indeed, one aspect of cricket that I have always loved is its sense of honor. Cricket is a very fair-minded sport, and if you play it you would never think of cheating. Often when your opponent does something extraordinary, your own team cheers him. That's just the way cricket is played all over the world.

I recall a conflict that took place in a match between India and the West Indies when I was growing up. The West Indian bowler bowled what's known as a "bodyline bowl," where the ball—bowled at lightning speed—comes close to hitting the batter's head. It was one of those Roger Clemens–type pitches, aimed at the head of the opponent.

When this happened, the West Indian captain, a player named Franz Alexander, walked out to speak to his bowler. He clearly reprimanded him for bowling in a way that could endanger the batsman and cautioned him against repeating it. But the bowler did it again. Alexander came to him the second time and now warned him. Batsmen didn't wear helmets then, and a direct hit could be debilitating, if not fatal. Alexander went back to his fielding position (he was the wicket-keeper, similar to the catcher's position in baseball) and the bowler once more bowled the ball at breathtaking speed, aimed at the batsman's head. At that point, Alexander walked up to him, took the ball out of his hand, and ejected his own teammate. I well remember seeing a picture in the newspaper of that ejected world-class bowler sitting in a train headed to Mumbai to be flown home. He was allowed to play in no more matches on that tour.

That was cricket. You played it fair and square.

In many ways, life was given to us—at least in theory—with such a strong moral standard. My buddies and I understood the moral standards of our culture, and we held to them rather innately. There were things we never had to discuss, certain boundaries we simply wouldn't cross. In relationships between fellows and girls, for example, we never would have thought of crossing lines of intimacy. We abided by the moral imperatives, and that counted for every one of us, as far as I knew. We would go out in large groups for an evening, boys and girls together, but none of the fellows had immoral intentions on those outings. Frankly, we had led sheltered lives and didn't know enough. Later, college days would lead some astray.

India prides itself on being a highly moral culture, so I knew early on that there was a moral framework through which I had to look at life. Yet I didn't know the "why" behind that framework. To me, it was merely pragmatic: you don't hurt people, you don't use them, you don't abuse them. Thus, I knew from the very beginning that the way my dad handled his relationship with my mother was wrong.

At the same time, I knew things weren't adding up in my own life. I don't recall connecting this to any kind of moral failure on my part; if I did, it must have been trumped in my mind by what I saw as a matter of survival.

My father's beratings continued. Yet now they came more frequently as I got older, at an age of adult responsibility.

"Why are you such a failure?" he would begin. This didn't come as a question but a character statement. "I could help you, if you succeeded only this much," he said, holding up his finger and thumb. "I could make a phone call and get you somewhere." I never felt this was an offer so much as it was a condemnation.

He knew correctly that I would never be admitted to a university with the grades I was making, so he saw community college as my only hope of salvaging a future. Hence, I was enrolled at sixteen, a year earlier than most students, to begin my shortcut to a university degree. Yet even this would short-circuit before long. The grading in India is very different from in the United States; you simply didn't score in the 80s and 90s. Forty was a pass, and 60 was a pass with distinction. Despite my father's plans for me and efforts on my behalf, my undisciplined study habits continued as they had. If I needed 40 percent to pass, I would study to earn 45 percent, and let it go at that. In some ways, I didn't know how to study. No one had ever taught me. On the other hand, learning wasn't an innate skill for me, and I wasn't very retentive.

Yet it wasn't just my passionate dislike for school that drove me away from studies. It was the depths of the emptiness welling up within me. Deep down, I knew there was no longer anywhere to turn for answers. I didn't even know if the answers to my deepest hungers actually existed. Life had simply stopped making any sense.

That frustration and hopelessness drove me with even more determination to the cricket field. It was the only place I could find that offered any kind of hope or reason to exist. I began skipping my classes regularly, wandering the streets on my bicycle, in search of a cricket match I could watch or take part in. And soon, I was absent for every class I was taking. I showed up only for exams and barely squeaked by. I was on a collision course.

One day, after cycling home, I turned into our backyard as usual, only to find my father standing in the doorway. He wasn't normally home at that hour, and the sight of him startled me. He stood with his arms stretched across the open doorway, as if to block my entry into the house.

"Hi, Dad," I said as innocuously as I could as I parked my bike against the neem tree in our backyard.

I felt his glare bearing down on me.

"How was school?" he asked.

A terror rose in my heart. He had never asked me such a question before. His interest surprised me.

"Fine," I answered as I approached the door. I tried to act as I normally would, but I couldn't help trembling as I got within his reach. He would not move to allow me to enter the house.

I was face-to-face with him now, as uncomfortable as I had ever been in my life. The moment of truth had come.

In an instant it dawned on me that my report card must have arrived. The absences!

He literally grabbed me by the scruff of the neck and dragged me into the house — and the torrent of anger my father unleashed on me was like none before. The beating began, and the hits and kicks were descending in unmitigated wrath. In the beginning, I raised my hands instinctively to protect myself, but it did no good.

Soon I had turned and was crouching, taking his blows on my back. With each attempted answer I gave to his raging questions, another hit followed. Once he got going, he didn't know when to stop. I knew I could no longer do anything against him, and I crumpled to my knees.

"Enough!" a voice cried. "Please stop! Please stop!"

It was my mother. She came between us, and my father relented while trembling and breathless with rage. He was also asthmatic and was now wheezing heavily. I could hear him and his heavy breath.

As I felt my mother's comforting warmth over me, it was as if a violent storm had ended, leaving devastation behind. Yet I remember sobbing and not being able to stop.

Some of this is still a blur to me, except that I know my mother came in the way of the beating and brought it to an end. I don't remember when my father stopped, nor do I remember how badly my mother suffered herself. I only know that if she hadn't stepped in, he would have done serious damage to me.

Just telling this story now, in written form, has been painful.

That night, I stood punished and facing a wall—a fitting metaphor of my life. My charade was over, but that had done nothing to free me. I was more imprisoned than ever by the pressing struggles within me.

My father's thrashings had never worked; they only increased my malaise. Yet a terrible truth had begun to dawn on me. I knew that in this one area of my life, he was at least partly right. I had never taken my studies seriously and, therefore, there was no future for me. I seemed destined to be an academic vagabond.

I was the one among our band of friends who had the least promise of a future. Sunder was obviously headed for a great academic career. He had been accepted to the prestigious Indian Institute of Technology on the outskirts of Delhi. My other friends on our cricket team all had something at which they were good.

But cricket was all I had. And all I could imagine for myself was a professional career in the sport. I wanted very seriously to play, not taking into consideration how tough it would be to make the lineup. What I didn't consider as well was that professional players at that time didn't make a living at their sport in India; their primary profession was in some other area. Some worked for the rail lines, others for firms that allowed them time off to play professional matches.

My dad obviously knew this. If he suspected that I had any such aspirations, he would have known it was no way for me to make a living. Now, more than ever, his haunting summation of my life came back to me: "You'll never make anything of yourself."

And now I was convinced: *He's right!*

That is probably why I've never held it against him. I *wasn't* doing well. And I *wasn't* making it. Why should I expect to have a future?

Still, his words carried a heavy, double-edged blow. First, he was right. And, second, this was all he had to say to me. He had nothing else to offer.

I don't blame my father for my failures up to that point in my life. But I do believe he made a mistake. I am a father myself, and I believe my dad should have taken me aside to talk. As best as he was able, he should have said, "Son, sit down, I want to speak with you. Tell me, what's going on inside you? Why are you living this lie? Why are you doing this to yourself? Where is it you want to go in life? And how can I help you get there?"

I think that, in general, many fathers don't want to have this talk. For whatever reason, they would rather avoid it. They seem to think that things will correct themselves. Or, they hope someone else will come along who can enter their son's or daughter's life and offer some answers and direction.

I have no doubt that the way my father related to me then was not uncommon for his time and context. And it was certainly true that, in terms of the culture, I was a source of shame for him. But the fact remains that he extended no genuine help to me. Nor was there any offer of hope. That was a heartbreaker.

Both my sisters had been going to a Catholic school all this time, by my parents' choice. One day, in an unusual event, a group of young visitors under the ministry of Youth for Christ was introduced at an assembly and were given the opportunity to present in song and testimony their faith in Jesus Christ.

I'm not sure exactly what my sister Sham was going through in her own life then, although she was much more successful in her studies than I was. As was typical, we didn't talk about very personal things. But my sisters became the trailblazers for the family, although they didn't exactly know to what degree. Sham loved music, and listening to the presentation this visiting group made undoubtedly piqued her attention. And at some moment during that assembly, something in her heart seemed to have been touched by it all.

As the program wound down, the speaker asked, "Who among you here today would like to have peace with God?"

Sham was one of those who raised her hand. Frankly, I don't know of anyone in India who doesn't want peace with God.

The Youth for Christ team followed up on the spot with the students who responded. They were so thrilled with Sham's "commitment to Jesus" that they invited her to join the Youth for Christ group, and some weeks later they asked her to share her testimony at a youth gathering. Sham was thrilled at the thought and agreed to do it, even though she had no idea what it all meant and what exactly to say. In fact, she didn't know what it meant to "give a testimony."

She got all excited about the evening and asked me if I would accompany her to that "Youth Rally"—a term quite foreign to her and to me. After much discussion back and forth, I agreed to go because she said there would be refreshments served after the event. So I, in turn, asked my buddy Sunder Krishnan to go with me. Sunder had a soft spot for Sham and he liked being with me; and, of course, the refreshments were no small attraction. So off we went, with no clue what we were going to. As it turned out, Sham didn't give her testimony at that particular meeting. Yet, while she was at the rally, it began to dawn on her that a new life had begun within. Thus began my sister's months-long process of settling in to what a decision for Christ meant.

The rally was held at an auditorium called the New Delhi Ministry Corporation. As was typical of an Indian auditorium, it was pretty plain: whitewashed walls and ceiling fans spinning to cool off the high summer heat. A lot of noise in the halls, cobwebs in the ceiling corners, green fungus here and there on the walls—it was just a typical public auditorium with acoustics better for outside sounds than inside ones. But there we sat waiting for the program to begin, and I was immediately impressed by the large number of young people who were there. I wondered, "What am I doing here? What is this evening all about?"

As the program began, the most unforgettable part of the evening left me completely amused. A soloist stepped up and, with an accordion wrapped around his chest, sang a song, "There Is a Balm in Gilead." I looked toward Sunder, wondering what on earth this song was about? I thought he was saying, "There is a bomb in Gilead," and my only hope was that we weren't sitting in Gilead! Putting my face in my hands, I shook in absolute bewilderment and smothered laughter, thinking that I had come to a place I knew nothing about and was listening to what made no sense, only so I could have refreshments at the end of it all. God's little twists of humor in the shadows still amaze me.

A few minutes later in the program, a man stepped up to the podium and began to speak. After listening a while, Sunder and I glanced at each other once more with a knowing look. We both were bored by this; in fact, we didn't much care for the whole scene. And to finish off what we felt was a wasted evening, no refreshments ended up being served either. Utterly disappointed, we left. There was only one bright light in the experience. There were some pretty nice-looking young people there, and that did serve as a possible reason to return.

Some time later, with Sham's trademark persistence, she asked me to go to another Youth for Christ rally. "This time," she informed me, "the young people will be singing. And I'm going to be one of the singers." She beamed with delight. Music was always an attraction for me, so again, for my sister's sake and Sunder's eye for her, we went.

As we walked into the auditorium that night, I was keenly aware of the struggle that was going on in my soul and of my continuing clouded thinking about Jesus Christ. Maybe the presence of some happy young people and a buzz of excitement put me on notice that all was not well with me. I knew something had reached the crossroads inside me, but I was not sure what to make of it in terms of a clear answer of what and why. I knew my real reason for wanting to be there that night: I was seeking an escape from my pain, and a reason to live.

I remember very clearly the speaker that night. He was quite different from the previous speaker, with not quite as dynamic a personality. There was a calmness about him and a saintliness to his demeanor. This man delivered his sermon in measured tones, carefully, deliberately, as if laboring to get across what he wanted to say. He was speaking on John 3:16: "For God so loved the world that He gave His only begotten Son, that whosoever believes in Him shall not perish but have everlasting life." At this point, it was more the man than the message that was getting through. I was truly drawn to him. He seemed so authentic, so caring. The message in parts was almost penetrating my soul.

His slow delivery (by Indian standards) made no difference to me. What I heard him say was planted within me to flower later. I faintly recognized truth, as God sought to break open my undisciplined heart. Although I didn't understand much of what this speaker was saying, it was enough to alert me to the fact that I was not right with the world and that God had the answer.

When he finished, he invited anyone who wanted to know Jesus Christ to come forward. I raised my hand—the only hand in the whole place to go up. About that time, a song began, with a group of young people singing. I rose from where I was sitting and made my way to the front of the auditorium.

Standing alone at the front of that big place made me feel a bit awkward. But inside, I was not wavering in the least. Somehow I *knew* this was what was needed—and what I wanted—in my life. A counselor approached me, and without hesitation I said, "I want to be like the man who just spoke." He opened a Bible, led me through the Scriptures that I needed to hear, and told me how I could have a personal relationship with Jesus Christ. "Yes, that is what I want," I responded, "but I don't know what to say or how to pray." He was a very kind man and led me in a simple prayer of commitment to Jesus Christ.

My halting prayer that night didn't seem to make a dramatic difference right away. It was more like a speck of salt being dropped into a vast tub of water. There was really a battle going on for my soul. Very little seemed different to the naked eye, but things were changing nonetheless. This is important to know. When someone from another culture hears the simple strains of Jesus' message, there is a vagueness in the beginning because you are not quite sure how it all fits into your culture's context. You just add anything new; there is never a subtraction. Something happened for me that would make a difference, but the road was still foggy. Nothing had emerged from the shadows yet. I left that night half aware of what happened but half in a blank about what it really meant.

All this time, my dad had been expecting me to attend Madras Christian College, like my brother had done. He foresaw me following in the distinguished path of my grandfather, who had been a student there prior to his professorship, and the path of my dad himself, who had matriculated there before going on to Nottingham in England. My mother also had gone to university in Madras.

As I made the leap from community college, I'm not sure why I chose to make the break from family tradition and attend Delhi University instead. Maybe it was because my friends were in Delhi. Or maybe I just was a homebody who didn't want to go away to college. In any case, my father pulled all the strings he could to get me into the university. His plan was for me to become a premed student and to go on to a career as a doctor.

Once I was admitted to Delhi University, it was my mother who went with me to enroll me and help me fill out the forms. That's the way it always was: my mom was the one who went with me to do such things, whether I needed to buy books or to get clothes for school. There was never a time when my dad went with me to do any of those things, as he did with my siblings.

By this time, everything was falling into a seemingly inevitable pattern that was becoming clearer to me by the day. There is an accepted understanding in Indian culture that you are assigned a path. Such a path is called a *marg*, meaning "the way." You hear a lot of talk about the way of devotion, the way of knowledge, and the way of meditation. And because *marg* is an assigned way, you don't question whether it's true or false. It is simply the way that's laid out for you.

To me, the way that was laid out ahead seemed littered with rubble and pitfalls. After only a few months at Delhi University, I began to repeat my pattern of not studying. I was already flunking my premed courses, and I didn't know what to do. At the community college, I had always found a way to get out of what was required, to meet only the minimum standards. Now I realized I didn't even have what it took to get by.

In retrospect, my father wasn't the only one who had reached the end of his wits that terrible day; something had reached finality in me as well. Whenever I considered the imposing figure of my father, I felt only the burden of what he represented to me: *Life has purpose, and mine clearly has none.*

Everyone else around me had success, but no matter how deeply I searched my life for a shred of it, all I saw was failure.

There is nothing ahead for me. That became my summation of all things, and I had no idea where to turn for hope.

Religion had not made any sense; I couldn't buy into the mythological stories of the worldview of my culture, and nothing seemed to have come from the prayer I had prayed after the youth rally. All the movies and plays I'd seen were just that—entertainment and make-believe. I didn't think for a moment that any of it was true. Even the learned Hindu priest who oversaw the shoveling of my friend's ashes hadn't offered any ray of hope.

"There are no answers," I concluded. *None.*

CHAPTER 8

THE LONGEST SHADOW

WHO AM I, AND WHAT AM I DOING?

I had been asking myself these questions relentlessly, day after day.

If you have the idea that life is something random; that there is no point to it, no purpose; that you just happen to be here—in existential terms, that you are a useless being floating on a sea of nothingness for whom in the end it all comes to nothing—then the idea of becoming *nothing* can seem better than that random *something*. It was the French existentialist Jean-Paul Sartre who said, "I've asked myself many questions and answered all of them. What I cannot answer is why I don't commit suicide."

I had heard some of my classmates speak of the unspeakable on several occasions. The word "suicide" was whispered, sometimes in jest, at other times mockingly, but we knew there was really no humor or sarcasm intended, especially as failure always seemed imminent.

Yet, they had no more reason to consider it than I. "Why put my family through any more of this?" I thought. "My father, my mother, my brothers, my sisters?"

I don't know when exactly I came to the decision. But when I did, I made it firmly and calmly: *A quiet exit will save my family any further shame. And it will spare me any further failure.*

Was I depressed when I made my decision? No. Was it impulsive? No, I had seen it coming for some time, perhaps always lurking in my mind as the final escape. Some cultures lend themselves more to the thought than others. My culture was definitely one of them.

When I arrived at the university that morning, I walked into the chemistry lab. No one was there. I did not hesitate in my mission. Somehow I got into the locked cupboard where the chemicals were stored. I pored over shelf after shelf until I came to some packets marked "poison." I grabbed several of them and stuffed them into my pockets.

I went directly home from the college and hid the bag in which I had put the packets. I had no idea what the chemicals were. They might have been some kind of acid, for all I knew, which could have burned through my insides. As far as I recall, that evening I played my usual game of cricket. What loomed in my mind, however, was foolish, very foolish—a coward's exit, really—but I had made my decision.

The next morning, one by one, each family member left for school or work. My mother, curious, asked me why I was still home, and I brushed her question aside, telling her that classes were beginning later that day. With the house emptied of my family, I went to the kitchen for a glass of water; it would help me to drink down the poison. Our house servant was there, tending to the boiling pots and simmering pans as he cleaned up from morning breakfast. So I changed my mind about carrying out my plan in the kitchen. I filled a glass from the tap and took it into the bathroom. I shut and bolted the door behind me and let the faucet run for a few minutes, while I wondered if I was really going to go through with this.

I hurriedly emptied my pockets of all the toxic packets. I opened them and emptied some of the contents from each, pouring them into the glass of water. The poisonous concoction began to effervesce, bubbling up.

I lifted the glass.

One last breath. I couldn't think of any reason to stop. The thought of my mother flashed through my mind, and it smothered my determination not to think anymore. "How is she going to react?" I wondered. "What will she do when she finds out?"

But I had to go through with it. I pushed all thoughts of my mother aside, and I swallowed the entire contents as quickly as I could.

My first reaction was nausea, because it was salty, very salty. Almost immediately, my body seemed to react to it, wanting to expel it.

Once it went down, I filled the glass again and clumsily poured in more of the chemicals. Fighting back nausea, I took another gulp. But I could no longer suppress the saltiness of the poison welling up in me. I began to throw up. I did not realize that, once the gag reflex had set in, I wasn't throwing up just the poison but also every bit of the moisture from my body. I was dehydrating fast.

Soon I collapsed to my knees. I tried clutching on to the sink, but I could barely hold on. I could feel my strength leaving me.

Impulsively, I called out for our house servant.

I had no idea whether he heard me. With all the noise coming from the kitchen, I gave up that he would hear me.

Suddenly, the door banged hard behind me. It was the servant, pushing against it. Another bang, and another. Finally he burst through, snapping the door off the hinges. He looked at me on the floor, then at the opened packets on the sink. He was completely unnerved.

"Take me to the hospital," I whispered.

I was rushed to the emergency room at Wellington Hospital. Much of what followed is a haze to me. But I do remember lying in a bed with needles in me while the doctors tried desperately to get fluids back into my body.

I tried to raise my hands but couldn't. My windpipe was so dry I couldn't swallow. I realized I could do nothing to help myself, or even to help the physicians and nurses. My muscle strength was completely gone. I could not even lift my arm.

As I lay there, with all the activity to revive me going on, I began to drift off. "If I am to survive," I wondered, "have I made myself an invalid? Will I need sustenance forced down my throat?" I didn't know what was going to happen to me, and suddenly I was fearful. I hadn't known how to live, and now I'd proven that I didn't know how to die. I had failed at both, and I feared where that might leave me.

WHEN I AWOKE, MY MOTHER WAS BESIDE ME.

I realized I was in the intensive care unit. Fluids were still dripping into me, and I sensed that a lot of time had passed, perhaps an entire day. A doctor stood by my bed, holding up my arm to insert a needle. As he let go, my arm flopped back down onto the bed.

I have to confess that all that followed is still very unclear to me. I never asked for any details then or after my discharge. For one thing, I wondered what had happened to the plastic packets of poison I had emptied. Did the servant try to protect me from my father and throw them out so that it wouldn't look like a suicide attempt but just a sudden gastrointestinal attack of some sort? He definitely did something with them to cover my tracks. None of us have ever talked about the incident. In fact, a few years afterward, when I did mention it in an interview with a magazine, the details seemed to shock my father. He wanted me to talk to him about the whole episode, but I wanted this to just be a thing of the past.

Another question haunts: how much did my mom know but not tell anyone? I know that in the times in which we now live, nothing is private anymore. And even this telling in print I do with great unease. The first time I have revisited the hospital where all this happened is at this point of writing, and the floodgates of memory have seemed at once unstoppable and blurred. My attempt to end my life was a sad, dark event. Moreover, it defined who I was—someone with no hope, no meaning—and I was embarrassed even to have my mother there with me in intensive care.

Two or three days passed before I began to feel any strength at all coming back. My friends were not allowed to visit because I was so ill. But they wouldn't have known what had happened. No one had told them why I was in the hospital. I was sure that only my mother—and perhaps my father—knew what had happened. All my mom told my buddies was that I was receiving the best of care.

A day or so later, a man named Fred David came by to visit. He was one of the directors of Youth for Christ, whose rally I had attended with my sister Sham and whose meetings I had just started attending. As Fred stood over my bed, he could see I was in no shape to talk. So he turned to my mother and handed her a Bible.

"I've brought this for you," he said, opening the book. He flipped through the pages until he came to a certain spot. "Here," he said, pointing to a spot on the page and showing it to my mother. "This is for Ravi."

They talked for a while as I drifted in and out. I was uncomfortable with any visitors, but I was glad Fred was there; his presence seemed to bring my mother some reassurance. Once he left, my mom decided to read the passage to me.

"He brought this for you," she said, showing me the Bible. She opened it to the fourteenth chapter of John's gospel: It told of Jesus in conversation with the apostle Thomas. She looked down at the page and began with this sentence:

"Because I live, you also will live."

The words hit me like a ton of bricks.

Live?

"Mom," I interjected, "please read it again?"

This "life" sounded very different from ordinary life. I had no real idea about what it all meant, and no idea of the context of the words. All I knew was that it spoke of something beyond what I had experienced.

She read the verse again.

"Who is that speaking?" I asked.

Later I found out the words were those of Jesus as he spoke to the disciples. He was responding to Thomas's question about where Jesus was going.

I didn't know the full ramifications of the verse. But to me, Christ's words in John, chapter 14, verse 19, were the defining paradigm: "Because I live, you also will live."

"This may be my only hope," I thought. "A new way of living. Life as defined by the *author* of life."

"Jesus," I prayed inwardly, "if You are the one who gives life as it is meant to be, I want it. Please get me out of this hospital bed well, and I promise I will leave no stone unturned in my pursuit of truth."

It was a simple, pragmatic prayer. Yet it would have immense ramifications.

I HAD BEEN IN THE HOSPITAL FOR FIVE DAYS WHEN THE ATTENDING doctor came to sign my discharge papers. I had finally regained enough strength to go home. As he looked over the documents and scribbled a few notes on them, he asked an odd question of me: "Do you really want to live?"

Live? I looked at him in surprise. He only continued to scribble.

Very sheepishly, I pretended I did not hear what he asked.

He stopped writing and turned to me with a sober expression. "Do you really want to live?" His expression hadn't changed.

The words my mother had read to me resounded loudly within me: *Because I live . . .*

"We can make you live again by getting this poison out," the doctor said, "but we cannot make you want to *live*."

... you also will live, said Jesus.

I let the doctor's question settle in—but I already knew the answer.

Upon my return home, I was glad I hadn't left a note. I didn't know if my brothers and sisters even knew what had happened. I don't believe they knew; but if they did, we never talked about it. As for my father, perhaps he was actually in denial, as he mustn't have asked any questions to have not known exactly what had happened that day. This was the quintessential expression of a cultural tendency to cover shame, and I was as much a part of it as he was.

Today, we live in a very different culture from the one in which my parents raised me. We never talked about my attempt at suicide, even years later, after our family had left India. Even my mom and I never talked about it. I wish we had.

The truth is, I have seldom relived it myself because of the intense sadness and embarrassment of my foolish act.

It took years before I could mention it to anyone, even those closest to me. The only one with whom I was comfortable talking about it was Margie, my wife. The best way I can explain this is that it has been like trauma from a war experience. To dredge up the memory is difficult, but to forget it would be unwise. I remember well from what I was rescued. If I'm one-on-one with someone now and they want to know about my experience, I don't really mind talking about it. But at the time, I kept it to myself.

Sometimes now, when I talk about it in India, I can see from the expression on my listeners' faces that they are uncomfortable. I realize I have to weave my telling of it in a way that helps people recognize that I'm aware this is a very uncomfortable subject. Yet I often wonder: have we done justice to our children when we have not allowed them to open up and share the deepest troubles of their hearts? On those rare occasions when I have mentioned my suicide attempt to an audience, invariably mothers have come up to me with tears in their eyes. They hardly speak a word. About all they say is, "I know what you're talking about. And I'm so glad you're out there talking about it."

Life presents very despairing moments for many. I am convinced that it is only the fear of the unknown that restrains the impulses of some. There is principally, therefore, only one reason I ever mention my experience in any sermon or talk. More often than not, there is someone in the audience who confesses to having wrestled with the thought of suicide, and I want more than anything else to give that person the hope that I was given—hope that only Jesus can give.

I was very clear in my mind as I left the hospital with my mother that I had made a commitment to Christ. It was the most striking and most noble-minded decision I had ever made. My life now belonged to Jesus Christ. He had answered my prayer. Inside me there was something new—a new vibrancy, a new meaning, a new hope, a new Ravi Zacharias. Of that I was absolutely certain. And I was going to plumb the depths of what this new life meant. There would be no turning back for me.

As surely as I had tried to take my life, I now knew something dramatic had happened. There was a supernatural element to my decision—all the details of which I could *not* discern then. I know for certain that I could not have conjured up such a change. My will simply did not have the capacity to make such a change; that had been proven again and again. But I knew that in those verses from the book of John, Jesus seemed to be talking about a new being and a different kind of believing, thinking, acting, and doing than what I'd had in my life up to that point. Purpose and transformation were now writ large in my heart.

I also marvel at how God was in the shadows then, for I could have done permanent damage to my body—but God protected me from it. What if there had been some neurological debilitation? That did not happen. In the shadows was the One who made me select the "right" poison, just enough to awaken me from my stupidity and steady my feet in the right direction. The wrong poison would have been catastrophic in every sense of the term. And now I want to tell you this: our servant's name meant "one who follows God." Certainly for that hour and for that moment he lived out his name and became God's instrument to save me.

Nothing—that had been my life before. Now I saw that the nothing was *not*—and that *something was.*

Nothing can never desire to be something, but *something* can desire to be something else.

I had found that something in Jesus Christ. Decades have gone by, and I have only become more certain in my heart and mind that Jesus Christ is who He claims to be—the very Son of God who draws us into a relationship with our heavenly Father, the author and giver of true life. The utter delight in my heart and the bounce in my step that followed my experience in the hospital day after day, year in and year out, could not be stifled by the tragedy and despair that had preceded. I was a new creation, and everyone who knew me now knew this. It is actually quite difficult for me now to even picture myself in those terms of the past.

The book of Proverbs says, "The path of the righteous is like the first gleam of dawn, shining ever brighter till the full light of day" (Proverbs 4:18). The dawn came in my life after my darkest hour, but how brilliant is that light that shines at that hour and only gets brighter with the years. That is the light of Christ. The songs I once heard my father sing—"Lead me, Lord, lead me in thy righteousness"; "Behold, I tell you a mystery"; "Abide with me" from my grandmother's funeral—all now became reflections of the wellspring of an inner life that sang for the first time with hope. Jesus Christ rescued a despairing young man in Wellington Hospital in Delhi on that unforgettable day.

Who am I? I could now answer it. "I am yours, O Lord."

A hymn by Charles Wesley perhaps most accurately describes my encounter with Jesus:

> *Long my imprisoned spirit lay*
> *Fast bound in sin and nature's night.*
> *Thine eye diffused a quickening ray;*
> *I woke—the dungeon flamed with light!*
> *My chains fell off, my heart was free,*
> *I rose, went forth, and followed thee.*

CHAPTER 9

A BOOK ON THE ASH HEAP

I CANNOT SAY ENOUGH ABOUT THE SIGNIFICANCE OF THE ROLE THAT YOUTH for Christ (YFC) played in those early days of my conversion. On the day that I tried to take my life, it was these friends who prayed for me. It was Fred David who brought the Bible to my hospital room (and, by proxy, the words that breathed eternal life into my broken body). It was all of these, both before and after my suicide attempt, who showed me that I meant something, and that God loved me as an individual. It was my relationships at YFC that gave me hope of coming back to a caring group. And it was they who, as time passed, gave me opportunities for leadership.

So there it all was, the unlikely strands that came together, weaving the small patch of fabric that was my conversion—a song that I chuckled at, a soft-spoken man who drew me to the message of truth, a group waiting to share the love of Christ with me in my time of greatest need, a Bible brought to my mother for me, and a passage of Scripture that sprouted in the moisture of God's sovereign grace. John 3:16 had given way to John 14:19, when Jesus said, "Because I live, you also will live." It all came together for me in the hospital room, but Youth for Christ is where those seeds were sown. I had now found a new home in my faith—a new home, which I made my hangout. In these important ways I could say I was finally *home*.

Youth for Christ was the residence of Fred David, who lived in a one-room apartment on the roof. The main part of the roof, called the *Barsati*, which literally means "the place where the rain falls," was where our group met once a week. Fred—an energetic, darkly complexioned Anglo-Indian—was the YFC director in Delhi. He was also very musically gifted, with a rich baritone voice, and he usually led the music at YFC gatherings, accompanying himself on his accordion. Although he was eleven years older than I, Fred would become one of my closest friends.

Then there was John Teibe, Youth for Christ director for all of Asia. He and his wife, Anne, lived in the upstairs flat of that residence. John was a long, lean Canadian from Calgary, Alberta, about six foot four, with an angular jaw and a permanently implanted smile on his face and personality. Along with Fred, John led most of the activities that took place at YFC.

If there was one place in Delhi where my Christian life was shaped, it was in that "upper room." Overnight, after my commitment in the hospital, it became the place where I spent most of my free time. Monday nights were Bible study, called "TAMI Club," an acronym for "Teens Are Most Important." I loved every minute of those Monday evenings, soaking up everything that was taught. Each new lesson increased my hunger even more, and I hated having the evening come to a close. My parents had a stipulation that we were to be home by 9:00 p.m., and I always made it back just in the nick of time.

One of the first things I wanted to do after I came to the Lord was to bring all of my best friends to Youth for Christ. Every Monday night, I gathered a group of my buddies from university, all of whom were willing to go, and they came with me to TAMI Club. Now that I had become a Christian, this was what I had to offer them. For all those years, my Hindu friends had taken me to their temples and festivals, and now I readily invited them to come with me—Sikhs, Hindus, Muslims, and Buddhists.

Religion was never an issue. Not one of those friends ever said, "I can't come; I'm a Hindu," nor was there ever any awkwardness or discomfort. We were close buddies—cricketmates and playmates from childhood, walking into each other's homes as if they were our own—and we were as open with each other as Indian youth culture allowed. In all truth, we wanted the best for each other, and I wanted my best friends to have the hope that I had. They had been such an inspiration to me—sterling young men and women, way ahead of me in studies, yet always maintaining a close relationship with me.

In those first few months at TAMI Club, many of my buddies made commitments to Christ. I was so brand-new to the faith myself, I didn't know the importance of following up with them on their commitments. I have always wished I'd had the wherewithal to do that. But a small core of those friends did follow through in their walk with the Lord, and they became tremendous young leaders.

Meanwhile, I was rapidly gaining a grasp on the basics of the faith: the life of Christ, the cross, God's plan of salvation, Christ's "Great Commission" to evangelize. During those intense months, as I gobbled up every morsel of learning I could, something changed in my life, causing an about-face I never would have expected: I became a voracious reader!

I had never been much of a reader, preferring to watch movies or discuss issues with people. I very rarely picked up a book out of interest—perhaps a Perry Mason novel by Earl Stanley Gardner or something similar from time to time. Then one evening, as I walked out the back door of our house, I saw something lying on top of the garbage heap in the alley. As I looked closer, I saw it was a book with no cover—an old, tattered copy of a volume I realized my dad must have thrown out.

Curious, I picked it up and read the title page: *The Epistle to the Romans: A Commentary* by a man named W. H. Griffith Thomas. I had no idea who this author was, but my hunger was so fierce that I immediately opened it and began to read. Over the next few days, I devoured that book—of all things, a Bible commentary! It became a treasure, as I used it to help lead the Youth for Christ Bible studies when my turn came. I still have the tattered copy of that commentary in my possession.

Just like that, I was plunged into a world I'd never known—the world of reading. One of the first volumes I was presented with was *The Cross and the Switchblade*, an amazing story of the conversion of Nicky Cruz the gang leader and of the work God was doing in the lives of such young people through the ministry of David Wilkerson. I loved the book so much that I began seeking out biographies.

I lapped up the stories of William Booth, founder of the Salvation Army; David Brainerd, the missionary to American Indians; and, most intriguing of all to me, C. T. Studd, the English cricketer who gave up everything to became a missionary. Studd had been the captain of Cambridge's cricket team, had turned down an opportunity to play for his country, and even refused his family inheritance—all to help take the gospel into China and India.

As I read about these inspiring lives, the old adage became true for me: "Fire begets fire." The standards these Christians set by their examples raised the bar for me. Though I later learned, as I grew in my faith, that these saintly lives weren't as perfect as their biographers made them out to be, the basic truths were undoubtedly in place, and their examples stoked my consciousness as to what the Christian life could be.

Anything I could lay my hands on with the gospel message I read. As I continued to grow in my faith in the years that followed, for whatever reason the first writers I encountered were mainly English: the Oxford don and apologist C. S. Lewis, the converted journalist Malcolm Muggeridge, and many of the Christian expository writers. I read everything I could of the works of F. B. Meyer, G. Campbell Morgan, and particularly James Stewart of Scotland, whose writings were especially powerful. As I stood in a downtown bookstore poring over Stewart's works, I thought, "Yes, this is the man I want to read." I don't recall anyone directing me to these writers; I just tried them out as I stood in bookstores, browsing through the shelves.

I also remained immersed in Bible commentaries, especially those by William Barclay. Commentators have the task of explaining to a biblical illiterate such as me what the Scriptures are all about, and—along with Meyer, Stewart, and others—Barclay skillfully guided me through a vast territory with great insight.

For the first time, I felt my mind being stretched—and I loved it. I realized that thinking could be fun, and with that simple realization I was sent headlong into the lifelong discipline of reading.

I was thumbing through the newspaper in our living room one day when I came across an item that left me reeling. It reported that a young man had doused himself with kerosene and set himself on fire. As I read further, I learned that the young man was from our neighborhood—a classmate named Yudhvir.

My immediate reaction was, *No!*

Yudhvir was one of my closest buddies, a cricketmate at college and a part of our group. We all knew he was headed for a bright future in the department store his family owned.

I was stunned. *Why would he do this? He seemed to have it made!* Ironically, Yudhvir's name meant "victor in battle." Evidently, he had lost a very important one: the desire to live.

I tried to imagine the tall, lanky kid taking the measures required to end his life in such a horrific way. Then I quickly realized: I knew exactly why he would do it. I had been there myself.

That was me just a few months ago.

I jumped on my bike and rode straight to his family's store, hoping to talk to someone. But when I arrived, the doors were closed.

That next day at school, some of my mates and I gathered together to talk. As I looked into my buddies' eyes, I saw they all were shaken to the core. I myself wondered: "If Yudhvir did this, and I had tried to end my life, who knows who else among us might be on the edge?"

I had to challenge them.

"Guys, listen to me," I said. "This is where all of us are headed. You need to realize, we're all searching."

I looked from face to face around the room. Each of my friends had taken my words at face value.

In the meantime, something significant had happened. A humble, very likable Indian man in his early fifties named Victor Manogaram, the director of India Youth for Christ, was coming to visit Delhi. John Teibe had mentored Victor, intending to one day pass on to him the mantle of the leadership of YFC Asia. Victor was never quite comfortable with that thought, although he never shirked it. You see, Victor continually battled an inferiority complex over having no education.

I don't know if Victor even finished high school; I don't believe he did. Yet he touched a great many lives through his simple preaching. Victor wasn't a complicated man, and what came through to his listeners was simple humor, simple gospel, and simple authenticity. He was deeply dedicated, and he never shrank back from his calling because of self-doubt. Instead, he said, his weakness required him to constantly seek the Lord's affirmation.

Christians and non-Christians alike were drawn to Victor for these very reasons. Both Fred and John knew the power in his preaching, and Fred tapped me one day, saying, "Victor is coming to speak this week. Can you organize a good gathering?"

At the time, our regular meetings drew about twenty to twenty-five young people. I glanced at the old typewriter on Fred's desk and told him, "Let me use that. I'll write a letter to everyone I know." I spent hours typing out invitations to all my Hindu friends, as well as to any name that was given to me.

On the night Victor spoke, we had a record gathering of fifty-three people — more than double the usual turnout. The place was packed in that tiny living room, and among those attending was my brilliant, scholarly friend Sunder. As Victor delivered his simple, plainspoken message, something stirred in Sunder. That night, he committed his life to the Lord.

Years later, I would read an observation by G. K. Chesterton that, to me, summed up Victor's impact. Chesterton says, in essence, that there is a dislocation of humility in our times. We have become more confident in who we are and less in what we believe. Our pride has moved us from the organ of conviction to the organ of ambition, when it is intended to be the other way around. In short, our confidence should be in our message and not in ourselves.

Victor Manogaram was a living example of Chesterton's caution. It was a truth I myself was forced to draw upon throughout my life. In the years to come, with that beaver-like smile planted on his face, Victor would muse, "I cannot believe that God used an uneducated man like me to touch a nuclear physicist in the making." Yes, that was Sunder's future career. He was going to end up as a leading expert in the area of nuclear safety in Toronto, Canada.

In turn, Sunder's commitment had a profound impact on his life and on our future friendship — we became soul mates. Of course, when Sunder's parents found out about his conversion, they were stunned. Both Mr. and Mrs. Krishnan were orthodox Hindus, and this was scandalous to them. His mother was absolutely outraged and blamed me, yet his father remained silent as he pondered what it meant to the family that the oldest son had turned his back on the religion of his birth.

Many years later, I was talking with Mr. Krishnan in their living room one evening as I waited for Sunder, when a subtle shift in tone took place. Very quietly, he asked, "Tell me, Ravi. What was it that led you to your decision?"

At first, I wasn't sure what he meant. "Uncle," I asked, "you mean, my decision for Christ?"

"Yes," he said rather diffidently. "What led you to — to Christ?"

I don't recall the precise answer I gave him. But I was intrigued that an adult — particularly this adult, for whom I had the greatest respect — would ask me this question. I had the sense that what I would tell him now would perhaps one day have meaning for him.

Sunder's salvation was only one of the exciting things that took place seemingly every day at Youth for Christ. One Sunday, I was hanging around the office when a friend asked if I wanted to go with him to meet someone that afternoon.

"Sure. Who is it you're meeting?"

"Kenny Gnanakan."

My jaw dropped. Kenny Gnanakan was the brilliant guitarist for the Trojans, one of the most popular music groups in India. How this friend had made contact with Kenny, I didn't know. But I jumped at the chance to meet this well-known musician.

As we spent that afternoon with him, I found myself sharing my faith casually but with visible effect. It was so effortless, I felt as if the Lord were giving me the words to say. Everything I had learned, it seemed, was on the very tip of my tongue. Ken at times seemed a bit distracted as I spoke, but I urged him, "Look, you've got to come to our club meeting tomorrow night. We'd love to have you."

He agreed to come, but we didn't count on him actually following through with the invitation. After all, this was *Kenny Gnanakan!* Yet, just as TAMI Club was starting on Monday evening, Kenny ambled in. That night, Fred David gave his testimony, and something wonderful happened. Kenny Gnanakan committed his life to Christ!

As it turned out, this was no fly-by-night experience for the talented musician. Kenny's commitment stuck, just like Sunder's, and it also would influence many. The die was cast; God's hand was on our lives.

The biggest challenge I faced after my new commitment to Jesus Christ was to find a church where the Bible was preached. As I went from one to another, I didn't understand many of the sermons I heard at some liberal churches. In one of the churches, the minister was obviously a brilliant man, but even as a newly converted teenager I knew he had very little to say on important matters. One of his sermons was titled "Adam, Where Are You?" and during his delivery, he stopped every few moments, looked out over the congregation and cried out in dramatic fashion, "Adam! Where are you?" It might have been more stirring to me had I understood a single thing he said in between these cries. Instead, I went away from most of his sermons bewildered and joking to myself, "If I were Adam, I'd hide from his preaching too."

One Sunday, John Teibe happened to be in the same church. The pastor's sermon that morning was "Something about Nothing," and its effect on me was no different from most of his sermons. As John and I walked out afterward, he draped his long arm around my shoulder and said under his breath, "Well, Ravi, at least we can say the title warned us."

I stifled a laugh. I appreciated John's humor over something I thought he might find offensive. But John didn't seem at all fazed by the "nothingness" he'd heard from the pulpit. Rather, he seemed to know that there was a great deal more to be said about the good news of Christ than what we'd just heard. I was eager to learn all of it.

Soon enough, I began to see how God was widening my glimpse of the Christian faith. A short time after my conversion, Bill Bright, the president of Campus Crusade for Christ, wanted to bring his ministry into India. When he applied for entry, however, the government turned down his visa. The reason for this, I'm sure, can be summed up in bureaucratic red tape.

When ministry workers in India learned what had happened to Dr. Bright, they grouped together with Christian leaders from overseas and appealed to my father. Not surprisingly, after a couple of phone calls all red tape had been cleared, and Campus Crusade came to India.

Why would my dad do this for Dr. Bright's ministry? First, there was his nominal Christian background. I believe that this, combined with his sense of fairness, prompted him to reason, "Why should this man be turned down? He had done nothing to hurt the country. It's not right." I remember the night Bill Bright was in our home for dinner —little did I know what a giant in the faith he was. Years later, his stature only grew larger in my eyes when I spoke, at his invitation, at the Campus Crusade international headquarters in San Bernardino, California. What a small world, and at the same time what a large picture!

My life soon began to take surprising new directions in other areas. For years, my father had been friends with George Varghese, the general manager of Delhi's largest hotel. Every now and then, my dad took us to visit Mr. Varghese, and I grew to admire the man. He would lead us up to the hotel's luxury suites and along the way introduce us to the other impressive executives, as well as to industry leaders from around the world.

As we sat down with Mr. Varghese in one of the suites, the hotel staff waited on us hand and foot. My father and his friend would be talking casually, when the door would open quietly and someone would bring in a tray of food of the highest quality. Of course, that caught my attention right away. Then, before we'd noticed, our half-eaten plates were whisked away — and along would come another round of sumptuous delights.

Those experiences with Mr. Varghese resonated within me. And after my first year at Delhi University, which I somehow completed despite my suicide attempt that March, I went to my father to talk about what I wished to do with my life.

"Dad, you know how I admire Mr. Varghese," I said. "I see all these big hotels, and I love the industry. That's what I want to do. I want to go into hotel management. I want Mr. Varghese's position."

I'm not sure what my father heard in this that told him I had even a remote possibility of succeeding. I'd been a failure in his eyes in so many ways. But evidently he heard something.

"OK," he said.

India is known the world over for its excellence in the service industry, and one of the industries that thrives in my homeland is hotel management. A great number of the people managing five-star hotels all over the world are Indian, and many were trained at the Institute of Hotel Management in Delhi. It is a renowned college, and some of its graduates go on to Cornell University, which boasts one of the world's premier graduate programs in hotel management.

I had my sights set on the Institute, and my dad pulled some strings to get me in. Once again it was my mother who went with me to enroll, but this time it didn't matter; I had been given a new lease on life, and I was enjoying it to the fullest.

About that time, a family we knew offered to let us use their BSA motorbike while they were on an overseas sabbatical. That bike became my transportation to the college, and day after day the twenty-five-minute ride was one of the most enjoyable journeys of my life. I can't say I didn't take risks, but it was a lot of fun zipping around and weaving through the traffic. And from day one, I excelled at the Institute, no matter what the subject. Business, economics, accounting, marketing, human resource management, reservation systems — my interest in all of them was keen. Food is a vast component of the hotel business, and I excelled there too. I had to learn nutrition, catering technology, food and beverage management, French and Continental cuisine, and yes, bar training (including mixing drinks, an aspect that was to shape a major life-decision for me later). Then there were the recipes we had to know backward and forward, some fifteen hundred for sauces alone.

I loved all of it, and my grades reflected my motivation. At the end of the first term—to my surprise and everyone else's—I stood at the top of the class. Every term after that, I consistently ranked first or second. I had never imagined that one day I would walk up to the principal's office of my college and see my name at the top of the list and hear my friends congratulating me—"All right, Zach, congrats!" I played cricket for my college, I performed brilliantly in my studies, and I longed for Monday nights. Life had taken shape for God's glory.

The program at the Institute was designed to take three years, with the idea that we would pursue a master's degree in hotel and catering. That was the goal for each of us: to place in a master's program at Cornell or in England, followed by a three-year internship at a top-tier hotel. With that visibly clear aim ahead of me, life suddenly looked hopeful. My heart was filled with the possibility that now I was going to make something out of my life. A very real career path had opened up in front of me, and I knew I would succeed in it. I had a role model in George Varghese, someone about whom I could say, "That's who I want to become." I had very high standing as a student. And, with my dad's contacts, I had every reason to believe I would one day be general manager of a large five-star hotel in India.

Along with everyone else, I wondered how such a turnaround could have taken place, and so swiftly. The key was that now I looked at life through a window of meaning. And that was the one thing I had been desperately longing for: *meaning*. Now everything in my life was packed with it: my studies had meaning, my family had meaning, my friendships had meaning, my sports had meaning.

All the things I had thought were the causes of my despair—my failing studies, my senseless wandering, my hopelessness—had actually been the *results* of my despair. The Austrian concentration camp survivor Viktor Frankl wrote, "Without meaning, nothing else matters. With meaning, everything else falls into place." If you can't see the *why*, you cannot live for the *what*. And as soon as I was able to answer the "why," even my failures began to make sense.

On weekend mornings at dawn, a buddy and I would go to the Raj Path to study for our exams. He would find one tree and I another, and we would plant ourselves underneath them for the duration of the day. We would arrive at six or seven in the morning and stay until five in the afternoon, calmed by the serene surroundings as we sat soaking up our college subjects. Early on, I would start itching to go home, but I would be too embarrassed to tell my friend, who was much more disciplined than I.

We fed ourselves with delicacies from the hawkers who came by, offering chicken kabobs, ice cream, nan bread, and certain "unpronounceables" in English. I was still pretty much at the mercy of friends when it came to spending money, but my college buddies were as wonderfully generous to me as my friends from the neighborhood had been. My friend and I ate during our breaks, watching the families come and go, picnicking or playing or renting boats to paddle across the long, shallow reflection ponds. Sometimes small bands would be playing, or a carnival would be held in the distance. As the sun made its way across the sky and morning turned to late afternoon, I was always struck by how very beautiful the place was. But even more beautiful was the change I sensed in me. I could lie on the grass and stare at the sky, with tears of joy streaming down my face. I knew the author of life!

The rapid changes taking place in me daily were beyond my power to describe. My father, especially, was astounded by the fact that I held a top ranking in my class. Yet, from everything I had learned in my life with Christ, I knew that He had not just changed what I did but what I *wanted* to do.

The love I had begun to feel within was of a depth that couldn't be spoken. It approached something like the beautiful love music in Indian culture. Love songs in India are of the deepest level, not lighthearted at all, with the words for "love" very carefully chosen. When an Indian talks about profound love, he may use the word *mohabbat*. The closest equivalent is probably the Old Testament word *yāda⸵*, when it is said that a man "knows" his wife. It is a rich word, used in the most intimate way.

That came close to my feelings about the turnaround that had taken place in my life in such a short time. I simply couldn't describe what had happened. One day, I had been a creature of despair, irresponsibility, and failure. Then I became a creature of hope, diligent and accomplished in the things to which I set my hand. To me, the reversal was staggering. Nobody fully understood the dramatic transformation on the inside. This was the work of God.

It was also a huge paradigm shift for me to suddenly see life—my own and others'—through the eyes of God. For years, I had looked at life the way a kid might work through a puzzling, new toy, taking it apart but not knowing how to put it back together again. He wonders, "What makes this thing tick?" So he takes a screwdriver and tries to unpack it, but with each piece he removes, it makes less sense.

Only Jesus could legitimately explain the multifarious strands of human personality locked within me. He could explain my emotional life, my actions, and my reactions. He could explain why I longed for human touch, and why it was actually the touch of soul that I was ultimately after. Without Christ, I still would have the gnawing undercurrent that had run through everything in my life and that had led me to the tragic choice that very nearly brought me to an end.

Jesus wasn't just the best option to me; He was the *only* option. He provided the skin of reason to the flesh and bones of reality. His answers to life's questions were both unique and true. No one else answered the deepest questions of the soul the way He did. And because Christianity was true, it was emotionally experienced. There was no greater example of this than my own life.

It was still some time before I could fully articulate the depth of change. My life had been punctuated by one failure after another, and there was a great deal of shame yet attached to that for me. The story of my early days was that only God's grace could have brought about this new life for me. This was a new DNA, a new birth. There simply was no other explanation. The songwriter George Wade Robinson said it well:

> Heav'n above is softer blue,
> Earth around is sweeter green!
> Something lives in every hue
> Christless eyes have never seen;
> Birds with gladder songs o'erflow,

Flow'rs with deeper beauties shine,
Since I know, as now I know,
I am His, and He is mine.
Since I know, as now I know,
I am His, and He is mine.

CHAPTER 10

EXTRAORDINARY MEN

THE CASUAL OUTINGS THAT YOUTH FOR CHRIST'S FRED DAVID AND JOHN Teibe planned for us were fantastic. Anything was an excuse for getting together and going out: a movie, a sporting goods store, a meal, a soft drink or snack. Fred and John were great at gathering up guys to do things that seemed natural but that also included conversations full of deep discipleship. For many of us, these lessons lasted throughout the years.

Those outings were perfect for relaxing, and whether we were nibbling on samosas or sipping cappuccinos, we talked about any issue of life that might have preoccupied us. Without fail, Fred and John brought those issues into perspective with a practical Christian theology.

Our main hangout was Connaught Place, Delhi's vast, circular outdoor shopping area near the city's center. Connaught is made up of a half-dozen or so blocks of curved buildings that face each other and form a circle, separated by streets that shoot out from the grassy central hub like spokes on a wheel. If you stand in the middle of that hub and turn slowly in a circle, you can see hundreds of shops lining the great mall, whose inner diameter measures almost a half kilometer. Each shop is owned independently, and many have doors and windows decorated with beautiful inlaid mother-of-pearl. Outside, on the sidewalks, street vendors set up their own tables or tents from which they hawk their treasures all day long. It is a vast and bustling place.

Only a block or two away from Connaught Place stands a multistory office building that houses the newspaper called the *Statesman*. It probably was during one of those Youth for Christ outings that I

learned the paper was founded by William Carey, the British missionary who landed in Calcutta in 1893. Carey developed the *Statesman*
for one purpose: to provide a voice for the common people. At the
time, some gruesome customs were still being observed in India. For
example, when a husband died and was cremated, it was customary
for his wife to throw herself into the flames and accompany him in
death. Another prevalent custom was throwing female babies into
the river. Carey was horrified by all of this and enjoined some famous
Indian reformers to help him fight the practices. Using the voice of
the *Statesman*, they were influential in curbing both these customs.

Casual lessons like this not only influenced my thinking but also
captured my imagination. As I sat in Connaught Place with my buddies, there before me, standing perhaps a dozen stories high, was the
tangible result of one Christian's commitment and determination.
The example of a historical believer's life had been brought closer to
home for us, and it fueled our own commitment.

The leaders of Youth for Christ not only gave us life lessons drawn
from the world around us; they also gave us opportunities to express
our beliefs and develop our gifts. Young men and women alike had the
chance to give their testimonies and to preach at rallies, club events,
and even in some churches, which was largely unheard of in India's
relatively formal religious culture. To no one's surprise, my buddy
Sunder's brilliance shone in this area too. Because he was such a great
student and extremely gifted at organization, he delivered strong,
well-crafted sermons. Sunder and I grew spiritually together, and our
souls were knit in numerous efforts of preaching and outreach.

Fred and John kept encouraging us in everything we did, and at
times our group's activities seemed to bustle as much as Connaught
Place. Of course, that suited me well. Several of us put together a
singing group that performed at various events, and, thanks to my
dad's influence, we secured an engagement to sing carols for Prime
Minister Nehru at his home. It took place on Christmas Eve, and
Nehru seemed sufficiently moved that he walked up to me afterward,
grasped my hand, and placed in it one hundred rupees for our group.

It was at this pinnacle of happiness in my life—succeeding in college and thriving with Youth for Christ—that I made a decision that
would affect everything. I had gone to my first YFC youth camp,
along with Sunder and both of my sisters, when Fred David gave an
illustration I would never forget:

A wealthy man walked into a village one day seeking to buy up all the homes. One by one, the villagers sold their houses to this man for a good price, except for a poor fellow who lived in the middle of the town. He simply wasn't willing to part with his home. The wealthy man offered a generous amount, but the poor man still wouldn't budge. Even when the price was doubled, the man said no.

Finally the rich man said, "Name your price. I'll give you whatever you want, because then I'll own the whole village."

"I don't want to sell to you," the poor man said. "I'm happy where I am, and this is where I want to stay." He continued to stand his ground, much to the wealthy man's disenchantment.

A few days passed and the rich man was seen strolling through town with his friends, showing them the village. When the poor man heard about it, he stopped one of the wealthy man's friends and took him aside. "Is this man telling you he owns the whole village?" he asked. "Don't believe him! The ground you're standing on still belongs to me."

Fred explained his story: "I believe the enemy of our souls must taunt God the way this poor man taunted the rich one. You see, if there is any part of our lives that we haven't turned over to Christ, the devil reminds him, 'No, that one *isn't* totally yours. I still have this patch of ground here.'

"Jesus is totally committed to us. And until we learn to be totally surrendered to him, we'll never find the joy of what it means to fully belong to him. That is the key to every believer's life—full ownership by Christ. Everything we are and want to be belong to him.

"The Lord wants to have *ownership* of your life. If there is anything hindering this from happening, I invite you to come forward now and lay it before Christ."

The words burned in me. I walked forward that night, as did Sunder and a few other close friends, and my face was literally on the altar as I prayed, "Lord, if there is anything in my life that you do not have possession of, I want you to take it. Whatever it is I have held back, I want to be totally yours."

I made my full commitment to Christ that night. Little did I know that, within two years, that commitment would have me heading somewhere I never would have imagined.

Around this time, our family started going to another church. I had passed by Centenary Methodist Church every day on my bike route to school and was always struck by the sign placed on the property outside. It read, "Trespassers Will Be Forgiven." Everywhere else in the city, the trespass signs read, "Trespassers Will Be Prosecuted" and "Trespassers Will Be Arrested." The simple difference in this sign had always struck me as profound.

Once my family started going to Centenary Methodist, we all became involved right away. I joined the youth group, my father sang in the choir, and my parents even joined the church. I had never been confirmed in the Cathedral Church of the Redemption, but at Centenary I was. It happened on an Easter Sunday, and I wore a white shirt and white trousers for the ceremony.

Why the switch in churches? There was a very significant ministry in India at that time which had begun to reach my dad—an outreach to executives called "International Christian Leadership," led by Cliff and Betty Robinson. My father had started going with the Robinsons to a weekly Bible study, and somehow Cliff was getting through to him, as was John Teibe from YFC. Once my father began to grapple with the issues of the gospel, he decided that we should go to Centenary Methodist.

The new pastor who came to Centenary soon after our arrival was Ernest Fritschle, an American and an evangelical. Not only was my deep hunger fed by Rev. Fritschle's preaching, but I also began to see more of Christianity's mission and purpose at Centenary. On one occasion, my father had a severe asthma attack. I will never forget seeing this pastor come into our house, weighed down by a big oxygen cylinder on his shoulder. He hooked it up to help my father breathe. He was a servant to his congregation, and by the look in my dad's eyes I could tell the process of God's breaking through to him was beginning.

I have some fond memories from that church. A weeklong campaign was held outdoors on the church property, led by Ian North, the evangelist for Ambassadors for Christ and a powerful preacher. As I sat on the lawn and listened to him night after night, I thought, "This is life as I never imagined it."

Sunday after Sunday, I could hardly wait to get to church. I even gave up my Sunday cricket matches with the college team so I could go. In fact, cricket's tug on me gradually faded, apart from reading the scores every now and then. Church had become that important to me.

One Sunday, as I walked in for the evening service, I saw a distinguished-looking black gentleman sitting on the front row. He looked familiar, so when the service ended I decided to approach him.

"Very nice to have you here, sir," I said.

"Very happy to be here," he answered.

"What brings you to our church?"

"I'm in town playing for the West Indies cricket team," he said.

That's when I recognized him. It was Conrad Hunte—one of the finest and most elegant batsmen in the world. Conrad Cleophas Hunte, *opening batsman for the West Indies*! As we shook hands, I didn't want to let go. It was as if the Lord were saying to me, "Here's one of the world's best cricketers, but his life is what it is because of what he has in his heart, and now you have the same." I was completely at peace, relinquishing a small dream for a greater reality.

IN MAY OF 1965, WHEN I WAS NINETEEN, YFC HELD ITS YOUTH CONGRESS in Hyderabad, historically a predominantly Muslim city, with Christian young people gathering from all across India and Asia. Although my parents couldn't afford to send me, I was able to go because of the generosity of Fred and John, who raised the money for several of us with an appeal to sponsors from overseas.

We'd heard about the preaching contest that took place each year at the Youth Congress. It was the highlight of the week, with one teenager from each delegation representing his or her group. Sunder was the obvious choice to preach for our Delhi crew, and I was taken along to lead the cheers. But, oddly, when the time came, Sunder wasn't able to go because of a conflict with his studies.

"Ravi," said Fred, "that means you're up."

"What?"

"You've got to preach. It's the least you can do after all I've done for you. India can't be the host country and have no representative from Delhi, the capital. You've *got* to do it."

"Well, what do they want? I can't just stand up and say anything I please?"

"It doesn't matter. Just preach something from the Bible that has gripped your life."

"OK, OK. But when?"

"About three hours from now. Hurry; go and get something prepared. And I'll be praying for you!"

Somewhat confused, I rushed back to my room and put my pen to paper in that hot, sparsely furnished school dorm. Sweating profusely as I wrote on a piece of paper, I muttered to myself, *"How* did I get into this embarrassing situation?"

At the appointed time, folding that paper into my Bible and putting on a neatly pressed white shirt and trousers to match, I hurried over to the tent where the contest was soon to take place. As I arrived, I saw the rest of the contestants in different stages of preparation. I went directly to the front table, where I was handed a brand-new Bible and concordance. "What's this for?" I asked.

"The rules are, you can't use your own Bible," I was told.

"OK, then let me at least take my notes out of my Bible."

"No, you can't do that. We give you the topic. Then you have thirty minutes to prepare and ten minutes to preach."

"You're kidding me!" I gasped.

"No. Those are the rules, and you'd better hurry or you won't have the time you need."

There were two hats containing prewritten topics. I dipped into one and opened it. It read, "Elijah."

"What's this?" I asked.

"You have selected the Old Testament character Elijah. Now go and prepare a talk on him."

I was on the verge of tears. "I don't know a thing about who this man is." My voice faltered as I spoke.

"Then pick from the other hat. You are given a choice of a character or a theme."

I dipped into the hat. "The Love of God," it read. I breathed a sigh of relief, for it had been the story of my life. The love of God pursuing a derelict, lost young man!

"You have thirty minutes to prepare your sermon."

I just put my head down and starting writing without looking up. After twenty-five minutes, I felt that what I'd written was pretty close to what I wanted to say. I hurried back to the tent, where all of the contestants were being introduced.

There was quite a buzz in the audience, and I recognized most of the judges as they took their seats on the panel. One was Jay Kesler, who later became president of Youth for Christ. There was also Don Ingram, the YFC director for Detroit, and Sam Kamaleson, who was probably the best-known Indian Christian at that time. Sam was a great singer who had a deep baritone voice, a powerful preacher of international fame, and pastor of the Emmanuel Methodist church in Madras.

Sitting next to them were others I recognized because they were the speakers for the week. The whole thing was nerve-racking.

I would be almost the last one to preach. One by one, young people stood and delivered their messages, each putting his or her own convictions and style on the theme. Some were stirring, but one girl in particular stood out. It was clear to everyone that she was the frontrunner. Finally my turn came.

Nervous, but excited as well, I stood up and began my message. At first I could hear myself talking rapidly, spitting out my words at a breakneck pace. But once I calmed a bit, the sermon seemed effortless. The thoughts I had scrambled to write down only minutes before came to me easily, so much so that the time allotment flew by.

Once I finished, my buddies gathered around, wide-eyed: "Ravi, we're proud of you." "That was a moving sermon." "God's hand was on you." Fred David was like a bigger brother with his arm around me: "The Lord had a purpose in this man! Thanks for your courage. God will honor you." I didn't know enough to be hopeful. The only thing I knew for sure was the peace I'd had as I preached.

Three days later came the announcement. "We have a winner," the judges declared, and the tent grew quiet. Everyone expected the girl to win, and I was so used to losing in my earlier days that it was no big deal to me now to hear some other name announced. And so the verdict came: They announced a young woman's name, and the place erupted with applause. I stood on my chair and cheered with the Indian flag, because she was from India.

But the head judge raised his hand to ask for silence. As the cheering died down, another announcement came: "Actually, we have a tie—there is a tie. We have another winner."

You could have heard a pin drop in that tent. Then—

"It is Ravi Zacharias."

My buddies went crazy. I was numb—utterly numb—and overcome with emotion. "I cannot believe what I am hearing," I whispered to myself.

I found out about the judging years later. The panel had been ready to give the prize to the girl when Sam Kamalesan spoke up. "I think," he suggested to the others, "we are seeing a young man today whom God has put his hand on. Yes, it's a tough call, and they are both outstanding young people. Let us make them equal winners and have them preach again."

This time the subject given to me was "the cross of Jesus Christ." I could not have asked for a more appropriate theme. This was no longer a competition to me; it was the proclamation of the most important message on the face of the earth—the message that in Jesus we have the offer of forgiveness, and the payment of the ultimate price for our lives to be restored to God.

At the end of that sermon, young people streamed forward to make their own commitments. Yes, they awarded me the prize—but it had lost its accolade in the light of the greater message that we could all be winners in Jesus if we received him into our lives by faith and with sincerity. And, yes, I would have been just as much at peace if the young woman had received the prize. With grace and generosity, she came and congratulated me.

As I look back, I don't know how Sam Kamalesan might have discerned my calling, or how the others might have been influenced by his insight. But their decision that day was a huge turning point in my life, the significance of which none of them—nor I—could have known.

Back home in Delhi, Sunder learned of what had happened. Ever since, he has joked, "I did you a great favor by not showing up." He did, but of course it was God's move, not ours. I had been the first one to be disappointed when we learned Sunder couldn't preach that day. Yet in a profound way, my best friend gave me the greatest opportunity I ever had. Had he not been prevented from coming to Hyderabad, I never would have preached, much less been considered for a prize.

THAT SAME YEAR, AN AMERICAN TEEN PREACHING TEAM CAME TO INDIA, led by a man named Jim Groen, who eventually would become director of YFC International. My buddies and I were so touched as we listened to those young Americans preach that we were inspired to do something similar.

"We need something like this in India," I told Fred David. "And it should come *from within* India. Young people from here need to be ministering to the young people here. I'd love to set up an Indian teen preaching team."

"Great idea," Fred agreed. But there was the question of funds. How could we raise the money?

Once again, I pulled a chair up to Fred's beat-up typewriter and wrote to everyone I could think of: missionaries, YFC workers who had once worked in India, American and English people whom I knew, Indian businesspeople who loved the Youth for Christ ministry.

Within a couple of weeks, the first gift came in—from a man named Brian Reeves in London. He sent ten pounds, giving us about 1/25th of what we needed. Other gifts soon followed: ten dollars, fifteen dollars, twenty dollars. When the time came for our first trip in December of 1965, my letter had raised the entire budget for our team, with nothing to spare.

We called ourselves the "First Indian Teen Team." Fred was going to lead the group, which included Sunder and me, who would do the preaching, and my two sisters (Sham and Prem), who would do the singing, accompanied by Fred and Sunder on accordions, my soft whistling in the background, and Kenny Gnanakan on the guitar. Kenny had volunteered to go with us to provide music on his guitar, although he said he didn't know any Christian songs. When we probed further, we discovered he *did* know the old Christian folk song "Michael, Row Your Boat Ashore," so he decided to play it wherever we went.

There was still an obstacle I had to overcome before going, and it was a big one. I had to get time off from classes at the Institute of Hotel Management. That was unheard of, even without considering the purpose for my request.

The principal of the Institute was an Englishman, Mr. Alex Simms, who at one time had been the manager of the Savoy Hotel in London. I knew he had a nasty reputation, but I was determined to be absolutely straightforward with him when I went to his office to request the days off.

"Mr. Simms," I said, "I have a dream that's coming true. I'm going to be a preacher on a team of five." I told him the four cities where we planned to go and the sorts of speaking engagements we were going to have. Then I made my plea: "I need a week off from classes."

My words were met with stony silence.

"Sir, if I had a letter from you," I continued, "I know that all my teachers would agree to give me the time off. I promise to make up all of the work. In fact, I would ask you to request the assignments from my professors."

Mr. Simms leaned back in his chair.

"Zacharias"—he always addressed students by their last name—"I've always been proud of you as a student here, with your honored accomplishments academically and your brilliance with the cricket team and all of that. I will grant you permission," he said, "but I will hold you to everything you say you're going to do. And if you don't do it, you're going to answer to me."

I could barely believe what I'd just heard. *It's going to happen!* As I walked out of Mr. Simms' office, I could have jumped and clicked my heels in midair.

It was no secret to my teachers and classmates why I was taking the time off from school. Yet they all celebrated with me. Even my Hindu buddies were happy for me, shouting, "Good luck, Zach. Have a great week!"

We did it all on a shoestring budget, traveling across the country on trains by third class (which was the lowest class). We hit four cities by train—Delhi, Calcutta, Hyderabad, and Madras—staying in people's homes and eating whatever they served. Sunder and I traded off preaching at the various events, deciding whose turn it would be according to whose style best suited the audience.

One of my first sermons was in Madras at Emmanuel Methodist Church. Sitting in the audience that day was Sam Kamalesan, the senior pastor who had graciously invited the team to host the service and me to preach. His presence did not make it easy. But we had a great service, and Sam became one of my true heroes.

Yet even more challenging would be my next engagement—to preach at Madras Christian College. In the school's eyes, I had credentials because of my family's history there, but our team had been warned that it was going to be one tough crowd. I sensed it even before

I stepped behind the pulpit. As I began speaking, a slow handclap was started by some, trying to silence me. I decided to just keep going. Soon the clapping died down, and I got the feeling that people were actually listening to me. It turned out I was right: when I gave the invitation at the end, the response was overwhelming—nearly one hundred in that audience of just over two hundred people responded to the invitation to turn their lives over to Christ.

It was an amazing ten-day trip, with Sunder and me preaching and Kenny and my sisters drawing in crowds with their music. And when it was over, hundreds of people had committed their lives to Christ. I realized I had preached twenty-nine times, from only five sermons I had written out to bring along.

Coming home on the train, however, I was struck by a strange feeling. I realized that during the trip, what I had to say was what people had wanted to listen to. Our team and our message had actually attracted crowds—and I found that unnerving. Through it all, I wasn't sure of myself, but I was very sure of my message.

The sensation wasn't so much a matter of ego but the fact that it was simply incredibly and unnervingly new to me—going from being nothing, a nobody, to being listened to by so many in different walks of life. Yet I couldn't quite be sure what was happening both in me and through me. I knew who I was in Christ because of my conversion, but in terms of my preaching, I was completely in the dark. It was all too new and too beautiful to fully absorb.

WE ALL WERE SADDENED WHEN JOHN TEIBE ANNOUNCED THAT HE AND Anne were moving back to Canada. The Teibes had spent nine years in India as missionaries with Youth for Christ. Now, John said, it was time for them to go back home.

On his last day in India, John took me to dinner. As I look back on it now, I think about all the things he had to take care of before departing, all the things that must have been running through his mind. But none of that ever came across in his time with me that evening. He took me to one of Delhi's favorite restaurants, Moti Mahal, famous for its tandoori chicken. And at one point, between bites of the three chickens we devoured (Indian chickens are small!), John said something curious to me: "I want you to know, your life is going to go one of two ways."

This took me somewhat aback.

"I believe that you either will make a very profound impact with your life and God will use you mightily," he said, "or you will be a colossal wreck."

It was a sobering thought—and quite an astonishing thing for someone to tell a teenager. But I know now exactly what John was saying. He was nervous because he couldn't see a place for me to continue to grow beyond my formative years at YFC. He knew that it wasn't the church so much that had spawned my growth as it was the Youth for Christ environment. John had seen all of us grow up fast in two years' time, but now, as we faced another stage of life, he wouldn't be around to guide us.

Most churches simply didn't give young people the kinds of opportunities we had been handed. First of all, it wasn't customary to allow teenagers to deliver sermons. Those opportunities came to us for one reason—the extraordinary men who led Youth for Christ. YFC had offered me a sequence of opportunities that were absolutely key at that crucial point in my life: Bible studies, youth rallies, camp, Youth Congress, and chances to share my faith. If it weren't for YFC and the men of giant character who devoted themselves to our growth, my friends and I would not have been rescued. Fred David and John Teibe invested in us everything they had.

After the humiliation of my suicide attempt, no one had ever sat down with me and said, "You've got something going for you. Can I help you reach it?" Fred and John were the first ones to help me see my way in the light. My mother had always supported me through everything—loving me, embracing me, and looking after me. But these men added the words to her touch. They saw something in me, and they not only encouraged it; they worked hard to see it come to fruition.

Much has come from their labors in Delhi in that short time. After being trained by John Teibe, Victor Manogaram, an Indian national, the humble man who was instrumental in Sunder's conversion, eventually became director of Youth for Christ in Asia. Kenny Gnanakan, the incredible musician, went on to study theology in Australia. He and I remain friends, and today Ken is the director of International

Needs, an important work that trains Christians for careers in trades, farming, and other vocations. Sunder has become the pastor of a large church in Toronto, Canada.

In later years, John Teibe and I have often talked about the brief time we had together in Delhi. All in all, it was only two years, and he marvels now at what the Lord did in so short a span. "I wouldn't know what to do to regain that kind of impact for Youth for Christ," he says. We agree it will take someone who can cross both cultures—East and West—to capture the minds and imaginations of Eastern young people.

SATURDAYS AT THE COLLEGE WERE WHEN WE DID ALL OUR BAKING, AND ON this particular day our class had baked some fresh dinner rolls and topped them off with a sweet buttery glaze. I also had made some tomato soup from a recipe I devised, and that afternoon I went by the kitchen to pick up some of the goods. I was taking them home to my family.

It was a beautiful day, and I spent the wonderful half-hour bike ride home navigating the weekend traffic. As I pulled up to the front gate of our home, my parents were out in the front yard. They were delighted as I held up the bag of food, and they came over to the gate where I stood, my mother calling for the cook to come and take the food inside and to serve the fresh rolls with tea.

We talked for the longest time as I leaned against my bike and they sat on the lawn furniture. We bit into the rolls I had made, fresh from the oven and enhanced with a touch of butter and homemade jam, and sipped on the tea as we enjoyed the glorious spring weather and the jasmine flowers in the background. We chatted as parents and son, indeed, as friends. I remember that day as one of immense delight in my heart, as I marveled at the deep pleasure of being right with all around me, chatting so casually and openly with both my mother and father. I had never dreamed of the day I would be in this setting, where both my parents were proud of everything that was happening in my life. I will never forget the look of utter fulfillment on their faces.

I think my father knew I had found my niche. Yet I would tell you the smile on that tough man's face wasn't just from a sense of satisfaction over my career path. He was reveling at the change he had seen in my life. It was a true change.

I know my dad could not have envisioned anything greater. And I believe such times were crucial in moving him forward on his own journey—although he would have one more major hurdle to cross in the years ahead.

PART 2

EAST TO WEST

CHAPTER 11

THE GIRL IN THE CHURCH

As excited as I was about my prospects in hotel management, just before I jumped in with both feet I found myself being tugged at the heart toward military service. India was at war with Pakistan, and a deep sense of duty had begun to emerge in me. A college buddy had also talked about joining the military, and we realized we shared a desire to become pilots in India's Air Force.

So with the blessing of our families, my buddy and I traveled all the way to Dehradun in the foothills of the Himalayas, where we would be tested and interviewed with several hundred other applicants. Only a top handful would be accepted. After a full battery of mental, physical, and endurance tests, I was overjoyed to learn that, out of the few hundred competing, I had placed third and my buddy fourth. The officers in charge seemed impressed, knowing I had good physical endurance because of all the sports I played.

That night, I called home excitedly, "I'm going to make it. All that's left is the interview with the senior officer tomorrow."

For the first time, I could tell by my dad's tone that he was proud. I was told there would be a big celebration party for me when I arrived home.

The next morning, I sat confidently in front of the senior officer — a gruff, heavyset man — ready for anything. After many questions about my values and my hopes and dreams, he startled me with a direct statement.

"Son, I'm rejecting you," he said abruptly.

"Huh?" I thought, dumbstruck.

"You're being turned down by the Air Force," he repeated.

139

I was stunned into silence. I had a hard time believing this. Before I could ask why, he explained. "This job is about killing, and psychologically you are unfit to kill."

What could I say to that? It hit me hard. He must have seen tears welling up in my eyes, because he said, "I'm doing you a favor, young man. Believe it."

When I stepped off the train in Delhi, a crowd of family and friends was waiting for me with garlands. Talk about a low point—it was absolutely humiliating! I struggled with it; but deep inside, my concern was for a reason other than another failure. I wondered, "Is this God stopping my steps?"

I pondered much on this for the next few days. Finally someone suggested I go and talk to a visiting missionary who was staying at the YWCA, a man named Russell Self from Canada. I gathered myself to go and see him, and I ended up pouring out my heart to him over my disappointment.

Mr. Self sat listening and nodding his head, and I thought, "He must be thinking, 'This kid is just taking up my time.'" Instead, he responded with sage counsel.

"We can be so sure of ourselves at times," he said, "that we don't know there are some doors we shouldn't be entering. God not only opens doors; he shuts them too. Sometimes very painfully."

"This has to be one of those times," I thought. But knowing that didn't lessen my pain.

"What we often miss," Mr. Self added, "is that some of those shut doors reveal the most important clues as to where God wants us to go."

What was the clue for me here?

"Remember this, from Psalm 37," he said. "'The steps of a good man are ordered by the LORD: and he delighteth in his way.' God has it all in his order, Ravi. I believe that's what you're to know from this." Then he opened his Bible, leaned forward, and read: "Commit thy way unto the LORD; Trust also in him; and he shall bring it to pass."

"Where are you reading from?" I asked.

"Psalm 37:5," he replied.

That was all I needed. The Word of God is so pointed, so reassuring, so comforting in our time of need, and so full of warnings when we flirt with the sin of our selfish desires. This was something so new to me—to hear words of such deep penetration into the soul.

I knew he was right. As I left the Y, I thought about the Air Force officer who had rejected me, and I realized he had been right too. Not only was I psychologically unfit to kill; deep down I knew I didn't have what it took to be a pilot. The young men flying in India's Air Force were doing all kinds of daring things in planes—things that simply were not within me to do. On my little bicycle, yes—but in the air, I don't think so! "Yes, God," I whispered as I walked out the door of the Y that day, "only *You* know the direction my steps are to go. I will trust You with them."

My buddy, who had completed his interview after I had completed mine, had thrown up his hands in triumph, certain, as I had been, that we would fly together in India's Air Force. Yet only he was selected for the National Defense Academy. Five years later, I would be heartbroken to learn he was killed when his plane went down in the Himalayas. That news sadly brought back so many memories of my friend—and it reaffirmed to me that God ordered my steps and that our times are in His hands.

As my father got closer to retirement (which comes at age fifty-five in India), he began to think more about career prospects for his children. He was still moving in powerful circles, and he must have wondered aloud about our futures while he mixed with people like Roland Michener, who was then the Canadian ambassador to India. One day Ambassador Michener suggested to him, "Why don't you consider moving your children to Canada?"

My dad must have been taken aback at that thought. It would be a profound move for our family. Yet again, it might be a good one.

"If you decide to do it," the ambassador said, "I will clear the way for you."

When my father brought this up with the family, we were astounded at the thought of such a move, yet somewhat excited too. As Dad explained his reasoning, I felt the sheer excitement of the possibility. Going to Canada? I would be that much closer to my dream of going to Cornell University. I could finish my hotel management studies there, get a general manager's job in a large hotel, and simply do what I wanted to do.

"I've put in the application," my father said. He hesitated for a moment, then spoke his concern. "Only we don't have the money to go."

I blurted out the first thought that came to my mind. "Dad, we can pray," I said. "The Lord can make it happen if He orders it. Why give up?"

I didn't usually speak that forthrightly in my father's presence, much less to his face. But I was emerging out of a shell, and I felt the daring of the moment, the daring of faith. "Why not have courage?" I thought. "If going to Canada is what the Lord wants for our family, we'll be able to go."

My father was still a year away from his official retirement at the time, so he couldn't make the move immediately. But he could send Ajit and me ahead to sort of scout out the land, with the idea of moving the rest of the family later.

"What would you two think of going to Canada ahead of time?" he asked my brother and me.

We were only too willing to go, for the family's sake. The question became, where in Canada should we go?

Ajit and I knew that John Teibe was from Calgary, so we decided that's where we would move. Then we talked to a friend, and she chuckled. "Why would you go to Calgary?" she said. "It's more agrarian. You should be heading to Toronto. It's much more cosmopolitan."

Just like that, my brother and I decided, "OK, we'll go to Toronto." At the time, that's how most of our decisions were made.

A few weeks before we were to leave, my father received some news from the Indian Airlines Corporation. He was informed that because of his government service over the years, he and his family were entitled to fly anywhere in the world that Air India flew, first class and free of charge. I just about hit the ceiling as I leaped into the air.

What a huge encouragement that was for our family! All of us would be able to make that major part of the move for free. Of course, more pertinently in my mind was that it was an answer to our family's prayer.

In May of 1966, on the day Ajit and I were to leave, the temperature in Delhi was 120 degrees. And, of course, there was no air-conditioning in our car as we rushed around trying to take care of everything before leaving; we could barely touch the steering wheel or, for that matter, sit on those plastic seats. When we finally were ready, we boarded the airplane, which was bound first for London before going on to New York and then to Toronto. To our great pleasure, we were escorted to the first-class section, where we were seated behind Mr. J. R. D. Tata, the principal owner of the Tata conglomerate and the chairman of Air India. That in itself was a thrill.

Five days and three international flights later, after a brief stop in London to see relatives, Ajit and I flopped, exhausted, onto our beds in a Toronto rooming house that a friend had secured for us at the cost of eight dollars a week each. But our arrival had not been without incident. As our plane had taken off from London for Toronto, Ajit grabbed my arm and gasped, "The plane is on fire!" Sure enough, as I looked out the windows I saw that one of the engines had flames coming from it. The pilot made a dramatic turnaround, and several minutes later, after what seemed like an eternity, we descended to safety with a heavy thud. The automatic extinguishers worked, and we breathed a sigh of relief, but you could imagine our thoughts at that time. The next day's newspapers read, "Plane ablaze circles London"—somewhat of an exaggeration, but no doubt capturing the risk for which my brother and I had volunteered.

Because of the foreign exchange restrictions established by the Indian government, we were allowed to bring from India only fifty dollars each, with a little over four hundred dollars to follow a month later. This amount in rupees was three times our dad's monthly salary, and we knew he'd gone out on a limb to get it for us—in fact, he had probably borrowed it. So we knew we had to be careful to conserve it all. It had to last us until we had found jobs and received our first paychecks. Starting with only fifty dollars each—with eight dollars each paid out for our room rent, and eight dollars each for a deposit—we were left in a rather precarious state in a foreign land, praying by the hour that we would soon land a job.

During those first few weeks, my brother and I could hardly wait until noon each day when we would buy our big meal of the day. We would walk over to the supermarket—called "Dominion"—and buy a hot dog for twenty-two cents. On some mornings, when we couldn't stand going without something to eat, we allowed ourselves some cornflakes at a greasy-spoon place. But essentially, we couldn't eat very much until we got jobs.

Early on that first morning after our arrival, I phoned the Youth for Christ office in Toronto and told them about our situation. "We came to Christ through Youth for Christ in Delhi," I explained. "Do you know anyone who might be able to show us around the city?"

The next day, one of the YFC leaders came by and picked us up. We must have unsettled him with all our rapid-fire questions, my first one being, "Is there an evangelical church nearby?" I had had only a brief experience in the church that was fully evangelical back home, Centenary Methodist, and I was anxious to go to one. As he drove along, he pointed out a Christian and Missionary Alliance (C&MA) church just a few blocks away from our rooming house. The sign outside read, "The Alliance Tabernacle."

"It's Wednesday," he said. "They'll be having their midweek prayer meeting tonight."

He took us to the parsonage to meet the minister, who wasn't home at the time, but his wife invited us to the service that night. Excitedly, Ajit and I went that evening—the formal name of the church, we learned, was "Yonge Street Alliance Tabernacle"—and we sat in the front row, even though we could barely hold up our heads from being jet-lagged. We went back the following Sunday, and after the evening service the pastor and his wife, Ray and Anita Deitz, invited us back to their house for a small bite to eat. I remember that night for two reasons: first, how gracious they were to have invited us; and second, how tired we were from jet lag, barely able to keep our eyes open while we waited for the food.

The following Sunday, the church was beginning its annual missions conference, and we were excited to attend it. To our astonishment, the main speaker was a missionary to India, a man named Edgar Llewellyn. He must have been just as startled when he saw us sitting there, two young Indians, in a Canadian C&MA church. It couldn't have been a common sight in the 1960s; in fact, in the whole of Toronto—now declared by the United Nations to be the most multicultural city in the world—there were only five hundred Indians at the time. Today there are five hundred thousand.

After that service, a retired colonel in the Canadian Army and his wife invited us to their home for Sunday dinner, so we climbed into the backseat of their Lincoln Continental. My brother and I felt as if we were sitting in a living room on wheels. As we pulled onto the street, the window next to my brother suddenly began to roll down—by itself! We stared at each other, each blaming the other with a glare that said, "What are you doing?" Of course, it was the colonel, using his electronic panel to give us some fresh air. We were being introduced to the electronic way of living, and I have to say, on that night, half asleep, we were relieved to be in our beds.

Yonge Street Alliance Tabernacle was not a large church. Although it seated about four hundred people, the average Sunday morning attendance was about three hundred. To Ajit and me, it was a fantastic church to be part of, with good preaching, good music, and a good group for the young people. During those first few months, some wonderful families were gracious hosts to us, feeding us and shuttling us around to see various parts of Toronto. I was fascinated the first time I saw an escalator in a shopping mall, certain that if I tried to board it I would miss my footing and have to be carried out. One couple who had been to India and had actually met my dad some years before took us on a memorable day-trip to the majestic Niagara Falls.

There were a few downsides to our initiation into the congregation, as you might expect with any immigrant experience. My brother and I were often introduced as "natives from India," which in our minds conjured up images of thatched huts, grass skirts, and spears in hand. It also began to grate on my brother that he was introduced as "Ah-ssszheet." "It's Ah*Jeet*, with the accent on the second syllable," he would think, "just the way it's spelled." I also got quite frustrated because my English was difficult for some people to understand. I spoke very rapidly, with a strong Indian accent, so I had to force myself to slow down and enunciate every syllable. But that's where my beloved English authors helped me. I found that C. S. Lewis was handy for much more than practical theology; as I read more of his works, my concentration on his command of language began to improve my fledgling efforts.

Still, we had some very tough days in Toronto at first, and sometimes I cried, wanting to go home. To this, my brother would just mutter, "Grow up!" At one point I actually went to the India tourist office attached to the Indian consulate to ask them how much it would cost to go back. The man I spoke with graciously sat me down and told me that everyone expects things to be a utopia when they first come. "It is lonely in the beginning," he said. "Stick it out, and you will find this will become a wonderful place to call home."

He was right—and sooner than I expected. Within a week of our arrival, Ajit secured a job at IBM. And when I went to an interview at the Inn on the Park, the manager who sat down with me was so thrilled with my qualifications and knowledge about the food industry that he wanted to hire me right away for their banqueting department. Then he saw my age on the application. "You're not even twenty-one," he said, astounded. "You can't work in a licensed dining room!"

Eventually I was hired as an assistant to the banqueting manager at the Westbury Hotel, a landmark hotel in downtown Toronto, just around the corner from Maple Leaf Gardens, where the Toronto Maple Leafs played hockey. My shift at the Westbury began at 6:00 p.m. and ended at 3:00 a.m., and although I loved the job, it was exhausting. My hard work, however, quickly earned my boss's trust. The Westbury had seven dining rooms, and almost every night I was helping run banquets that served a thousand to fifteen hundred people. The banquets ended around midnight, and afterward I had to take inventory, tally up everything that was sold or left, lay the groundwork for the next day's banquets, have a late dinner in the kitchen with the chef, and finally catch the subway to go home. Sometimes I left so late that the subways weren't running, so I had to take a bus, which was especially hard during the winter.

After a while, I realized that the prospect of going to Cornell was becoming cost prohibitive. So I trained my sights on a fine hotel management institute in Toronto called Ryerson, and I enrolled with less than a year's worth of work left to earn the degree I'd started in Delhi. Later, when my boss at the Westbury heard about my studies, he suggested, "Why finish the rest of the year at school? Just do your practicum here. We'll train you, and in eighteen months you'll be a banqueting manager." I would gladly take him up on his offer.

One of the highlights of my job at the top-tier Westbury was working alongside its nationally famous chef Tony Rolden. Tony was a very fine Spanish gentleman in his forties, a straight-up fellow who had served in World War II, and we had a great relationship from the very beginning. Tony really knew how to serve great food, and due in part to his reputation, the players for the Maple Leafs and some visiting NHL teams came to the Westbury after their games to enjoy his fabulous roast beef dinners.

Every night, after the banqueting work was over, Tony made a meal for both of us. He had a great culinary touch. All food, according to him, had to be delicately spiced, retaining the freshness of the food's taste. For me, spices were made to find delectable combinations. So every meal involved an exchange of ideas and knowledge between us. Sometimes the managing director of the Westbury, Mr. Stanway, joined us, but on most nights it was just Tony and me. Once we had firmly established our working relationship, Tony said he loved working with me and that he counted on my theoretical knowledge of planning, menu compiling, cost management, and so forth.

"You know, Ravi," he said one night, "you have one thing I don't have. You're an educated man. I know as much of the kitchen world as I possibly could at my age—really, everything there is to know. But I'm not educated. I want to make a proposal to you."

"What's that?"

"Let's go into business together."

Tony wanted to start a restaurant—a great one. By this time, he had become the best-known chef in Toronto—indeed, one of the best in Canada—and he had the money to finance a start-up. He was ready to go out on his own, and he was asking me to do it with him.

"You be the brains behind it," he offered. "I'll be the hands."

Here was yet another dream of mine coming true—and in a rather astonishing way. In just a few months' time, I was being asked to partner in a business with one of the nation's top chefs. It sounded like a great career move to me, with great appeal on many levels. So, night after night, Tony and I sat down over that late meal and talked things through.

"If you really want to make it," I told Tony, "it's got to be distinctive. And that has to come in the areas of soups, sauces, breads, and desserts. You've got to come up with the best in these main four areas. You can have superb quality in the main courses, but only if you've got top-notch soups, sauces, breads, and desserts will you keep them coming in."

Soon we were drawing up a floor plan, featuring an open area near the entryway where a large soup tureen would be visible, with steaming signature soups aromatically seasoning the air. For months we planned and schemed, every night advancing the plot further than before. Once again, my future seemed to be coming into a much clearer view.

Yet, one of the downsides of the hospitality industry is that your time is not your own. You work long hours, and your most intense times are during other people's holidays and celebrations, such as Christmas and New Year's. I never forget that whenever I'm in a hotel. Whether I'm there only for a meal or for an overnight stay, I'm always conscious that my ability to relax is because someone else is working.

During one stretch in a holiday season while at the Westbury, I hadn't been able to go to a Sunday church service for several weeks because of my work schedule. Any time I did have off, I used to take a bus to Fort Wayne, Indiana, to visit Fred David, who had moved there with his family to go to a Bible college.

In the midst of that rough period for me, the area youth committee for the Christian and Missionary Alliance planned a weekend "Youth Symposium," and, having learned of my preaching prize at the Asian Youth Congress, they asked me to speak at it. After the service at which I preached, my brother and I were walking out of the church when a girl stopped us.

"Ajit, I'm offended," she jested. "You haven't introduced me to your brother."

That's when I saw Margie Reynolds (Margie pronounced with a hard *g*) for the first time. She extended her hand and our eyes met, and I thought, "What a sweet face. And such a lovely girl!" It was a moment that would carve itself into my memory. On that day we met, everything changed, which is hard to describe when you have never felt that way before.

I knew right away that there was much more to this girl than just her lovely appearance. Margie was sharp, and the better I got to know her, the more things I loved about her. She was a remarkable conversationalist—very well-read, intelligent, solidly informed, and able to talk about virtually any subject. She especially loved history and had read book after book on all kinds of historical subjects.

And it was so easy to be myself with her. I found I could talk to Margie about anything—from history, to fun things, to theological doctrines. I could laugh with her, crack jokes, or be serious. The only things this girl knew absolutely nothing about, I discovered, were movies and modern music. She had never heard Elvis Presley sing or even heard of Jim Reeves, my favorite country musician. No, she didn't even own a record. Her family was mind-bogglingly strict on those matters. But I learned that for every book I had read, Margie had read a dozen more.

To my amazement, I found out that this bright, attractive young woman had never dated anyone. Her mother had encouraged her to go out with certain young men from the church in group situations, but Margie was never interested. And it would be another two years before she and I were officially allowed to date.

Though we were immediately interested in each other, Margie's parents weren't for it. First of all, she was sixteen, while I was twenty. And second, why would the Reynoldses let their daughter date a stranger from another culture and background who worked in the hotel industry, of all things, where your time was not your own?

Margie tried her best to get their permission for us to see each other, but her parents just wouldn't allow it. So we settled for seeing each other at church. Yet this soon became for us less a capitulation than a strategy. I did everything I could to be there, no matter what the event, just to chat with her. And we made the most of every occasion, from worship services to prayer meetings to youth gatherings—and especially youth group outings.

There is an old Puritan sermon titled "The Expulsive Power of a New Affection." It's an odd-sounding title, but its central message is that when you have a new love, it expels all old loves. With Margie, I gained a new appreciation of how a new love expels all other lesser ones. After we met, neither of us had any interest in going out with anyone else. Yes, I may as well use the words: I was smitten! What's more, that condition has remained in me to this day.

Margie and I had absolutely no doubt in our hearts that we loved each other, but there was the continuing issue of her parents' feelings. And then, of course, there was my future. Did I truly want to make the demanding hospitality industry my life's calling when my priorities and my "heartbeat" were changing toward other things?

Finally, Margie and I had to come to a decision: we left everything completely in God's hands. If we were to be together, the Lord would have to change her parents' minds. I prayed each day that God would turn around their hearts, for I knew I loved her deeply. And I truly believed that the God who had ordered my steps would be the one who would lead us there too. We both wanted their blessing, without which we knew we would have no peace.

I DON'T THINK OLDER CHRISTIANS CAN EVER FULLY KNOW WHAT AN important role they play in the affirmation of younger believers. When you're just a youth, it means so much to have someone who's farther along the road say to you, "I see something in you, and I want you to be encouraged in it."

Ray Deitz was that man for me in Toronto. As the pastor of Yonge Street Alliance Tabernacle, he and his wife, Anita, were wonderfully kind to Ajit and me. Ray baptized us, affirmed us, and showed great faith in me especially. A little over two years after Ajit and I had first shown up, Ray even asked me to join the church board. So, there I was, all of twenty-two, making decisions with men twice my age. Ray also asked me to help lead the youth, so I served on the executive committee of the youth group as well.

Then, with the help of others, I formed a youth preaching team of about ten of our young people. That's when I was really off and running. We held services all over southern Ontario, and on two occasions we drove to Fort Wayne, Indiana, where Fred David was now the minister of music in a church. Fred had set up a "youth rally" weekend where our young people would be able to preach, and to my great delight Margie went along on that first trip. She was always my biggest cheerleader, showing pleasure every time she heard me speak, and it was so encouraging to look out and see her beaming back her affirmation.

Back at the Alliance Tabernacle, Ray Deitz gave me repeated opportunities to preach, and every time I did, people said the same thing to me afterward: "You know, Ravi, the Lord has gifted you with evangelism." This was encouraging to hear, but I didn't know what they were talking about. To me, I was just preaching. So I would nod a sincere thank-you, and sort of write it off in my mind.

Yet, in truth, I did know that a special sensation rose up in me as I preached. I had an intense urge to persuade. From the very beginning—in both Delhi and Hyderabad—I knew I wanted to preach to people who were on a quest, people whose minds were challenging what they saw around them, who were hurting inside, and who needed someone to speak to those issues. Now God was shaping that call in me, using a small church, a newfound love, and a pastor who cared.

In my own heart and self-analysis, I was still just a kid from India who had been transformed by my new life in Christ. I truly hadn't the faintest idea of what lay ahead, because I had no one to look to, no one who was modeling the gifts that others were seeing in me. I simply was at peace where I was with Christ and with Margie, that new "gift in the making" that helped make each dawn another wonderful day to be alive.

CHAPTER 17

"I AM CALLED TO THIS"

MY MOTHER STRUGGLED IN TORONTO—OH, HOW SHE STRUGGLED. Everything was foreign to her. She and our three younger siblings had arrived six months after us, in December, and right away our mom ran into the inevitable culture clash. For example, Margie's mom took her to buy some snow boots to wear during the hard winter, and the saleswoman who was helping her tried to lift Mom's sari above her ankle.

"No, no," my mother chided and half chuckled in embarrassment, and in her strong Indian accent, she continued, "you cannot do that. Please, please, no, no."

The woman sighed and told her, "Well, if you want snow boots, you're going to *have* to do it."

"Then please let *me* do it."

Mom wasn't going to allow anyone, not even another woman, to see her calf muscle.

Ajit and I had prepared for their arrival by renting a home from a family in the church where our whole family could live. Yes, we had saved up enough money to do that. I remember the night my mother and younger siblings arrived. We stocked up the fridge with ginger ale, juices, and muffins—things that would be both foreign and welcoming to them. Once they arrived, I began to feel more of a sense that Toronto was home.

Despite my mother's struggles, she was determined to get an education while in Canada. She trudged through the snow to attend classes in special education because she wanted to teach mentally challenged children. And she succeeded, earning her teaching certificate and a position at a school just a few miles away. I was so proud of her.

A few weeks after her job began, she came to me with a request: "Ravi, I want you to explain hockey to me."

"Hockey?"

"Yes," she said with no explanation.

In Toronto, National Hockey League games were telecast every Wednesday and Saturday nights, and I thought that might be the best way to teach Mom. So each week, we sat together and watched an NHL hockey game. As I explained the sport as best I could, she would take notes, and whenever a goal was scored, she always wrote down the name of the player who scored or of someone who had made an outstanding play.

Only later did I learn that one of the children in my mother's classroom never spoke. He would sit through the entire school day, silent and introverted. So Mom had decided to talk to his parents to find out what his favorite occupation was at home. "Watching the Toronto Maple Leafs," they had told her.

Every Thursday morning then, after the Wednesday night game, my mom tried to talk to the boy about the previous night's game. "What did you think of that goal by Paul Henderson?" she would ask. He would suddenly light up with excitement if the Leafs had won or react in disappointment if they had lost. Bit by bit, she drew him out of his shell, until the day finally came when he spoke to her. By sheer determination to hear this lad speak, she endured even that in which she had absolutely no interest.

Margie's mother was, and is, a very friendly person, and she and my mom hit it off right away (this, despite the Reynolds' feelings about Margie and me). I had already told Margie that without my mother in my life, I would never have made it, and Margie could relate to this right away because she had come from a very close family. As Margie got to know my mom, she could see that the Lord must have had a special place for her because she had lived through so much, endured so much, and had never once complained about it while we were growing up. My mom only began to talk about the difficulties of her life once she got to Canada, and it's a testament to her affection for Margie that she confided much in her. In fact, there were some things she shared with Margie that she had never even shared with me. On one occasion, she told Margie a rather startling story. "I was committed to be engaged to another man, you know?"

"What?" said Margie.

"Yes, my parents arranged it all. I had never met him, but I was told some things about him. Then the day drew closer and closer, but nothing was said. The engagement was all set. Then the day came and went. One day, I said to my mother, 'What happened? Why did I not get engaged?' 'Oh,' said my mother, 'some time ago, while he was riding in a rickshaw, he suffered from a heatstroke and died.'"

Margie was stunned. "And they never told you this?" she asked.

"No. That's the way it was, growing up in those years."

When Margie shared this with me, I asked my mother, and, sure enough, with some hesitancy she told me the story. What does one say to an episode like that?

Because the Reynoldses weren't in favor of our relationship at first, Margie would occasionally slip over to our home, where my mom was always cooking Indian food for the family. If you ever walk into a home where Indian food is being prepared, you'll never be able to deny where you've been, as the aroma of the spices and sauces works its way into your hair and clothes. So, whenever it was time for Margie to walk home, we always hoped the fresh air would remove any scent of curry over the course of the two-mile walk. But it never worked. Mrs. Reynolds always knew where her daughter had been.

Our family's humor took some getting used to for Margie. Admittedly, some Eastern humor is almost juvenile—verbal slapstick, I suppose. A little bit like *Dumb and Dumber*. So that when Indians have a laugh, it can seem to be at childish things. But it really isn't childish; it truly is child*like*. Sometimes when my family broke up over something, Margie would whisper to me, "I don't know what's so funny about that."

"Margie," I would explain, "it loses something in the cultural translation."

In turn, I have to confess that when I watched *I Love Lucy* with Margie's family, I would say the same kind of things to her. Who would ever think of beds traveling across the room by vibration each time a train went by? But after a while, it grows on you, and the laughter comes naturally.

My dad didn't arrive until the next year, when he was able to officially retire from Indian government service at the age of fifty-five. That was a big move for him. Indian law did not allow my dad to take his money out of the country, so even with the retirement package he received from the Indian government, he needed to work when he arrived in Toronto. He went through interview after interview, but no one wanted to hire him because of his age. Eventually, he took a job at Eaton's, which was at that time Canada's largest department store, selling shirts. What a comedown it was for this powerful man! In India, he had people waiting on him night and day, at work and at home. Now he was climbing up and down a ladder on the sales floor, trying to please choosy customers.

He finally found a marvelous job as an employment manager for a large company. But the shift in my dad's life had registered somewhere within him. It was the beginning of God's process of humbling him.

Like my mother, my dad had great affection for Margie, just as he had for my sisters. She seemed to draw a natural tenderness out of him, and he always called her "Margie-girl." Yet, my dad still remained my dad. Whenever he would come to hear me preach at church, it always made me more nervous and self-conscious. I would see him tilt his head back to listen, and boy, was I terrified! He was not always complimentary either (though I'm sure that all the while, deep inside, God was doing a profound work in his life). To our father, we kids were always representing the family, so he continually wanted to shape us to his way. After I delivered a sermon, he might say something like, "Do you have to shout so much?" "Why do you have to tell a humorous story in a sermon?"

I would feel a stab in my heart, because that was just my style, and I was still learning to preach. Most of the time, I thought to myself, "Please, just let me be." I just endured it.

A few years later, sometime after Margie and I were married, the magazine article appeared that mentioned my suicide attempt—a story printed without my knowledge. My dad was horrified and embarrassed by it. I was just as embarrassed and didn't want to talk to anyone in the family about it. But by this time, Margie had established a close enough relationship with my father that she decided to talk to him about the subject. At the end of their discussion, his comment to her was so defining of him.

"Oh, well," my dad said, "I suppose if God could use people who are murderers, he could use someone who tried to commit suicide."

Beyond that, the issue has still not been discussed among our family.

Not long after my buddy Sunder graduated from MIT in Boston, he moved to Toronto and married my sister Sham. Around that time, his own parents followed my mother and father's pattern by relocating to Toronto, where they moved in with Sham and Sunder, not far from where we lived.

Sunder's mother still held her son's conversion against him, and she arranged her Hindu idols prominently in their room in Sham and Sunder's home (and they are still there today). But Mr. Krishnan still seemed very curious about the faith that Sunder and I had embraced. Every time I visited the Krishnans, Sunder's dad found a way to get me alone so his wife couldn't hear us talking.

"I just finished reading C. S. Lewis," he would say. "What do you think of his book *Miracles*? And what about the other one, Ravi, *The Screwtape Letters*?"

We would talk until he heard his wife approaching, and then he would quickly change the subject. But he never missed an opportunity to speak about Lewis or other subjects revolving around Christianity. I realized that the powerful seeds of the gospel, sown back in our homeland, had never left this very fine gentleman, one of the finest men I'd ever known.

In those days I loved to cook, and I utilized my passion whenever I could, most often for our church. I prepared a lot of food for youth events, sometimes feeding two or three hundred on special occasions. One summer, I worked at a Bible conference for the Christian and Missionary Alliance, cooking for all the campers for the entire summer. The Westbury let me have the time off, because they knew that both the cooking and the church were passions for me.

However, I'd never heard of sloppy joes, cole slaw, or macaroni and cheese—the usual camp fare. My specialty was French cuisine, so I went with what I knew, and those campers reaped the rewards of my culinary studies, enjoying a multitude of sauces, potato dishes of all variations, Yorkshire puddings, and all kinds of Continental specialties. It didn't quite add to the camp atmosphere, but it certainly made for table conversation.

I wasn't able to eat that way on my own income, of course. Besides, I was spending most of my money in those days on books. My mind was hungrier than ever, and books had become my biggest expense; I quickly learned to look for newspaper ads for used books and would end up first in line. And, by reading as widely as I did, very often one author would introduce me to another. It was C. S. Lewis, for instance, who led me to G. K. Chesterton, who had been such a tremendous influence on Lewis. Chesterton stood out for me because he had the ability to stretch my imagination, as did my old favorite, the biblical commentator James S. Stewart. Stewart expanded my thinking by constantly making historical references, literary references, and references to the heroic journey God has for every Christian. And then there was one of my favorites, Malcolm Muggeridge. Language to him was the gateway to the imagination, and I found him to be right about this.

At times, my mind seemed nearly to explode with the voracious hunger I had. I began to realize that I desired more than what books offered. So I looked into studies in theology, and I learned that Toronto Baptist Seminary offered part-time classes to people like me, whose work schedules required flexibility. I could take their classes during the day, while I continued my great job at the Westbury at night.

But I found it exhausting to work at night, take classes during the day, try to keep up at church, and see Margie as much as I could. In the end, however, exhaustion wasn't the reason something had to give. I had begun to look at life differently, for a variety of reasons: my love for theological study, my passion for preaching and the increasing number of invitations I received, and, not least of all, Margie's great love. It changed everything about the way I viewed the career ahead of me.

The hotel catering business was about maximizing margins in every area, about figuring out ways to sell more food and liquor—especially liquor, where the profit margin was larger. I was encouraged to get customers to order liquor with every course, from aperitifs to liqueurs. I remember days at the hotel when I saw some pretty pathetic sights and had to ask for security to come and usher people to cabs, or when I had to listen to the sorry tales of those who were trapped in the lifestyle. I began to think that, whatever one's conviction in this matter, enticing someone to consume more was not what I felt I could live with honorably. Margie would often ask me that question as well. Yet, in her usual, gentle way, she knew how to raise it without an accusatory feeling but rather to prompt me to think through the issue carefully.

Now, with another passion slowly pushing aside my love for hotel management, I could no longer deny it. I decided to look beyond the part-time classes I was taking at the seminary and consider going to Bible college full-time. With this decision, I knew I'd have to face the encouraging, talented man who had been helping me map out a bright future.

One night, as Tony set our plates down for our post-banquet meal, I said, "Tony, my friend, I have something to tell you."

He anticipated what was coming. He seemed to listen with interest as I told him about theological training, about my passion for preaching, and about the requests I was getting to speak.

Before I could finish, he put his hand on my shoulder.

"Ravi, I've known for a while where your heart is," he said, smiling, yet with a bittersweet look. "You have to do what's right. Taking away the passion of your heart would be to change you in the wrong way."

And so, with that, just twenty-eight months after Ajit and I landed in Toronto, I would start classes in theological training at Ontario Bible College.

My father struggled terribly with my decision. This was the last big hurdle in my life he had to cross. "What are you going to do there?" he demanded. "And how are you going to support yourself once you're out? Have we financed all your education for you to just become a preacher?" In his mind, the ministry was just not for the intellectual or the successful. After that initial outburst, he backed away and didn't speak to me for five weeks.

I didn't rule out his questions—they were a legitimate reaction. In fact, I *didn't* know how I was going to pay my bills. My parents couldn't support me—so I would have to take on work to supplement the small "love offerings" I made from preaching engagements. I lined up a few things, but as the day to begin college approached, I knew I wasn't going to have enough.

On the weekend before classes started, I drove eight hours to Fort Wayne to preach at Fred David's church. I got back at around 4:00 a.m. on Monday morning, with my first class to start at nine. Yet I still didn't know whether I would even go to the college that morning, because I didn't have the minimum amount needed.

As I walked into my room, I found an envelope lying on my dresser. When I opened it, I saw that it was from my younger brother, Ramesh, with a note and a sum of cash. Ramesh had written that he wanted to help me pay for my first semester's fees. He had been working part-time, and something told him that I needed help.

My brother's gesture touched me deeply. And I took it as being from the Lord. I walked into Ramesh's room, where he was sound asleep, and I offered a prayer of thanks for him.

Something of enormous significance to our family happened about five weeks later. In spite of his toughness, my father had always been spiritually minded to a certain degree. When he arrived in Toronto, I could tell that John Teibe and Cliff and Betty Robinson of the International Christian Leadership executive ministry in Delhi had had a deep influence on him. Yes, Dad had sung in the choir, and he knew all the right words—but it was not from a heart that had been conquered yet. He was still only halfway there.

Some of my family was sitting in church one Sunday evening when the invitation was given to publicly respond to Jesus Christ and to say you were willing to follow him. Glancing around, I was surprised as I detected conviction on my father's face. It was an expression of determination he put on whenever emotion was creeping up.

That night, it came across his face as the invitation was given. He had his head down, trying to hold in the conviction. He had done many things that would have shown the world that he had a spiritual side to him. But deep inside, his pride had always been an issue. My father never, ever, wanted to look vulnerable. His position, his speech, and his personal carriage all revealed an inner strength. Now something was happening. He was touched in his innermost being by a message that cut to his heart.

He was restless, and then with a bent countenance he stood up and gave a sideways look. In what must have seemed like an eternity to him, he walked forward to the altar in the famed People's Church in Toronto. This was his moment of truly humbling himself before God.

In my heart, I felt the world's weight lifting for him and for our family. It was a new dawn, a new gift from God—my father's salvation. Only a high-powered Indian would know what this meant in terms of the surrender of pride. All the ramifications of position and prestige keep you from doing anything like this in India. At least at that time it was so; it was a rare happening. But God took one through the eye of the needle—what is not possible with man *was* possible with Him.

I knew that, when this happened, there was no turning back for my father. For the first time, he made a public confession that he was determined to serve Christ with all his heart. From that point on, my dad became a transformed man, probably more than any person I ever knew. His life, his temperament, his language, the way he treated my mother—everything changed. He was truly transformed from above. God gave me a brand-new father.

"How wonderful, Lord," I said inwardly. *How absolutely wonderful!*

In time, he became an elder in the church and an active Gideon in the worldwide organization. He also was asked to join the church board. His pastor commented on how he would come to my father, seeking wisdom for making tough decisions. And my dad loved his family more than ever. He was the typical grandfather, never coming to his grandchildren empty-handed.

I had always loved my dad—but more so than ever after that. Was it hard for me to get close to him, even after this? Yes, I am sorry to say it was. That was just my hesitant personality; I was always nervous that I would disappoint him. But that was not him—it was just me. Our hearts would become knit (and especially later, at a timely moment granted to us by God), even though my heart was nervous. That's the best way I can put it. My dad soon began to cheer me on in my Bible college days as I prepared for ministry.

And so, from that room in the Wellington Hospital in New Delhi in 1963, to the church altar in Toronto in 1968, not just a world without but a world within had been traversed. The physical geography part of it had been easier; for the terrain of the soul, only God was big enough.

It would have been hard to miss Koos Fietje. He stood out easily on the campus of Ontario Bible College—a tall, lanky Dutchman about my age who was deeply committed to the Lord, a trait that was immediately evident to all who met him. The first time Koos and I met, we knew right away we would be friends.

It was friends such as Koos and Roy Tibbit, who eventually would work for Wycliffe Translators, that made my time at Ontario Bible College such a powerful experience. These friends were a new breed to me, each of them hungry, each sharing a passion common to mine. Again, it was a case of "fire begets fire," as God shaped me through their friendship, their deep commitment, and their serious focus.

There were also some fine men who taught me at OBC, many of them serving as surrogate father figures. Anywhere I went on campus, it seemed, I could sit down with a professor or administrator who was willing to mentor me—someone who could help me, who could show me whether the direction I was headed was wrong or right.

And still, there were books. I remained a habitual browser, and now I could do it freely in the college library. I remember clearly the afternoon between classes when I came across a writer who would become a timely mentor. The English revivalist Leonard Ravenhill stirred me deeply through his book *Why Revival Tarries.* I started reading it in the library, and his fiery style and powerful pithy statements so grabbed my attention that I simply couldn't put the book down. I could hardly wait for a class lecture to be finished so I could hurry back to Ravenhill and read another ten or fifteen pages before the next class started.

You can talk a lot about God, Ravenhill wrote in essence, and you can know a lot about God, yet you can know very little of God in your relationship with Him. I did not want that to happen to me. I remember one paragraph he shared about prayer, quoting the famed Saint Chrysostom:

> The potency of prayer hath subdued the strength of fire; it hath bridled the rage of lions, hushed anarchy to rest, extinguished wars, appeased the elements, expelled demons, burst the chains of death, expanded the gates of heaven, assuaged diseases, repelled frauds, rescued cities from destruction, stayed the sun in its course, and arrested the progress of the thunderbolt. Prayer is an all-sufficient panoply, a treasure undiminished, a mine which is never exhausted, a sky unobscured by the clouds, a heaven unruffled by the storm. It is the root, the fountain, the mother of a thousand blessings.

He then quoted E.M. Bounds: "No erudition, no purity of diction, no width of mental outlook, no flowers of eloquence, no grace of person can atone for the lack of fire. Prayer ascends by fire. Flame gives prayer access as well as wings, acceptance as well as energy. There is no incense without fire; no prayer without flame."

Thoughts such as these, as well as Ravenhill's own writings, more than any other during my Bible college years, shaped my thinking about prayer, preaching, and the importance of getting near to God.

When I mentioned Ravenhill's book to a friend, he said rather casually, "Oh, yes, Leonard Ravenhill. He preached at my church in London, Ontario."

"He did?"

"Sure, he preached six or seven times. In fact, my church has his sermons on tape."

I could hardly believe my good fortune. "Could you get those tapes for me?"

He did, and the more I listened to the tapes, the more profoundly I was moved to want to be the kind of man Ravenhill described—one who was needed in Christ's church for the church to be what God intended it to be. I listened to those tapes every night in my room, causing my mom to say at one point, "Don't you ever get tired of that man's voice?"

Even though my years at Bible college were great ones, I had no idea where I was going with the education I was receiving there. I knew I wasn't called to be a pastor, because I was more inclined toward a persuasive style of preaching. Over time, people's past encouragements about my gift for evangelism began to come more into view for me. Still, I didn't know any evangelists I could just walk up to and say, "Would you hire me?"

There was yet another surprising benefit for me from Bible college. Once I decided to pursue theological training, something shifted in Margie's parents' feelings about us. My choice to go to Ontario Bible College seemed to change their whole perspective; they must have seen that I was serious about my commitment to the Lord. Here I was, with a promising business career that I loved and enjoyed, giving it up to go into ministry.

Now they openly welcomed me into their home, inviting me often. And as time went by, I could sense their growing love for me. The day even came when they gave us their blessing to begin dating formally. What a day that was!

Yet, ironically, once I started at the college, I saw less of Margie. We had only a few hours each week to be together, because I had taken on part-time jobs and weekend work to pay school bills, and I kept Sundays clear for preaching engagements. Supplemented by full-time work during the summers—once I sold life insurance, and another time I worked in a warehouse, loading and unloading trucks and trailers—it would provide just enough income over the next four years. Yet Margie had begun her own training to be a nurse, and so sometimes the moments we had together were only about an hour a week. After my classes ended on Friday afternoon, I would come by in my red Volkswagen and pick her up from the nurses' residence, take her to her parents' house, then spend the weekend preaching, and return home just in time to pick her up and drop her off at the nurses' residence before going home to begin a new week.

Despite those limitations, I enjoyed being invited to the Reynoldses' house for Sunday dinner when I wasn't away preaching. Sundays in their home was all about the Lord's Day, with hymns playing in the background. We would enjoy a big meal, and Margie's mother was a born hostess when it came to this. Mrs. Reynolds served some of the finest Sunday meals, usually a traditional roast beef dinner with mashed potatoes and gravy and all the trimmings. Often she would make my favorite—butterscotch pie—which makes my mouth water now just to think of it.

As soon as Mrs. Reynolds got home from church, she and the family would start spreading the goods on the dining table. Like his daughter, Mr. Reynolds was a fantastic conversationalist, able to talk about any subject (except sports!). After the noon meal, we would all sit around talking until three or four o'clock, and maybe take a nap on the couch, with the sound of firewood crackling from a lovely fire in the fireplace. Then we would rouse ourselves to go to the evening service, and afterward it was back to the Reynoldses' for some cold meats, cheeses, and fresh kaiser rolls. Those were the days when I could eat and not worry about putting it on. Now wisdom gives caution to the taste buds. When I first met Margie, I weighed one hundred forty-one pounds—and at six feet tall I had a beanpole stature.

It was after I had finished preaching at our own church one Sunday that I was introduced to an older woman, a retired missionary to Vietnam, named Ruth Jeffrey. Mrs. Jeffrey and I exchanged a few pleasantries, and she complimented me on my sermon before she posed a question to me that at first seemed to come out of the blue.

"How would you like to preach in Vietnam?" she asked.

"Well," I stammered, "I've never thought of it. Why do you ask?"

"It's a desperate situation there, as you know," she said. "I believe there are people in that country who need to hear what God has given you to say." It was late in 1970, and the war was at its height.

"Why me, Mrs. Jeffrey?"

"I've heard you preach," she said simply.

She spoke very confidently and very knowledgeably. As we talked further, I let the idea roll around in my head. And the more we talked, the more appealing it became.

"If you feel God would want you to go," she said, "what would you think about a trip next summer?"

Summers were my only opportunity to make money to pay for Bible school. When I explained this, she suggested, "Well, what if someone were to underwrite the trip for you?"

"Who would do that?"

"I'll tell you what," she said. "Why don't you look into the cost, and let me know how much it would be. We can pray about it."

I found out later that Mrs. Jeffrey was the descendant of a famous missionary to China, Jonathan Goforth. Her confident manner in church that day had reflected her heritage. So I took her up on the suggestion and talked with a travel agent, who came up with a figure of $3,600 to cover my travel to Vietnam and the fees I would need to go back to school. I wrote to let Mrs. Jeffrey know, but I didn't hear back from her right away, so I put it out of my mind.

A few weeks later, a check for $3,600 arrived in the mail. It was accompanied by a note from a woman named F. Carol Brown from New Jersey.

"Somebody shared in my prayer group your need for this, so you can go to Vietnam and preach," she wrote. "May God bless you!"

I was utterly shocked. Who was this stranger who was paying my way? That was a lot of money at the time. God had to be in this, I realized, so I started thinking very prayerfully about how I should prepare.

※

WHEN I LANDED IN SAIGON IN MAY OF 1971, I COULD NOT HAVE FELT more alone. It suddenly hit me that I was in a war-torn country. Had I considered the dangers?

I was deeply in love with Margie. I had wanted to get engaged to her before leaving for Vietnam, but I'd been nervous about doing that while facing a mission like this one. I could tell that her parents had wanted me to give her a ring before I left. But I just didn't feel right

about it, just in case anything untoward were to happen. Now I felt
the conviction of my decision even more.

That first week, I stayed in a missionary home in Saigon, and I
have to admit that when I went to bed those first few nights, I cried.
A U.S. soldier apparently sensed my loneliness when he was visiting
the missionaries, and he came to visit me in my room.

He looked around my quarters, glancing over my desk, where lay
a Bible, a sermon book, a picture of Margie, and a small tape recorder
for sending messages to Margie and my family.

"What brings you here?" he asked, pulling up the lone chair as I
sat on my bed.

I told him my story. As I did, I thought, "If God has it in mind for me
to minister to the American troops here, it would be a great honor."

Instead, at that moment, I was ministered to. The soldier listened
thoughtfully as I talked. When I finished, he looked at me and asked,
"Can I sing for you?"

"Sure, I would love that."

He began to sing: "When you walk through the storm, hold your
head up high...." He had a magnificent tenor voice, and I listened
with a rest that gradually crept into my soul. I was so grateful for this
young man's kindness. He ended with the words (adapted from the
original song) "You'll never walk alone when you walk with God."
How timely it was in my need to have a man like this — a soldier
fighting a war — taking the time to hear the lonely heart of a stranger
from another culture and to minister so caringly.

That Sunday, I preached my first sermon in a church in Saigon.
After hearing me speak, some soldiers asked if I would address their
troops at the nearby base. Soon, the invitations to preach started to
mushroom. I was speaking at military bases both American and South
Vietnamese, in hospitals to the wounded, in prisons to the Vietcong,
and even to pastors and missionaries.

I remember one Sunday morning service very clearly. I delivered a
sermon that day to four hundred airmen, who all stood in their uniforms throughout the service. They were about to leave on a mission,
and the chaplain leaned over and whispered to me, "Many if not most
of these men will not be coming back."

As that service ended, the soldiers sang, "It Is Well with My Soul."
The sound of their voices and the sight of them standing there on the
very edge of mortality made a profound impact on me.

The very next day, one of my host missionaries came to me, excited because invitations to preach were coming in from the fringes of the country. "It's wonderful," he said, "but I don't know how we're going to get you to these places."

It was decided I needed an interpreter, someone who also had transportation. Up to that point, I had been using a different interpreter in almost every locale, and it was somewhat frustrating to adjust to. But as the national leaders began seeing the impact, they arranged for an interpreter—one suited to my style—to travel with me for the three months that remained. The one chosen for this task was Hien Pham, a Vietnamese young man only seventeen years old. He was designated to drive me from to place to place on his motorbike.

When the distances were too great, the U.S. military helped us get to our destinations. This included time spent with the Koho tribe, among whom we had some of our greatest responses to the gospel. My interpreter with the Koho was a missionary named Helen Evans. She was one special lady, and the Lord formed a bond between us such that I started to call her "Mother." We have kept in touch to this day, as I send her a Mother's Day card, and on my birthday she sends a card written "to my son."

One of the first places my young interpreter Hien and I went to was Long Bin, the military air base. From there, we were taken into some of the most dangerous areas of the country, flown by helicopter gunship or by transport aircraft of the U.S. military. The most troubled area we visited was about twenty miles away from the demilitarized zone. There at night, the skies were lit up with an amber color from flares and firepower all around.

On occasion, I saw the awful sights of some bodies lying dead on the ground and others strewn across fields after an ambush. On some nights, Hien and I went to bed knowing our own lives were in danger as we fell asleep to the sound of gunshots. We heard a lot of stories of killing and death, and we saw the results of the destruction daily. We went into military hospitals, where soldiers' bodies were badly burned or horribly maimed. Yet, with everything I saw, God kept reminding me continually that He was taking care of us and would protect us, and that I was there on His mission.

Vietnam was a world turned upside down. In the villages, even among the missionaries, men and women all slept in the same room. Hien and I once slept in a room with a pastor's four daughters, at other times in rooms with many more females than that. Oftentimes it was on the floor. In almost every place, we had to change our clothes in the dark, with everyone present, and go to the bathroom in open fields. This was all somewhat discomforting, but what could we do? Privacy was at a premium.

Actually, with a war raging, this proximity to everyone brought a small sense of security. Still, I realized quickly the price that these missionaries were paying for being there. They not only had to manage with very little, but their lives were in constant danger, and they lived with only the bare necessities to protect modesty and dignity. Some paid with their lives. I grew to love them and admire these courageous men and women. Many a soldier would not have made it if it hadn't been for the spiritual and emotional support given by the missionaries.

The experience was all so disorienting, so hard to know what was going on at times. I often wondered, "Can I take this? Am I going to be able to endure it?" I continually had to remind myself, "This is *all* for God." What else could I console myself with?

At one point, I was scheduled to preach at a pastors' conference just a few miles from the infamous My Lai, the site of a notorious incident where an American soldier lost his restraint and killed innocent men, women, and children. Only a few minutes into my sermon that day, Hien stopped interpreting. When I turned to see why, I noticed that he was visibly fighting back tears.

The Spirit of God had come upon him, and Hien could no longer translate. I had to stop my sermon as a handful of pastors came forward and began to minister to my friend. Then something strange happened. Virtually the whole roomful of pastors came pouring forward, dropping to their knees in prayer.

It was a shock to me. Later I was told that when Hien stopped interpreting, he said, "What this man is saying to us is true. We need to take the Word of God seriously. We need God in our land. It is we, the church, that is the problem." The whole place had come under conviction. I realized the meeting was over—at least the meeting *we* had planned—and we all knelt and prayed for a couple of hours. For the first time in my life, I was tasting the drops of revival, that moment when a group is touched from beyond the ordinary speech or word of a person.

It began to happen in a lot of the places where I preached—among soldiers, tribal folk, Vietnamese nationals, and even among the missionaries and church leaders. I remember speaking at a Bible college where God stirred the hearts of a handful of young men, and they also fell to their knees in prayer. Every time, I was intensely aware that I was unfit to be there. I wondered, "Why are all these people reacting this way? What is it that's affecting them so?" Sometimes Hien and I would have to stay up for hours after the meeting, counseling young men who were struggling in their faith or those who had questions about God for their lives. Sometimes it was a pastor, sometimes a soldier, sometimes a tribesman, sometimes a monk.

Hien was not with me at one point on the journey, a frightening three days when I stayed in the former school for missionary children in Dalat in the highlands. My host missionaries had to leave me there so they could attend a conference, saying they would be back for me after the three days. As they pulled away in their vehicle, I was left all alone in the deserted school.

In the early days of the conflict, the Vietcong had stormed into that same building, and terror had struck. Now that terrible history plagued me. Every sound at night would wake me up, and I slept with the dresser pushed up against the door. It was a long three days and three fearful nights for me before the missionaries finally returned.

When they arrived, the plan was to drive down to Saigon so I could be at their annual workers' conference for the entire mission field. About five of us piled into the jeep, and once we got on the highway, we drove through several remote areas. During one stretch, one of the missionaries turned to me and said, "We're about to enter the most dangerous area of Vietnam."

That shook me. I thought, "Why would she tell me that? Why couldn't she wait until we'd gotten through, and *then* tell me?"

As we drove through the area, suddenly our car began to sputter and chug, and then it died. Just like that, we were stranded on the side of the road—four missionaries and me, with not a soul in sight. Terrified, we opened the hood and poked around, trying to locate the problem, but nobody could find anything wrong. We tried everything, hoping that whatever needed repairing would be fixed as we fiddled around. We tightened what was already tight and loosened what was already loose—but nothing worked.

After a while, a white jeep appeared behind us, coming up the road we had just driven. As it got closer, we tried to look friendly and waved to them to stop, but when they came upon us they swerved around us and sped away.

We all let out sighs of frustration. Yet we couldn't blame them. They must have thought, "Why would *anyone* stop in the most dangerous part of Vietnam?" They probably were afraid of an ambush.

We had no choice but to stand by the roadside and pray. Then someone tried the engine again, and this time it started. Immensely grateful, we quickly climbed back into the jeep and continued down the road.

But after driving a few miles, we came upon the white jeep. As we approached, we saw that it had been overturned, and the bodies of the four passengers were strewn across the side of the road, bullet-riddled and dead. In the distance we could see the Vietcong still scurrying away. We realized that we couldn't stop—we had to drive on.

God has an appointment with each of us, and it is critical that every man and woman know this. He will stop our steps when it is not our time, and He will lead us when it is. This is a reassuring truth to know for every believer, and a necessary trust for anyone who ministers in areas of great risk.

It came into sharp focus for me— and became a turning point in my life—on the day Hien and I stood at the gravesite of six missionaries. They had been killed when their compound was stormed just a few years earlier at the hands of the Vietcong, in an act of cold-blooded murder. As I gazed down at the markers bearing their names, some of whose children I knew, and noted the short duration of their lives, I thought of their courage. They had given everything. This was all real, for the sake of the gospel.

It was a moment of commitment for me. I prayed solemnly, "Lord, I want to be what You want me to be. I'm willing to preach wherever You send me, at whatever cost."

The trip ended up being full of such commitments. I was making them daily as I went along. Looking back now, I see that my life grew in ways I would never realize until years later. In those memorable days of my life as a young preacher, God was preparing me to be willing to court danger in the years ahead.

I came back from Vietnam a brand-new man. The trip had permanently sealed my calling, and I realized, "I am an evangelist. I am called to do this—to be in places at risk, places where people are willing to hear." I couldn't tell you how or where exactly the calling came, but I knew it had happened. And I never looked back.

I DIDN'T HAVE TO EXPLAIN ANYTHING TO MARGIE. SHE HAD RECOGNIZED God's call upon me long before I did. When she met me at the airport at the end of August of 1971, it had been almost five years to the day I first saw her. Three weeks later, I gave her the engagement ring. She was to be the soul mate of my life.

Upon my return, I was asked to preach at the People's Church in Toronto, the largest church in Canada at that time, about what I had seen in Vietnam. Over the following months, I received a lot of encouragement from the pastors there and elsewhere, as well as from missionaries who came through Toronto while on furlough. Of course, Margie was still my greatest support. Sometimes she was able to accompany me on preaching engagements, and occasionally she even sang, which I loved. I was transfixed every time I heard her sweet, lovely voice and her beautiful playing of the piano.

With my birthday coming up, Margie wanted to surprise me, so she called Tony Rolden at the Westbury. Tony was overjoyed, insisting, "Bring him here. I'll take care of both of you."

I was indeed surprised when we pulled up to the hotel, because we surely couldn't afford a meal there. I was finishing up my last year at school, and we were saving our money to get married. But I couldn't have been more pleased. As we enjoyed our roast beef dinner that magical evening, Tony came out of the kitchen and sat down at our table. After that, the waiters were buzzing around us all night long, attending to our every need. It was an unforgettable evening. Tony assured me that I was doing what was written in my soul.

Several years later, long after we had left Toronto, I read a headline in the newspaper: "Canada's Premier Chef Dies." Tony had been of that reputation. In the intervening years, he had become head of Canada's association of chefs.

I still think about my friend a lot—in fact, almost as often as I peek into the kitchen of any hotel where I'm staying. And every so often, Margie will say to me, "I'll be surprised if you go home to meet the Lord before starting your own restaurant." The thought still brings a grin.

As the date approached for my graduation from Ontario Bible College on the last Saturday in April of 1972, I was asked to preach at the ceremony. The program usually involved testimonies, but this year the administration came to me with a request: "Ravi, we want you to preach." It was a great honor. Koos Fietje, Roy Tibbit, John Saynor, and I—close friends all through college—graduated together, and that day we made a pact that we would pray for each other every day, and that God would remain first in our lives. My dad and mom also were there that day to celebrate with me God's goodness and all that He had brought about in our lives to bring me to that point.

One week later, Margie and I were married, with the full blessing of our families. Now a dream I could never have dreamed for myself was coming true. It was one granted to me from above. As I looked at the invitation, I chuckled—two cultures had met. In India, we always put the full names of the couple and the full names of the parents. So it read—embedded in the heart of the invitation—"Frederick Antony Ravi Kumar Zacharias, son of Mr. and Mrs. Oscar Tobias Joseph Zacharias, and Margaret Jean Reynolds, daughter of Mr. and Mrs. Herbert Lindsay Cochrane Reynolds ..." I remarked that anyone who read that invitation had already paid the price of a time commitment to pray for us.

Three years after I left Vietnam, I was reading an article in a missions magazine about a revival that had taken place there. The author was describing the roots of its beginning, tracing it back to a young Indian who spoke at a Bible college in Nhatrang, where a group of Koho young people had responded to his invitation to follow Christ wholeheartedly, and from there had begun the revival.

What a surprise to read that. *Yes—I remember those college students!*

During the time of our meetings in Vietnam, I had seen nearly three thousand people come to know Christ. As I read on, I discovered that, in the months after I left, the blessing continued, and significant numbers of Vietnamese and tribespeople had come to know Christ.

I put the magazine down in utter amazement. God had used two young men and one veteran missionary as His instruments for national impact. Of course, the groundwork had been laid for decades with great sacrifice on the part of so many. That's the way revivals come.

Now, as I think of this period in my journey, I have to think of where my life might have gone had I made certain turns in the road. If I had been admitted to the Air Force in India, I would never have met Margie. I wouldn't have had the balance that she brought to my life, to bring so many things back together for me. If I had joined Tony Rolden in his venture, I would never have gone to Vietnam and recognized my calling to reach people for the Lord, even in areas at risk. As the Lord had orchestrated it, though, I had gone to war after all—but for a purpose different from the noble one I had as an eighteen-year-old. He had led me to speak hope to people at risk, in the most challenging of circumstances.

God had been in the shadows all along. Every step of the way—from the beautiful girl I met and married, to the school where my theology was shaped, to the committed buddies God gave me, to the calling of an evangelist, to the individuals who affirmed me—everything was being put back together. It was as if all the dismantling I'd done with the first seventeen years of my life was being given back to me, but this time the Lord was putting it together with His unerring hand.

When God puts a broken life back together, He removes the scars because He builds from the inside out. And when God steadies a faltering life, He puts you on *His* footing.

CHAPTER 13

THE LONGEST JOURNEY

DONALD COGGAN, THE 101ST ARCHBISHOP OF CANTERBURY, ONCE SAID that the longest journey in the life of one's belief is from the head to the heart. My own life was testimony to this fact. The truth that had gone into my head had rescued my heart from its turmoil.

Allow me to elaborate a bit on Coggan's maxim. If we say that a sexual union is sacred—if marital love is exclusive and cannot be compromised—then it stands to reason that if you violate that sanctity, your emotions will be in keeping with the violation. Likewise, if it is rationally sound that Jesus rose again from the dead, the heart should delight that this life is not the end. Or, if it is rationally sound that the home is a gift of God, then family life is emotionally invigorating. In short, if the reasoning is sound, the feelings will follow. Feelings follow belief; belief, then, should follow truth.

I would add that the converse to Coggan's statement is just as true, namely, that the longest journey is also from the heart to the head. And so came my hunger to know the great depths of truth behind my faith. It led me to further disciplined and in-depth study as I pursued a Master of Divinity degree at seminary.

The president of my denomination, however, wasn't pleased to hear about my plans. After my trip to Vietnam, Dr. L. L. King of the Christian and Missionary Alliance (C&MA) had taken notice of my preaching and evangelistic work. Upon my graduation from Ontario Bible College, the C&MA—in the person of Rev. William J. Newell, the district superintendent—put me on staff as a full-time itinerant evangelist in Canada. The stipend of six hundred dollars a month doesn't sound like much by today's standards, but I was thrilled to be paid to do what I had been doing on my own since my days at

173

the Yonge Street Alliance Tabernacle. This district was operating in the red, and to bring me on with a salary (the first time the C&MA had salaried an itinerant evangelist) was an act of faith on the part of Rev. Newell. I remember my dad's gratitude to him, "Thank you for investing in my son." Not to be outdone, Rev. Newell replied with a twinkle in his eye, "I plan to capitalize on it." How true his words would become—and in a short time. After one year, the honorariums from my preaching exceeded the salary, so, at least for my part, I did not add to the district's financial concerns.

The itinerant life had come naturally to me. Now, as I was poised to begin seminary training, Dr. King cautioned me: "Many an evangelist has gone to seminary and lost his sharp edge, Ravi. They come out jaded, or softened in their zeal. I'd hate for you to lose your sharp edge."

"Dr. King," I assured him, "if I ever begin to lose my evangelistic verve, I will be the first one to pull out."

The teaching at Trinity Evangelical Divinity School in Deerfield, Illinois, was fabulous, and I could not have asked for a better faculty. There is an old rabbinic saying that you have two sets of parents—the ones who brought you into the world, and the ones who brought you into the knowledge of the Lord. Thankfully, I have had both in my life, and the people who taught me at Trinity qualified supremely as the latter.

My biblical passion was fired by two Old Testament professors, Dr. Walter Kaiser and Dr. Thomas McComiskey. Both had earned their PhDs from Brandeis University, among the best schools in Old Testament studies, and they gave me a love for the Old Testament. But the two professors who would prove most influential in the direction my preaching would take were my mentors in philosophy and apologetics, Dr. John Warwick Montgomery and Dr. Norman Geisler.

Dr. Montgomery was as tough a man as they came, with seven degrees, three of them doctorates. It was difficult to find a secretary who would work for him. In fact, people who worked on the school switchboard placed a red ring about his button, so they would immediately know when he was calling them and could be mentally prepared not to make a mistake. I know this because my wife was one of those switchboard workers. Giving Dr. Montgomery the benefit of the doubt, I would say that quirkiness sometimes accompanies genius.

I'll never forget the first time I dared to ask him a question in class. All this apologetics stuff was quite new to me, and I asked, "Dr. Montgomery, would you please define 'circular reasoning' for me?"

He stared at me, and then with a touch of sarcasm said, "My friend, circular reasoning is reasoning that goes in a circle. Does that help?"

"To be honest with you, sir, no," I answered quickly. "The reason I'm asking you is because a critique I read of your apologetic method says you indulge constantly in circular reasoning. What I want to know is, what are they talking about?"

Again, he just stared. He might have been thinking, "Did this guy just get off the glass boat? Or does he just not know what not to ask in class?"

But after that exchange, Dr. Montgomery took a shine to me. He submitted to a scholarly journal a paper I cowrote with a classmate, and he later asked me to accompany him on a trip to East Germany for a two-week Reformation tour, to follow in the steps of Luther. Between our financial constraints and my feeling intimidated by him, I was inclined to decline, but it was Margie who finally put down the deposit for the trip and pushed me out the door. I saw a different side to Dr. Montgomery on that trip. He was not only encyclopedic in his capacity, he had a tender spot to his one-on-one teaching approach. Many a time, I would see him sitting next to a member of the group, engaged in a casual teaching mode.

Dr. Norman Geisler was a hero to me from Day One. Studying existential philosophy and taking numerous other philosophy courses under him made a huge difference in my approach to argument. Dr. Geisler inspired me with the confidence to walk into any lions' den and believe I would come away victorious for the gospel. His best gift to me was his twin loves, the Bible and philosophy. He loved the Word of God and never shied away from any attack on it.

As you might imagine, the study load at Trinity was so incredibly heavy that it kept me pinned to my desk for virtually every waking hour that I wasn't in class. That was true of every semester, but especially the first term of year two, when I had to master two languages simultaneously, Greek and Hebrew. The biggest challenge was giving my marriage due time, let alone developing other friendships.

As it happened, two doors down from us in student housing lived William Lane Craig and his wife, Jan. Bill would go on to become a leading evangelical philosopher. In those days, he and I joked about what we called our "fellowship around the garbage dump." Around nine thirty or ten every night, we would empty the trash in the dumpster behind our apartments, and that was about the only time we found to talk about our studies and its challenges.

Through it all, Dr. L. L. King's caution came back to me many times—almost constantly, in fact. When you're dealing with criticism of the New and Old Testaments, you're facing tough attacks on the Scriptures by some great intellectuals. And you have to be honest with yourself in bringing your own integrity to these matters. You wonder, "Did the walls of Jericho actually come down so dramatically? Did these walls even exist? Is the book of Daniel actually predated prophecy and not postdated history? What are the realities here?"

The problem is that you're diving deeply into this kind of critical material for three to four weeks before you even get into the actual text of the book you're studying. Then, once you do start into the book, it can easily become to you just a text for analysis and not the Word of God in all its life-altering power.

I stayed on my knees a lot as those days proceeded. And, thankfully, I had professors—men full of great intellectual integrity—who were sensitive about keeping the primary focus on God's Word. One of those men was Gleason Archer, who had written a book-by-book defense of the Old Testament, challenging the critical attacks against it. Because of its yellow cover, it was branded by us seminarians as "The Yellow Bible." He gave me tremendous confidence in responding to the textual critics with the declaration that the text we have for Scripture is authentic.

My experience at Trinity points up one big difference between Islam and Christianity: Islam shuns a critique of the Quran. If you ask the hard questions of the Quran, you risk being branded, and, in some cases, you even risk your life. The Christian, however, has always been willing to subject the Bible to the severest analysis and is able to come out, knowing that it can survive the blade of the skeptic. Examining those tough issues at Trinity, I only grew in my love for and trust in the Holy Scriptures. I think of what I gained there as summed up in Jesus' words, when He said, "The Scripture cannot be broken," and, "Thy Word is truth," which He declared in prayer to the Father in John 17.

In the fall of my second year at seminary, I was asked by Elmer Fitch, one of the district superintendents of the Christian and Missionary Alliance, to speak at the pastors' conference in that area, which opened up many opportunities for me to preach. From that point on until the time I graduated, there were few weekends that I was not out speaking. The benefits were twofold: I graduated from Trinity debt free, and it kept my passion and calling alive so that I did not become too buried in academia.

Also, during my second year Margie did not come back to Trinity with me after Christmas. Instead, I joined her in Toronto in February for the birth of our first little one, Sarah. Our medical coverage was in Canada, and so Margie stayed there, awaiting the arrival of this gift from God. It was a joyous moment for me to see our daughter in Margie's arms, and my heart nearly burst as I held Sarah myself.

The day after her birth, my brother-in-law Sunder took me out to dinner, and halfway through our meal he asked, "Well, what does it feel like to be a father?"

Exhausted, I groaned inside, thinking, "Why does he want to be philosophical now?" I joked my way around the question, and after dinner I went home to get some sleep.

Sometime past midnight, the phone rang. "It's Sarah," Margie said, trying to remain calm. "There's a problem with her blood count."

Our daughter had an ABO incompatibility. She was allergic to her own blood, and her body was creating antibodies against it. When the mother's blood type is O and the child's is either A or B, such a situation can arise. Because Margie's type is O, she had antibodies within her circulation against A or B. Normally these antibodies remain contained, but sometimes they can leak through the placental barrier and enter into the baby's bloodstream. In effect, Sarah in her type A now had antibodies counter to the very blood type circulating in her, and she was in a deteriorating situation. That night, I paced the floor, wondering, "Lord, what is happening here?"

Sarah's situation got worse the next day, and this continued in the days that followed. Finally, by the fifth day, it had reached crisis proportions, and the doctors were contemplating a total-body blood transfusion.

What does it feel like to be a father?

Suddenly I had found out.

If you had put Sarah in a room next to a dozen other babies on their first day of life, I'm not sure I could have picked out my daughter. I had barely held her in my arms before this crisis arose. But she was our very own offspring, and I loved her—and so every nerve in my body hurt in response to this threat. The next time I saw her, she had been placed under fluorescent lights as part of her treatment, the rays counteracting her body's reaction to her blood. It was a sight that broke my heart.

Our baby Sarah came out of that experience healthy. But from that first moment, I gained an appreciation of the analogy God has given all of us: that we relate to him as a child does to a father. And seeing life through the father's eyes is a different kind of seeing. There was no room, not even an inch, for selfishness—it all had to go out the window. I also learned from Day One that you may have your plans for your children, but they have their plans for you.

It was a ground-level reminder that training in theology was about more than doing battle with Bultmann and Barth.

DURING THE SUMMER BREAKS AT TRINITY, I BEGAN TAKING LONG overseas engagements to preach for the Christian and Missionary Alliance, while Margie went back to Toronto to stay with her parents. It was during one of those breaks—in the summer of 1974—that the denomination asked me to go to Cambodia.

Here was a nation on the cusp of the darkest time in its history. For decades, there had been only a handful of known Christians in the whole country, and now it was under siege by what would become one of the most vicious regimes in the history of the world. The C&MA asked me to preach there for five weeks.

I was making the necessary preparations to leave when my father approached me with a letter he had written to me. He asked me to open it only when I arrived in Cambodia. When I did, in my dimly lit room in Phnom Penh where I was staying with missionaries, I read words I never could have dreamed would come from him.

My dad told me how thrilled he was that God had called one of his children into the ministry, and that it spoke volumes to him. Then, in open language he had never used with me, he said how sorry he was for the hurt he had brought into my life. My dad knew how to use words, and he chose the right ones. He did everything he could to bridge the gap.

It meant everything to me. And now tears rolled down my face as I considered all that God had done. At one time, my dad had looked me in the eye and said I would never make anything of my life, that I would end up an embarrassment to him. I knew, better than anyone, that *only* God could have brought about this change in him. The Lord had changed our relationship—by changing both my father and me.

This moment could well have been another story in one of Jesus' parables on the return of the prodigal. Only here, it would take on a different twist. It would be something like this:

There was a young man who, determined to go his own way, asked his father for his inheritance and in a fit of despair left his home. His father, outraged by this, slammed the door shut, pushing the son out of his home, and asked him never to return because he was shaming the family by his demands and his disrespect. The son went into the far country and squandered his inheritance by making a sport of life. Then, when he had come to nothing, he went to the top of a hill to jump and to end his life.

Just before he reached the top, he fell on his face—so hurt and destitute of any help. When he opened his tear-stained eyes, he saw a cross. On that cross there hung a man, who looked at him with eyes of compassion and mercy and said, "Come to Me, and I will give you eternal life." The young man struggled to his feet to get to the cross, and he felt a strong arm supporting him. It was the arm of the one who had paid with his life.

The tears were gone and a new life infused, and a lamp and a map were given to this young man to walk by the truth. As he descended toward the bottom of the hill, he saw another man bent over, weeping and asking for forgiveness. The young man recognized the voice. It was his own father. The young man opened up the map and shared the light of the lamp. Together they embraced, knowing that the same man on the cross had brought them both there, because the home had been locked to the son and lost to the father.

With the help of the map, they walked back to the locked home. The shadow of the cross was on it. The lock had been removed, and what awaited them there was the one who had been pursuing them all along. The light of the risen Savior welcomed them in.

The words of my father spelled the gospel: *reconciliation*. We were brought together and made one by God. Nothing could compare to those affirming words from my dad.

The good hand of the Lord continued in His grace to us. And there was another important relationship that, in his marvelous way, God shored up for me on that trip to Cambodia. In order to get to Cambodia, I had to change planes in Thailand, and as I carried my bag through Bangkok Airport, who did I see standing before me among all the Asians but a tall, lanky Dutchman.

"Koos?"

He grinned. "You thought you could go through Thailand without seeing me?"

"Koos Fietje!" I shouted, embracing my old buddy. "I didn't want you to come all the way down to Bangkok for just an overnight. You're up country."

"No, my friend," he said, "you don't know how I've longed for this time of fellowship." He grabbed my bag from me and stated, "We're going to talk till you leave."

Koos had been serving in Thailand as a missionary with Overseas Missionary Fellowship. When he had heard I would be coming through, he phoned back home to find out when I would be in the airport. Now he whisked me off to his nearby hotel room, and we spent the night catching up before my flight would leave the next day.

As we lay on the two beds, arms behind our heads, we talked about the journey God had put us on since we first met. It had been a wondrous path for each of us and our families, and we marveled at what God had done since we'd last seen each other. After a while, though, I began to detect the slightest hint of melancholy in my friend's voice. I could tell he had serious things on his mind.

"I have this feeling, Ravi," Koos finally said. "I think God is calling me to a very serious commitment," he said.

"Yeah?"

"I feel him calling me deeper. And, well, I get the sense that my life is going to change dramatically. I think that someday—I don't know when—God is calling me to pay the ultimate price."

It must be said that many passionate young Christians count the cost of such a sacrifice when they first commit to Christ. But once you're actually in harm's way, you never really want to think about the possibility. Koos had always been outspoken about his faith. I knew that his actions were consistent with his words, and that there could be some in this foreign setting who would not take kindly to his preaching.

"I'm just telling you," he said, "because I need your prayers."

"Koos," I reminded him, "we made that commitment to each other, and we will honor it."

With the last hour we had together, we prayed for each other. I was more thankful than ever for this friend whom God had given me and who, after all these years, was still an example to me.

When I arrived in Cambodia, there was a devaluation simultaneously of money and of life. It was a land in chaos. If you went shopping, you had to take a briefcase full of cash because the money was reduced to almost nothing. No matter what I might have been told, I couldn't have been prepared for the pervasive darkness that hung over that country.

I had been duly warned that it would be very difficult preaching there, so I prepared myself for that. After one of my first meetings, in the city of Phnom Penh, I asked the interpreter to dismiss everyone except those who wished to commit their lives to Christ. He did—and a large number stayed seated.

I assumed there had been a misunderstanding. So I asked the interpreter to repeat the direction, and he did—twice more—but still a vast majority of those in the room stayed. By the time I had finished, a sizable number prayed to receive Jesus Christ into their lives. That was very significant, given Cambodians' historical resistance to the gospel.

In the city of Battambang, I was taken to a large public arena, where I spoke to a packed crowd, and great numbers of people came to the Lord. One of them was a man who'd been a Buddhist priest for twenty-eight years. As the masses of people pressed forward to commit their lives to Jesus, I quickly realized that what had happened in Vietnam four years earlier was happening now in Cambodia. By the end of the first week, we had lost count of the number of people who had given their lives to Christ.

We talk a lot about heroes of the faith, but there was no doubting the faithfulness of my two interpreters. Son Sonne was the director of the Bible Society in Cambodia, and Chhirc Taing was a colonel in the army—and both were putting themselves at great risk in serving Christ.

On my last night in Cambodia, these two men took me out to the best hotel in town, Le Phnom, for a dinner that I will never forget, one where I came face-to-face with the reality of what ideologies can do to people. Le Phnom was where most foreigners were staying because the city was fast deteriorating. My distinguished interpreters ordered a curry dish for me, and they had the same. As I took my first mouthful, however, I knew something was wrong with the food. It tasted very strange. I did not want to offend them, but I did not want to eat this meal either. Then I plunged my fork into the curry again and heard a crackle. When I raised the fork, a large cockroach lay impaled in the prongs. My tablemates saw it and gasped. Chhirc turned red with embarrassment; Son got teary. "This is the best we have now," he said. "Please forgive us, Brother Ravi."

"You needn't be embarrassed," I replied. "But if you don't mind, I will just have some bread and skip the meal." By this point, I had spread my food on the plate to see two or three roaches in it, and the same was true in their dishes. They just moved the roaches aside and ate the meal. Cambodia is called "A Gentle Land," but what communism in its rabid form had done to its people staggered the imagination. Millions were killed on that watch.

When the murderous Khmer Rouge gained power, Colonel Chhirc's name was on their "Ten Most Wanted" list. The Christian and Missionary Alliance urged him to flee, offering to escort him out of the country, but he refused to go, opting instead to send his family out. If I remember correctly, his wife refused to leave without him.

"If I am able to lead even one person to Christ by staying, it will be worth it," Chhirc said. He remained, and hours after the Khmer Rouge marched in, they took him from his home and executed him for having stood against them. Son Sonne was taken out to the high seas and drowned.

The horrible dinner we had that night pales into insignificance in the light of what was demanded of these dedicated men. I would never forget them. Their examples remain as lights to the church in Cambodia—servants who gave their all for the benefit of those who would come after them.

We count many costs in the Christian life, and God in his way prepares us for them all. Still, the heart is never fully ready to face a significant loss.

I was in Detroit on a preaching engagement and was fast asleep in the pastor's home when I was awakened by the phone ringing. I looked at the clock, and it was 3:00 a.m. I heard footsteps coming toward my room.

Suddenly I grew fearful, remembering that my mother had not been well when I began the trip. She had been in the hospital.

"Ravi, it's for you," the pastor whispered into my room. I walked to the hallway and picked up the receiver. It was Margie.

"Your dad called, Ravi," she said amid tears. "Your mom just passed away."

It was a rude, rude shock. None of us had expected it. *My mother —gone.*

I returned to my room and sat up in bed, wondering, hoping that this was just a dream. How could this happen? As the sad news began to sink in, I quickly packed my bags and immediately rushed home.

Mom had been a diabetic and dependent on insulin for years. After we moved to Canada, her new doctor had switched her from insulin to an oral medication. It not only didn't work, but she developed congestive heart failure and then suffered a stroke. Now, the Lord had finally taken her.

Isabella Manickam Zacharias died early, at the age of fifty-seven. It hit all of us very, very hard. We hadn't had a death in the family since my grandmother had passed away years before, when we were children in Delhi. Now my father met me at the front door of our family home, and he looked stricken.

That night, as we sat in the living room consoling each other and absorbing the shock, my father turned to me and said, "Son, I want you to preach at her funeral."

It was another clear affirmation from him. Normally in such situations, the oldest is given that responsibility. Now he was asking me to represent the family for the gospel's sake. My brothers and sisters were supportive of this decision, and it was a tender moment for all of us in the family. Ironically, it was then, more than ever, that I wished my mother were there. And in a real sense she was, for had it not been for her, I wouldn't have been there, to say nothing of her own hope in Christ.

Coming up with the sermon for her funeral was not easy. The words simply wouldn't come. To think something and then to verbalize it makes the reality concrete, but I had an awful time trying to make that bridge. I finally went to my dad and said, "All I can think about is that Mom is gone."

"Why don't you get down on your knees," Dad gently suggested, "and ask the Lord to help you."

As I went to my knees with only that thought—"she's gone"—I sensed the Lord saying to me, "If you must insist that she is gone, at least finish the thought. 'She has gone—*where?*'"

Ah! The thought was completed in my mind. "*Home,*" I said. "She has gone home!" Home to be with the one who made her. What a difference to know that!

When our family gathered at the funeral home, we all were moved as our father wept with remorse at my mother's casket. Margie remembers it well as she heard him whisper, "Oh, Belle, oh, Belle," and then cry out, "will you ever forgive me?"

It was a cry that covered years, and it was not for show. In all our hearts, we knew what was behind his cry.

Our dad's remorse was a reflection of both his conversion and his heartache. Someone has said that our sin scorches us most *after* we have received forgiveness, and not before. Once you realize how much you've been forgiven, you see how great that forgiveness really is. In that moment at Mom's casket, the hard truth fell upon my father that his chance to remake his love with my mother had lasted just six years. It also showed me that deep inside he was a good man who had been seduced by power in his earlier years—but the Lord had restored him in his latter years.

Our mother's death left a lot of people brokenhearted. Her boss, the principal at the school for the mentally challenged, spoke to me of her "pristine character." He told us that her students cried at the news of her death. And my brother Ramesh struggled terribly in the days that followed. I wouldn't be surprised if some days he still has to pull his car to the roadside to cry over Mom.

As Margie and I drove back to Deerfield, Illinois, after the funeral, I gazed out the window and muttered, "The world isn't the same anymore." The cars looked different, the trees looked different— everything was changed. I felt great sadness also because our children would never know my mother. I have often felt that loss for all of my children. My mother's personality would have made a profound influence on them. But it was not to be.

She was a special lady.

A few years before, my mom had quietly asked me to handle her estate. I was the only one she spoke to about it, and she said she wanted to leave a large portion to me and to my younger brother, because I was in theological training and Ramesh was in medical school. The others were already well settled.

"Mom, that's not good," I told her. "Just distribute it evenly. You don't want to create any tension. I think you should trust the Lord in this, and leave it up to Dad. Let him manage it when the time comes." She agreed, but only reluctantly. I could tell she really wanted Ramesh to finish medical school, and she knew of his need. As for my future, she had monetary concerns.

Then she told me that for all those years, she had continued giving to the Saint Philomena shrine in gratitude for Sham's "healing." Mom wanted this to continue after her death.

"Mom," I told her, "who do you think healed Sham? Do you think it was the grace of God, or do you think it was some other source?"

"No," she said, "I think it was the grace of God."

"Then why don't we just give it to the Lord?" I said. "I'll make sure that this gift happens for some cause in India where love and mercy are offered in Jesus' name." She nodded. And so on her behalf, after she was gone I gave to several ministries she had appreciated. It was a fitting act for a woman whose entire life had been devoted to giving.

SHORTLY BEFORE I GRADUATED FROM TRINITY IN 1976, DR. KING OF THE Christian and Missionary Alliance flew to Chicago to see Margie and me. He had a proposal for us.

"We would like you to commit the year 1977 to speaking around the world," he announced.

I almost fell over in my chair. *Around the world?* It was a daunting notion.

"We'll send all of you—you, Margie, and Sarah."

That made it sound a little less daunting. But only a little.

"It would be for forty-eight weeks," Dr. King said. "You'll take off from New York on New Year's Eve and begin your work in England. Then you'll work eastward, through Europe and the Middle East, and finish on the Pacific Rim. You'll be home the next December."

When we accepted, I had thought, "With Margie and our little one along, it will be OK." But it was the toughest year of our lives.

We spent that year staying in spartan bed-and-breakfast establishments or in the more restful missionary guest houses, the three of us usually confined to a single room. And in those eleven months, I preached 576 times.

Our lives were put at risk on many occasions. In one Middle Eastern country, Margie was menaced by a rude, perverted gesture by a hotel employee. It shook her terribly, and I was very upset by it but didn't know what to do. Our host missionary immediately went with me to the hotel manager, and when we reported it, the man was instantly fired. If he had tried it with a Middle Eastern woman, he could have lost his hands over it.

The situation became only more nerve-racking after the man's firing. He phoned me in our room to ask me to retract the story. I refused, and we had to be moved to a different hotel for our safety. That night, even in another hotel, we received threatening phone calls—a few words spoken in Arabic before the caller hung up. Around midnight that same night, two-year-old Sarah woke us up with a bloodcurdling scream from a bad dream. Margie and I realized that Sarah had absorbed the tension of the day, sensing that things were not right.

We had another unnerving experience in Thailand. We were dropped off at the wrong bus stop, miles from where we were supposed to be—in the middle of nowhere, on the side of a deserted highway. We spent an hour in a torrential rain with only a tree to shelter us. Little Sarah ran a temperature of 105 degrees, and there was no help to be found. Finally, after walking to seek assistance, I was able to bring back two rickshaw drivers, who took us to our destination—but only after we circled in the rain for at least another hour as they looked for the address we'd been given. Little did we know that the buildings in that city were numbered not by their geographic order but by the chronological order in which they were built.

Sarah developed a serious ear infection during that chaotic episode, and years later would require very serious surgery that threatened facial paralysis. Although she would lose hearing in that one ear, through the hands of a skilled surgeon her face would remain undamaged. I am so grateful to the Lord today for the healthy, lovely lady Sarah has grown up to become.

There were many other difficulties and severities over the course of that year, and our young family incurred the cost of them. At the same time, thousands of people came to Christ. In Hong Kong, at the end of the trip, I spoke in open-air meetings, in halfway houses, and in prisons where people sat on death row for selling drugs. On our final day, as we packed for home, I knew the trip had changed me as nothing ever had. I thought, as John Wesley once had, "The world has become my parish."

After that very tough year, we went back home and settled into a wonderful domestic life in Niagara Falls, about seventy-five miles from Toronto. Margie and I enjoyed those years immensely, and in 1978 we welcomed our second little one, Naomi. I loved what I did as an itinerant preacher, because whenever I got home from a trip, I was *home*. I could be with the children and with Margie and enjoy our family. I did all my studying at home, and if I needed a change from sitting at my desk, I simply took my books to the next bedroom and studied there. I took breaks for lunch with my family, and later in the afternoon I would take a short nap—only thirty minutes, but necessary for the demands of a full study day. Then I had tea and worked until dinner in the evening.

It was in the midst of this idyllic family setting that I received a call from the Christian and Missionary Alliance headquarters in Nyack, New York, the evening before I was to leave for a speaking engagement in New York City. Dr. King wanted to meet with me after that event.

Given the price my young family had paid on our previous assignment, I have to say I was wary of what the C&MA president might want to talk to me about. Midway through that dinner with Dr. King in New York, he brought up the subject that was on his mind. "We've got people graduating from seminary who don't know how to lead people to Christ," he said.

Safe so far. Then—

"I'm looking for an evangelist to teach in our seminary," he continued. "I want your impact here, Ravi, with our ministerial students. I want the passion and conviction of evangelism in their training."

As he spoke, I thought about my young family back in Ontario. Moving them away from the life we were enjoying was the last thing I wanted.

"Dr. King," I answered, "I'd like a little time to pray. I need to seek the mind of the Lord on this."

I will never forget the response he gave me—and Dr. King could be quite imposing.

"Young man," he said, "the call of the church *is* the call of the Lord. And we as a church are calling you."

If ever there was a decision in which my will had to be forced to the task, it was that one.

Margie's concern went beyond our family's welfare. She was worried that I would lose my primary calling—to preach—and she desperately did not want to see that happen. Yet, a year later, we were in Nyack, New York—just up the Hudson River from New York City—and, sure enough, even after just a short time span, I already sounded more like a professor when I preached than an evangelist. That was only the beginning of our struggles during that period.

Living in the suburbs of New York City was very expensive, even back in the 1970s and '80s. I had my salary from the seminary, but it wasn't sufficient to support a family—and thankfully the administration understood that. You had to find other means of supporting yourself, or else have both spouses working, and I didn't want Margie to go through that, especially with our growing family. So we decided I would continue my itinerant work, speaking almost every weekend, as well as chairing the Department of Evangelism and Contemporary Thought at the seminary and carrying a full teaching load. Also, once a month, I took a weeklong engagement anywhere around the globe. I might be in Australia, Malaysia, or Singapore for five days, then come right back to a full teaching slate of three to five classes, covering a broad range of subjects: the early history of evangelism, world religions, evangelistic preaching, history and theology of worship, Christian apologetics—everything I could bring to the task of the chair I held.

Meanwhile, Margie carried the major responsibility for our home in my regular absences, alongside that of being a mom to our three children, as Nathan, our youngest, had now arrived.

To complicate matters, the seminary grew to five times its size during my time there. The student-to-teacher ratio ballooned so dramatically that my responsibilities became a difficult task to manage. Sometimes when I spoke from the lectern or pulpit, my head would be spinning from sheer exhaustion. I would be in conversation with faculty or friends and completely lose my train of thought in midsentence.

At home, as I ate dinner, I would wonder if the arm I lifted to feed myself was actually my body, or just some appendage independent of me that was moving of its own accord. Or I would come home, lie down on the floor to rest for a few minutes, and be sound asleep immediately, which was very atypical of my personality. Also, my voice had always been naturally husky, but now it became raspy—an affliction I still have. I wasn't used to lecturing for three hours at a stretch, and I developed a vocal ulcer that caused my throat to be in constant pain. That ulcer is with me to this day.

I had become worn to the core and wondered, "How can I keep this up?"

The truth was, teaching *wasn't* my calling, and carrying two full-time loads was taking me on a collision course with my ebbing health and strength. Margie knew I was struggling, and neither of us was at peace. It was a very tough time for our marriage.

During this stressful time at Nyack, I received an urgent letter from Overseas Missionary Fellowship. When I opened it, I saw the black border around the page—and I almost dropped it.

Koos had been killed, martyred for his faith.

I was stunned. One of my closest friends, with a wife and several children—a brother in whom I had seen Christ—now dead.

Throughout all the years, I had remembered our pact. And then I remembered afresh his last request for prayer.

It had all been for this moment, I realized. The Lord had been faithful to prepare my friend. And now he had called Koos home.

Of all the experiences I had at Nyack, it was the students' faces that come into sharpest relief now. Margie and I had found some companions for our journey there—Bill Crockett, the professor of New Testament; his wife, Karen; my boss Wendell Price, who was a true Christian gentleman; and Roy Johnston, who worked at the Christian and Missionary Alliance headquarters and had first interviewed me for work with the Alliance, and his wife, Carol, who were truly sent by the Lord to minister to us. But for me, my closest friends became my students, because I saw something in them and envisioned what they could be.

Three young guys in particular—Rick Pease, Steve Goodwin, and Kerry Bowman—all were passionate for Christ. They were sharp students and deeply committed, and I worked personally with each of them. I pointed them to role models and put them in the hands of other mentors. Then, when they were ready, I raised money for them to go to Europe on a mission trip, an event that defined the pattern for each of their lives.

These young men were special, and we all have stayed in touch over the years. Steve Goodwin, a brilliant guy, went on to serve many mission terms in Hungary and Germany. Kerry Bowman became the pastor of a large church in Indianapolis. And Rick Pease became CEO of a Japanese corporation in the U.S. named Enkei. He is now also on my board of directors. From time to time, Rick reminds me, "The greatest gift you ever gave us was to trust us enough to send us to Europe. It changed our lives."

My reward in all this was seeing their lives shaped to the calling Christ had given them. Yet now, recognition began to come to me from unexpected places. My first honorary doctorate was from Houghton College, a school in upstate New York, and it came as quite a shock to me. The president, Dan Chamberlain, wrote in his letter offering the degree, "In recognition of your pioneering impact in international evangelism." The honor was mostly for introducing apologetics into many countries in the two-thirds world.

Two other honorary doctorates came to me after that—one from Asbury College and the other from Tyndale College and Seminary (my alma mater, formerly Ontario Bible College) in Toronto. But the one from Houghton was particularly special, because for that ceremony my father bought me my colors to wear in the commencement exercises. It was a proud day not just for me but I'm sure for him too—a man who stood, as I now stood also, in the long shadows of those who had preceded us.

While in Canada, my father had begun to experience some heart problems, having already suffered a heart attack while in his fifties. Now, at his doctor's advice, he was scheduled for bypass surgery. Margie and I were still living in Niagara Falls at the time, and so when he phoned and said he had elected to have heart surgery, I asked if he would like me to take him to the hospital. He was most appreciative. I arrived on the morning of the admission, and we spent the day talking very intimately about life and danger and eternity. It was a very precious time for me with my dad, and it ended up being significant as the most meaningful time I ever had with him.

Dad had been nervous all that day, with an unsettled feeling about the operation. As he was being wheeled in for the surgery, he reached out and grabbed my arm, asking, "Son, would you pray for me?"

I did. It was a parable all its own. I spoke of our family's love for him and our gratitude for him, and that, no matter what, he was the dad who would always live in our hearts. There was a nervousness in him, because he was not in the best of weight or health, and heart surgery was still relatively new. As I left, he said, "Please give my love to little Sarah."

The next time I saw my father, he was on a respirator. He had emerged from the surgery unconscious and remained in that state for four days, a machine moving his chest up and down. He had been a heavy smoker earlier in life, and the surgeons who operated on him hadn't known the extent of the damage to his lungs.

On the fifth morning, Ajit came to be with him. I was getting ready to drive the seventy-five miles to come as well, as we were taking turns at his bedside. But before I left our house, the doctors came to Dad's room. That's when they turned off the respirator, and our father stopped breathing. Ajit looked at the nurse and asked, "Is that it?"

"I'm sorry, sir. That's it."

Dad was sixty-seven when he died; he survived my mother by just five years. Ajit phoned to give me the news. It was particularly hard on him, being so close to our dad.

My father had changed greatly in those few years after his late-in-life conversion. At his funeral, the vice president of the company where he worked, a Jewish man, commented, "In the death of Oscar Zacharias, we have lost not just our employment manager; we have lost the conscience of our company."

It was a moving tribute, and fitting of my dad's principles. Yet it paled next to the traits we children had come to see in the recent years of his life. As overbearing as he had been during his heyday of power in Delhi, he had become gentle and conciliatory during his latter years in Toronto. He lost all his pomposity and became very soft-spoken. We were only sorry that my mom didn't get to enjoy those years.

There were wonderful things about my dad that had seemed buried throughout his life, things that appeared clearer in retrospect. He had set aside everything he had built up in India—his position, his influence, his reputation—in a single moment to provide his children with better opportunities. To me, apart from his decision for Christ, that was the most telling fact of his ending years. To go to a strange land, to suddenly plan your life around your children's lives—it told me that this was part of his innermost desire for us all along.

I thank the Lord that Dad's death did not come before he had a chance to see what Christ had done in all of our lives. I'm convinced the changes my father saw in his children led directly to what the Lord did in his life—that it was a part of what ultimately led him to find peace on his journey.

Still, there was a coming event that he didn't live to see, which I wish he had. I was teaching at Nyack in 1983 when I received a phone call I never could have expected.

"Mr. Zacharias, my name is Leighton Ford, and on behalf of Billy Graham—"

That stopped me in my tracks.

"—on behalf of Billy Graham, I would like to invite you to speak at an historic conference for evangelists this year in Amsterdam."

I was awestruck by the offer. Later in the conversation, I had to ask, "Mr. Ford, could you tell me, how does Dr. Graham know about my preaching?" I didn't realize that Billy Graham even knew I existed.

Evidently, Dr. Graham had become aware of me and was following my ministry through some tapes he was given by Leighton (who is Dr. Graham's brother-in-law), an evangelist himself with the Billy Graham Evangelistic Association. Now, at the encouragement of Leighton, Dr. Graham wanted me to speak to a gathering of four thousand other itinerant evangelists, "the cream of the world's evangelists." It was an unbelievable opportunity, and a humbling one.

The topic I was asked to address was "The Lostness of Man." I had always spoken from an outline, and the message I put together was based on Romans 1. But Dr. Graham insisted that everyone who preached write out their sermons beforehand in their entirety, so they could be interpreted simultaneously into several languages.

I was very tired when Margie and I landed in Amsterdam, but I had to be whisked directly from the airport to meet with the team of interpreters, who were speaking languages from all over the world. It was such an extraordinary setting; all around me, I saw religious leaders connected in an intricate network—Bill Bright, Luis Palau,

Michael Green, John R. W. Stott. Many political leaders also graced the occasion. Finally, as I was having a bite of lunch, Billy Graham walked up to my table and extended his hand.

"You've got a powerful sermon, Ravi," he said, "one of the finest I've ever read." You can imagine the thrill that rippled through Margie and me over this man's comments about my sermon. I later learned that, in his kindness, Dr. Graham says this to everyone. But that's the kind of man he is—he wants to encourage. Whatever the other person has done, it is "the best I have heard."

The only way to describe my preaching experience at Amsterdam was *sheer exhilaration*. Seated before me were fellow evangelists from over one hundred nations. It was sobering to look out at the faces of four thousand others who were doing what I was doing. Yet I had shaped my message for them, around the theme we all had in common: without Christ, we are all lost.

The Lord anointed that day. As I finished, I stepped from the podium, grateful, first of all, that I hadn't blundered. And I was touched by the affirmations that came from some of the finest people whom I admired—Dr. Graham, Leighton Ford, and Cliff Barrows. In fact, Billy Graham was to follow me in the program, and as I finished preaching, he leaned over to Cliff and said: "This is what it's all about. I don't have to preach my sermon now." That is the humility of the man. But it was he that everyone had come to hear, and he preached in his own unique and powerful way. As I sat on the platform, listening, I knew it was an historic moment for me and for the thousands of others present.

Before I left Amsterdam on that occasion, something very curious struck me about the event. I pondered that there were so few people who were operating in the arena of apologetics. Most of the preaching in evangelism was geared to the "unhappy pagan." "What about the 'happy pagan,'" I thought, "the one who has no qualms about his life?" Life was about to change for me in my heartfelt desire to preach to the skeptic.

I would be invited back to preach at Amsterdam in 1986, this time to a gathering of ten thousand evangelists, an event that would go down as the largest gathering of nations in history. My first impression upon returning was the impact that had been made the first time I preached there. Total strangers grabbed my hand and said, "I was here in 1983 when you preached on the 'The Lostness of Man.' It changed my life as an evangelist." Many of these men were ministering in tough settings around the world and had received a fresh sense of their own calling through my message.

That was so reinforcing to me, especially because all I remembered from 1983 was being thankful for not humiliating myself. Chesterton's words had never been truer—that our confidence lies in our message and *not* in ourselves.

This time, Dr. Graham assigned the subject "Preaching across Cultural and Religious Barriers." I titled my message "Communicating in Babel"—and what an honor it was to speak to ten thousand of the world's evangelists. I believe these two conferences are among the greatest legacy Billy Graham has left. He reached out to us ordinary evangelists and affirmed us in our call. And through it, for me, God was again in the shadows, marking my path for the future and opening up the world.

CHAPTER 14

VERITAS

FROM AMSTERDAM IN AUGUST OF 1983, I HAD SCHEDULED A STOP IN INDIA to speak at a small conference of Christian and Missionary Alliance pastors. It was a humbling experience. Some of these men were bare-foot, and others had no change of clothes. As I spoke, many took notes on a single piece of paper, because it was all they had to spare. In many of their homes, the children didn't have books for school.

Yet, these were the cheeriest of men. On the day I left, they sang a song in Hindi that they had composed for me. It brought tears to my eyes to leave them.

At Amsterdam, I had seen some from the middle class and a few from the upper-middle class who were evangelists; now, in India, I was looking at those who worked in rural communities, barely mak-ing an adequate living to feed their families. I felt a storm of emo-tions within me. I realized there was so much facing the church in its efforts to make an impact on culture and society.

In the plane on the way back home to Nyack, facing a new bat-tery of classes, I told Margie, "I don't know why I'm doing what I'm doing." What I had seen and heard at Amsterdam had shown me that there still was not much outreach to the intellectual, nor were there many evangelists who had the training or access to reach those opin-ion makers of society. The combination of a proclaimer and apologist was very rare, especially the cultural evangelist-apologist. I also knew that many of the evangelists in my homeland of India were speak-ing mainly to one group of people. They weren't reaching upward. "Somebody has got to reach *them*," I said. At the same time, it was disheartening to see that so many of the devoted ministers in the land of my birth were untaught, untrained, and unprepared. I concluded I had to do something about it.

"I wish there was some way to raise money to start a ministry," I told Margie, "something both to reach the educated and to train preachers and others in apologetics. But more than that, to help the needy as well. If we could just get fifty thousand dollars, I believe we could build the base for such a ministry."

Margie had always had as much vision for the Lord's calling in my life as I have. But now she asked, "Where would we get *that* kind of money?" My wife had never held me back from any calling the Lord had placed on our lives. Her glance now told me she only wanted me to think sensibly, and of my limits. "Do it, but do it wisely!" is the essence of what she was saying.

I knew she was right. Margie had recognized the need as clearly as I did. We agreed we wouldn't tell anyone about our vision or the support that would be needed for it. We left it in the Lord's hands.

Almost immediately after my return, I informed the seminary administrators that I would be leaving, giving them a full year's notice; it would coincide with the end of my official contract with Alliance Theological Seminary. The administrators were disappointed and tried to talk me out of it, but I waved off every question. "I'm just in the wrong fray," I explained. "I know I'm battling in the wrong places."

Once they accepted my resignation, their only request was that I not tell anyone I was leaving until they could find a replacement. That made for two very difficult vows of silence on my part: no one could know the seminary's need, and no one could know Margie's and mine. But that mattered little to me at the moment. Once I handed in my resignation, one of the greatest stones I ever bore rolled off my shoulders. Although, in a strange way, I believe the Lord had been shaping me there for an important task as well.

After Amsterdam, invitations began pouring in from all over the world, far beyond what Margie and I could manage. Suddenly, the international scene was opened to me in ways I could not have imagined. The opportunity Billy Graham had given me to preach had provided a platform that couldn't have come any other way.

Margie and I sensed that this was the beginning of God's answer to our prayer. Still, we couldn't envision how it might come to pass. One weekend in November of 1983, as we were wrapping up an engagement at an event called the "Laymen's Conference" in Vermilion, Ohio, I made a request of the audience.

"We know that most of you are driving back to Cleveland after this," I said, "If you wouldn't mind, would you please pray for Margie and me? We're seeking God's wisdom on a certain matter."

A few minutes later, I was carrying our bags through the hotel lobby when a man who had attended the conference approached me. He was direct, yet soft-spoken, in his words.

"Ravi, I did as you asked just now," he said. "I went to my room and got on my knees, and I asked the Lord to reveal to me the wisdom you need. I asked Him if there was anything I could do to help in the decision you're making. Now, I don't know what that decision is, but the Lord did impress on me that I could help. He's led me to give you a check for fifty thousand dollars."

I gulped. I could not believe this. Nobody just blindly gives that kind of money to someone they don't know. Was it a joke?

"Sir, you don't even know me," I protested.

He looked me in the eye and said, "I'm going to trust you."

"And your name?" I asked.

He handed me his card. It read, "D. D. Davis Construction Company."

I didn't felt comfortable accepting that amount of money from a stranger, so I explained to Mr. Davis that I would rather meet with him first to explain the burden on our hearts. Then he could think about it. If I was going to be in his vicinity in a few months' time, I suggested that we could talk then.

"You don't have to come," he said. "I have a plane. I'll come and visit you."

So there we were, one week later, sitting in the White Plains Hilton across the Hudson River from Nyack, explaining to this stranger and his wife the vision we had for a ministry to reach intellectuals, opinion makers, and "the happy pagan."

As D. D. and his wife, Velma, listened, tears began streaming down his face.

"I'm not an educated man, Ravi," he said, "but I know how to make money. I've made a lot of it, money I'll never spend in my lifetime. There's money to be made on the streets of America, and all you have to do is pick it up. My problem isn't making money; it's wisdom in *spending* it. I want to get behind you.

"In my business, I construct refrigerated buildings, refrigerated trucks, cold-storage warehouses. And I've built them in places where people would starve otherwise, because they don't have a way to preserve their food.

"Ravi, what I'm doing in the food industry, you're doing with the gospel. You saw those people at the conference. They have no reach to the kinds of places you're going. You're the one who's going to take it there. Get your friends together, and let's meet with them."

Margie and I felt a bond immediately with this humble couple, and together we selected a weekend on which to begin our work together. We convened in January of 1984, Margie and I having asked our closest friends to come to Nyack to join us and hear our vision.

I shared how we envisioned a ministry that would communicate the gospel effectively within the context of the prevailing skepticism. It would seek to reach the thinker and to clear all obstacles in his path so that he or she could see the cross, clearly and unhindered.

"The presuppositions of the majority of this world aren't the same as Christians' presuppositions," I pointed out, "and many of their questions are honest ones." I told them I wanted to address those struggling people—the Thomases of the world—who saw life as not making sense. If the church didn't place true value on a person's questioning, then we were effectively absolving ourselves of any responsibility to that person. At the same time, if the skeptic's questions weren't honest, we had to address them in ways that exposed his or her dishonesty. Apologetics had to be about much more than answering questions—it had to focus on questioning the questions and clarifying truth claims.

Although the target audience would be the educated, such a ministry would necessarily keep as its aim every stratum of a culture's population. We would need to keep in view at all times the four arenas where society's values are shaped—academia, the business community, politics, and the arts.

We immediately allocated a portion of our budget to help needy pastors in India, such as the ones I had been with after Amsterdam '83. We bought motorbikes and scooters to help with their transportation needs, purchased books and paid school fees for their children's education, and provided money where needed for struggling families. We all agreed that any attempt at apologetics is ineffective unless your heart is also made tender to the physical needs of the world. I quoted someone who once said, "If you speak to a hurting world, you will never lack for an audience." In terms of an apologetics ministry, our approach would be to go to places on the basis of our strength and the inviting body's need, rather than on their strength and our need. In other words, we would not try to create opportunities but would respond to the needs and opportunities brought before us.

I had proposed a different name for the ministry other than my own name, but after everyone pondered it overnight, they advised, "No, Ravi, so much has happened with people in ministry having gone astray. If you give this ministry your name, it will stand up behind your integrity, or fall with the lack of it."

It was a scary thought to me. My character behind an entire organization? Yet I knew it was only right.

Ravi Zacharias International Ministries (RZIM) began in August of 1984, in Toronto, Canada. Today our headquarters is in Atlanta, Georgia, and we have offices in Canada, India, Singapore, the United Arab Emirates, and England, with several other bases planned. We purposely restrained growth at first, but over time the ministry expanded as the Lord's calling led.

As I moved out of the cloisters—from an anonymous role to a visible one—I was grateful that God had put people around me whom I loved, admired, and trusted. They would be needed for the increasingly heavy load and burden. For example, death threats were suddenly an issue. I was going into hostile countries more often, and I received phone calls from people wanting to get at me, especially from the Muslim world. At times, I suspected people of attempting to take me into places where they could do harm to me. In some Islamic nations, I had to be surrounded by bodyguards while addressing audiences, small and large. Yet, I have to say, even if those bodyguards had not been there, I still would have gone.

Whether you're in a visible position like mine or embedded like Koos Fietje, you have to learn that you cannot claim a path just because it is less intimidating. You must keep in mind that God does have an appointment with you, that there is a cost to serving him. At the same time, you have to be wise and not careless. To deny the reality that there are some places where you cannot go is to play the fool. More important, if you have not learned to pay the smaller prices of following Christ in your daily life, you will not be prepared to pay the ultimate price in God's calling.

Shortly after the fall of the Berlin Wall and the gradual opening of the Communist Eastern Bloc in Europe, I was speaking for Campus Crusade in Los Angeles. As I finished, I was motioned aside and introduced to two men from Russia. One was an interpreter; the other was General Yuri Kirshin, chief historian of the Center for Geopolitical Strategy in Moscow.

"Dr. Zacharias," the general said through his interpreter, "I am impressed with what I have heard. I would like to invite you to come to Moscow. We would be pleased to have you lecture at the Center, and also at the Lenin Military Academy."

Frankly, I was awed. The Cold War was still on, and the Soviet regime had not yet been dismantled. I had met with political and military leaders before, but I sensed that this was a significant opportunity.

In turn, almost casually, I invited General Kirshin to our ministry's upcoming "Founders Weekend" at the Greenbriar Inn in West Virginia to speak to us about what was going on in the Soviet Union at the time. To my great delight, he accepted and came to the event. What I hadn't planned for was that on the final night of our conference, a World Series game between the Atlanta Braves and the Toronto Blue Jays was on television. At the end of the evening, the ballroom was vacated almost immediately, with people scrambling to find a TV and watch the game.

Instead of addressing our founders, the general spent the rest of the evening talking with me through his interpreter at the front of the ballroom. Our conversation lasted well into the night when, finally, I had the privilege of leading General Kirshin to Christ.

"This is such a wonderful thrill," he said through tears. "It is unbelievable that I am having this experience!"

Now it was my turn to visit the general in his milieu. Margie and I traveled to Moscow, and my first engagement for the general there was at the Lenin Military Academy. It was a tough environment. Throughout my lecture, one of the officers kept giving me the choke sign. It was exasperating, to the point that I wanted to stop speaking and get into a verbal slugfest with him, but I thought better of it.

As soon as I finished, the officer shot to his feet and demanded, "All your talk is about God, God, God. What on earth is this you're talking about?"

My response to him was simple. "Sir, are you an atheist?"

"I am."

"If you don't know what it is I'm talking about, then how can you deny it?"

"What do you mean?"

(Atheists say that the term "God" is meaningless, yet they don't bother to know what it is they're denying.)

"It doesn't make sense to say you are an atheist," I pointed out, "if you do not know what you are denying."

From there a fascinating discussion ensued, with one young officer standing before the gathering and giving a courageous defense of his faith. "I know Jesus Christ," he stated, "and I know what this man is talking about." He was the lone officer to do so.

Later, at the hotel where Margie and I were staying, there was a knock on our door. It was the young officer, his hat in his hand. "I want you to know, sir," he said, "that I have been praying for years that someone would come to the Academy and present a defense of the Christian faith." We invited him in and had a moving conversation. His goal was to be the first Christian chaplain in the Soviet military. Margie and I prayed for him to have the strength he clearly would need for such a task.

As we drove with General Kirshin to the Center for Geopolitical Strategy, I told him about the young officer's visit. "I admire your courage for hosting that event," I said.

"No," he answered, "the courage was not mine. I could hide behind this event as an academic challenge that I wanted to present to the class. The real courage was in that young man who stood up. That's the kind of courage it is going to take to win this country."

The Center for Geopolitical Strategy in Moscow is twelve stories in all, eight above ground and four below. Every Russian premier or president has graduated from the Center, from Mikhail Gorbachev dating back to General Mikhail Kutusov, who fought against Napoleon.

When we arrived, the meeting room was filled with professors formally dressed in their imposing military uniforms. As we began our interaction around a table, they were all staring me down. The iciness of the atmosphere practically hung from the ceiling.

I told them stories right out of their own books. One was of Joseph Stalin, who at one time had been a seminary student but decided to renounce his faith in God. Stalin wasn't his true name, but a name given to him because it translates in Georgian as "man of steel." Stalin could will people into a different worldview with his piercing eyes. Even Lenin was afraid of the iron fist when Stalin took the helm.

The professors were clearly becoming uncomfortable at my comments and had to appear as defending their belief in "the State." They began to challenge me, one by one, with one of them saying, "I know all about your God! I saw my grandmother murdered by a German soldier who was wearing a belt that read, 'Gott mit Uns' ['God with Us']."

Finally, I said, "Gentlemen, before we go any further, let me tell you a story. This morning, my wife, General Kirshin, and I were walking along on this bitterly cold day in Moscow, heading to our first engagement, when we encountered a man wearing only slacks and wielding a huge machete. He ran straight up to us and stared at me, standing perhaps two feet in front of me. He lifted his blade, and I thought this was the end. Instead, he froze. Then he moved on, yelling and screaming. Prior to that episode, my team was attacked by a band of gypsies. Moscow has become one of the most violent cities in the world; the Russian mafia is controlling the land, and you know it.

"In this room are men who have labored very hard to prepare freedom for the people. But you are not able to prepare the *people* for freedom. Look at what is happening. After years of imposing an atheistic worldview from above, what has been produced? Unparalleled lawlessness in the land. You could not change the human heart."

I was addressing ideologies, worldviews, human nature, the human condition, the depravity of the human heart—and the setting allowed me to illustrate it profusely. I ended by sharing my testimony, how as a teenager I had given my life to Christ because of the emptiness and meaninglessness I saw in my life. I contrasted this with a description of Stalin's last moments on earth, when he clenched his fist toward the heavens, threw his head back, and was gone.

When I finished, there was pin-drop silence in the room. The whole demeanor had changed. They were especially silent when I was sharing my own conversion story. As the session closed, the professors lined up to shake my hand, the sternest of them taking Margie's hand and kissing it.

As the school's director bid me farewell, he presented me with a copy from the Center's library of Charles Dickens' translation of the New Testament. He told me, "Dr. Zacharias, I believe that what you have said to us here today is true. But it is very difficult to change after seventy years of believing a lie." There was a sadness in his eyes as he made this admission. They had set a course in history that was based on a lie.

Indeed, his comment told a tale in itself. It was a tragic story of how an entire culture can be shaped by the impact of a single ideology, with lie after lie perpetrated for decades. Ironically, the chief newspaper, *Pravda*, in reality a vehicle of falsehood, actually means "Truth."

After the event, General Kirshin took Margie and me to a meager dinner. He was very quiet, reflecting on all that had been said. I decided to tell him a story of how a foreign dignitary had come to confront Stalin, asking him over dinner, "How long do you intend to keep torturing your people and expect them to still follow you?"

Stalin's response was plain. He called for a live chicken to be brought to the table. He clutched the bird by the neck and began to de-feather it until it was completely denuded. Then he placed it on the ground. Stalin grabbed a piece of bread, got up from the table, and started walking away.

The chicken hobbled behind him and began nuzzling up to his trouser legs. Stalin reached down with a crumb from the bread, and the chicken pecked away at it.

"Do you see this chicken?" Stalin asked his guest. "I inflicted pain on it. Now it will follow me for food the rest of its life. People are like that. If you inflict pain on them, they will follow you for food the rest of their lives."

As I finished this story, I saw tears running down General Kirshin's face. He knew the cost of atheism was enormous. The Soviets had sacrificed their own people at the altar of power. It was not religion that had been the opiate of the people, but irreligion that had drugged them into the illusion of power and the reality of self-destruction.

I do not know how or exactly when, but after this visit to Moscow I noticed a gradual change in the nature of the invitations I was receiving. God had begun to set the table for me to address the political world, and in 1993 I received an invitation to Bogota, Colombia. There I spoke to members of the judiciary on the importance of having a moral framework.

While I was there, a tall, distinguished-looking man asked to see me at my hotel the following day. I had no idea who he was until I awoke the next morning and saw the hotel surrounded by military tanks. As I opened the door to my room, I saw bomb-sniffing dogs in the hallway. I thought maybe a bomb threat had taken place, but I soon learned that the hotel was being cleared for my visitor.

He had been the main figure in tracking down and capturing the biggest drug lord in Colombia. Now this man's life was in full-time jeopardy. Over breakfast, he told me, in fluent English, "I have been asked to frame a part of the legal system here. After hearing you speak, I would like to have your thoughts."

"Sir," I told him, "you will never be able to find an answer for your society until you find the answer for yourself."

He looked intrigued. We talked further about how a worldview that is incoherent within will only yield to an incoherence on the outside. What life is about defines how life must be lived.

I asked, "Do you know who God is, and what life is all about?"

"No, sir."

"Would you be interested in finding out?"

After breakfast, we went up to my room and continued talking. An hour or so later, he bowed his head and trusted in Christ.

It has been gratifying since then to see this humble man have a powerful impact on his country and in the area of international law.

Apologetics is not just giving answers to questions—it is questioning people's answers, and even questioning their questions. When you question someone's question, you compel him or her to open up about his or her own assumptions. Our assumptions must be examined.

If you're predictable in your approach—if your listeners know where you're going—they will turn you off. If you hand people outlines, they're already ahead of you, just filling in blanks. If you tell them they need love, they already know that. The task is to find the means to stretch their thinking in unpredictable ways, to take them in directions they are not expecting to go. Sometimes it is through an argument, sometimes through an illustration, sometimes through a stretch of the imagination. But you've got to take them in a radius of directions, like the spokes of a wheel. That is an Easterner's natural way of thinking, while the typical Westerner's way is more linear.

While I was naturally inclined to the "spokes" idea, it had helped me to enjoy thinking. I realized that was what Chesterton had been doing for me all along. Later, I saw that this approach had done something important for me—helping me to better respect my audience, to see that if this kind of thinking enthralled me, there are bound to be others who are similarly enthralled. Yes, logic is linear, but its implications are radial.

⁜

By 1990, THE LOAD OF MINISTRY HAD GOTTEN SO HEAVY THAT I DECIDED TO take a sabbatical for the first time since I had started in the ministry. I spent part of that year at Cambridge University in England with my family, and it was a very special time for us.

I was invited to be a visiting scholar, and I decided to focus my studies on the Romantic writers and the moralist philosophers. While at Cambridge, I also had the privilege of sitting under some great minds in other disciplines. I heard Dr. Stephen Hawking lecture, witnessing one of history's greatest scientific minds come to terms with his own philosophy of life, struggling between agnosticism and theism. My professor in quantum physics was Dr. John Polkinghorne, a latecomer to Christ, who provided me with some powerful ammunition for my ministry in the years to come. And I studied under some of the world's finest philosophers, many of them skeptics and some radically so. I knew that if I was going to face the challenge of atheism and secularism, which were becoming the reigning worldviews in the West, I needed to hear it from the toughest sources.

My professor of philosophy was Don Cuppitt, who was president of Emmanuel College at Cambridge. He was an ordained Anglican minister, as well as an atheist, and in lecture after lecture he lashed out at the Christian faith. To me, his attacks were flimsy because they seemed so personally motivated. I often thought afterward, "That's it? That's the best bullet he's got? He thinks this is piercing the armor of Christendom?"

Day after day, this man reserved his greatest wrath for Christianity. His larger premise was that all theologies were nothing more than anthropologies. In short, what we believe in our culture about values, we translate and sublimate into a religion.

But one day, as he lectured on Hinduism, I saw that his statements were completely false. "In India, for example," he declared, "there is a demeaning of women. This has gotten translated into the religion, and it is why Hinduism has become a male-dominated religion."

I was shocked at how little he knew of that religious worldview or of the Indian culture, for that matter. So I challenged him.

"Dr. Cuppitt, your premise is entirely wrong," I said. "Are you aware that in Hinduism, the transference of divine power is actually matrilineal? It comes through the feminine deity Shakti. And one of the most powerful deities in India is Kali, the goddess of Calcutta, for whom that city is named.

"I'm afraid your facts are simply wrong. They certainly don't support your premise that all theology is anthropology. And that premise clearly doesn't hold true about Christianity. It was the women to whom Jesus revealed himself after the resurrection. Why would he have elevated the testimony of one whose witness would not even be counted in court?"

He was rather shocked. He wasn't accustomed to that kind of direct challenge in the classroom. But from our exchange, the class went on to have some fascinating discussions, and a bit of backpedaling from the esteemed professor was in order.

In many ways, my sabbatical at Cambridge was a return to the idyllic early days of our family's life. The time we spent strolling in the evenings and enjoying the surroundings of that magnificent campus was precious. We even added an English border collie to our family, naming him G. K. after G. K. Chesterton. And, of course, there were the fabulous bookstores in Cambridge. Every time I walked into one, I was so overcome by the thrill of knowledge that I had to sit for a moment and gather my thoughts. Then I would begin, browsing through shelf after shelf after shelf.

Cambridge was also significant because it was there that I wrote my first book—*A Shattered Visage: The Real Face of Atheism*. (It has recently been republished under the title *The Real Face of Atheism*.) The title was based on a poem by Percy Bysshe Shelley called "Ozymandias":

> *I met a traveller from an antique land,*
> *Who said—"Two vast and trunkless legs of stone*
> *Stand in the desert ... Near them, on the sand,*
> *Half sunk, a shattered visage lies, whose frown,*
> *And wrinkled lip, and sneer of cold command,*
> *Tell that its sculptor well those passions read*
> *Which yet survive, stamped on these lifeless things,*
> *The hand that mocked them, and the heart that fed:*

And on the pedestal, these words appear:
My name is Ozymandias, King of Kings:
Look on my Works, ye Mighty, and despair!
Nothing beside remains. Round the decay
Of that colossal Wreck, boundless and bare
The lone and level sands stretch far away."

As I wrote the book, the picture I saw in my mind was of a seemingly endless desert, such as I once saw when I rode for an hour on horseback in the Egyptian desert, the barren sands stretching in every direction, almost disorienting the mind. I imagined coming upon a broken statue lying on its side—showing that demigods come and go and that nothing remains of them except their own opinion—a desolate, once-upon-a-time individual. This image was a metaphor for atheism: always trying to dance on the grave of theism, never realizing that in the Christian worldview there is *nothing* in the grave. Our Savior is risen. Atheism is just too philosophically bankrupt to answer life's tormenting questions. History is replete with power-mongers who have come and gone.

(That book, *The Real Face of Atheism*, has now lasted in the arena of sales for over fifteen years.)

My experience at Cambridge that year had reaffirmed to me an important task in apologetics, namely, to unmask the skeptic, because his problem with God isn't an intellectual one; it is a moral one. The famous atheist Bertrand Russell stated that he didn't believe in God because "he didn't give me enough evidence." I suggest that his problem, and that of many others like him, was not an absence of evidence but the suppression of it. Russell himself admitted that throughout his life, and in all his thinking, he never landed on love. How could a man who never found love tell you what life is all about?

Yet, the demand for morality comes equally from the skeptic, not just from the believer. The host of one of my speaking engagements at a university was driving me to the airport when he informed me, "My wife brought our neighbor to the meeting last night. She's a medical doctor—and not a believer."

"What did she think?"

"She was very quiet afterward, and I asked her about her reaction to your lecture. She thought for a moment and said, 'Very persuasive. I wonder what he's like in his private life.'"

Everything the skeptic had heard was being framed through a moral perspective. I was fascinated by her reaction, for even in her skepticism she made morality an evidence of truth. Yet, a skeptic has no metaphysical basis for such morality. By her reaction, the doctor had demonstrated that deep inside our souls, God's reason keeps surfacing unwittingly to the skeptic.

In 1993, an event took place that put me on the track of apologetic evangelism from which there was no turning back. It was the "Harvard Veritas Forum."

The idea of the forum was born out of a discussion I had had in an elevator with a businessman from Ohio, who wanted to bring the Christian faith before some of the finest minds of our time in order to have it tested and challenged. Kelly Monroe, a dedicated young woman who does pioneering Christian work on university campuses, asked me to be the forum's inaugural speaker. Kelly, author of *Finding God at Harvard*, was and is one of the most effective workers on the academic scene.

The first Veritas Forum was scheduled to take place at the busiest time on the Harvard calendar, the weekend of the Harvard-Yale football game. No one was sure what kind of turnout we might have. The venue would be Harvard Law School, and that evening, as I stepped to the lectern, the place was packed to overflowing. Every seat was taken, with students and faculty sitting on the stairs, on banisters, and on the floor next to the podium where I stood. That night was made more memorable to me because I had injured my back in Scotland the week before and herniated a disc. I had been in bed for a week, and this was the first day I was on my feet, walking with great caution lest I reinjure it. In that weakness, I delivered two lectures on successive nights: "A Critique of Atheism" and "A Defense of the Christian Faith."

The response both nights was tremendous. Each time I finished, students and faculty stood to their feet and applauded. It made a profound impact upon those who were there. Some even deemed the lectureship and its impact quite historic. For that, the credit should go to Kelly and her team for their hard work behind the scenes and for the seeds that had long been sown leading up to the event. After the first lecture, young Christians came forward to tell me that, up until then, they had felt forced to lie low in their beliefs. Now they had been given the robust confidence to present their faith again. In fact, on the final night, I was joined on a panel by some Christian students who were eager to answer the questions of their schoolmates. It was a remarkable evening. Their brilliant young minds engaged the challenge to faith from every direction.

Not long after that experience at the Harvard Veritas Forum, Chuck Colson contacted me. He had heard the taped lectures, and he strongly encouraged me to put them into print. "Ravi, you cannot leave it just with the talks," he said. "This has to go out to readers."

With his encouragement and his suggestion to Word Publishing (now called W Publishing Group), the book became *Can Man Live Without God*. In it, the lectures I delivered at Harvard were put to print and even expanded upon. (The question-and-answer sessions, which had been so robust and lively, we left unedited and intact.) In this book, I traced what happened to the world after Nietzsche announced the "death of God." The publisher had expected the book to last for twelve to eighteen months on the shelves. After eleven years in print, it is still my bestselling book.

I have received letters from readers in Germany, the former Soviet Union, and former Eastern Bloc countries, including one from a former atheist professor in Albania who said the book changed his life. He was so thrilled that it had been translated into Albanian because that was the most atheistic country in the world. Now the minister of religion in Albania has had the book distributed to every university faculty member. Newscasters, actors, politicians, university students, and homemakers write moving letters of how the book has changed their lives. I marvel that the circumstances that brought *Can Man Live Without God* into being could only have come through the grace of God.

The Harvard experience opened to us the university campuses of North America and, indeed, around the world. Following the forum, invitations to colleges just took off. I have spoken on almost every major campus—Berkeley, Princeton, Cornell, you name it. If we haven't been to a major school, it is more often than not because we haven't yet had the time to accommodate the request.

I had seen for years that the university scene was one of immense need. University students all over the world are longing and hungry. Now, as I look back over the past twenty-one years, I can't help wondering what would have happened in North America were it not for campus organizations such as InterVarsity, Navigators, Campus

Crusade, and others that took the university challenge seriously. Yet, the need remains and is ever-increasing, even as ideologues in professorial positions often berate or ridicule religion in general and Christianity in particular. The lines have become clearly drawn, and it is up to the thinking Christian to train the mind, take seriously the questioner, and respond with intelligence and relevance. I can honestly say that on every campus we visit, the response is beyond what we ever expected. Yes, truth is on the scaffold, as James Russell Lowell wrote, but the scaffold *is* swaying the future, and God *is* in the shadows, keeping watch—keeping watch upon His truth and upon His own.

chapter 15

ONE DESTINATION

THE FOUNDING OF RZIM EXTRACTED A MUCH GREATER COST FROM ME than I would have thought. I have to say it changed me more than I shaped it. First, let me share its downside.

You start an organization to help support and free you, but, especially in the formative years, the reverse takes place. You end up creating an organization that you support. Today, RZIM employs about a hundred people full-time in six countries, and for years a lot of that burden fell on my shoulders. I remember the early days, when I'd come home from a trip to India and sit down with my secretary and my administrative assistant. As we looked at our bank balance, I realized we weren't going to be able to meet payroll, to say nothing of the bills on hand. During that crisis, I wondered, "Have I traded one set of financial burdens for another?" Now I was responsible not only for *my* support but also for the needs of so many here and overseas.

If I could have done things differently in those days, I would have taken the role of leadership much more seriously. I didn't realize how much it takes to lead. On the day RZIM was officially launched, I went to bed at night, wondering, "Do I know what I'm doing?" I never envisioned that our ministry would grow as it has.

If you have a very particular individual calling like mine, you can become so focused on it that you lose sight of the bigger picture. I'm convinced that the most difficult task in leadership is to build the right team—and we now have a fine one at RZIM, but it hasn't been without its bumpy roads. The biggest price you pay is when you do not choose the right people for certain tasks. That is not to impugn them; it's just to say it's not fair to you and even to them. You can pick a wonderful person for a job, but if he or she is not right for the task, you're in double jeopardy.

This is where Billy Graham excels. He apparently is comfortable with his limitations, and over the years he has put together an incredible ministry team. Down through the years, people haven't recognized the genius of his leadership.

Conversely, you can become so focused on the bigger picture that you forget the individual call that God has placed upon you. I have always underestimated what God was trying to do in my calling. And when you underestimate that, you are at fault, because you do not prepare adequately. I'm a preacher and writer, not an administrator. But inevitably you must administer your role as a leader.

After twenty-one years—with millions of miles traveled, thousands of conversations with people, the constant press for development and fund-raising, continual apologetic study, intense open forums, and threats on your life—your restfulness is deeply affected. I have to admit that it has sapped my lightheartedness about life. I changed from being a typically happy, "take life as it comes" sort of guy (and a practical joker, remember!) to one who's very serious. I've become more driven than I ever wanted to be, and more impatient. That's not a natural trait for me.

Margie has often expressed sadness that I have lost the humorous side of my personality. Although it may sound odd for me to say this, that may be one of my biggest regrets. In the early days of my preaching, I used a lot of humor. It's an effective way of lightening serious issues and yet getting at them from an additional angle. But once I got into major philosophical issues, I decreased my use of humor until I dropped it altogether. People's expectations seem to be different in the realm of apologetics, and that probably had a lot to do with it.

My children have always shown great affection for me, but I'm sure that deep inside they probably think, "We wish Dad had remained the way we'd known him before." More and more since 1984, our children have had to see their father as spearheading a ministry in a continual growth pattern. When you're in the kind of position I took on, expectations are always rising, with people wanting more of you, and gradually you no longer have freedom to socialize as you want. You have to plan not only your days but also your hours. It's a reality my family has graciously coped with. Those wonderful days when I could study at home, enjoy lunch breaks with my family, take thirty-minute naps, and have afternoon tea are long gone.

But there is a brighter side, a much brighter side than I can fully state. The rewards of this ministry have been immeasurable, too numerous even to name. One thing that has never changed about me is my continued pleasure in a handful of close friendships, whether old or new, and my years in RZIM have provided me with treasured ones. In fact, bonds with close friends have become especially important to me during these heavy ministry years. There are a handful of people I feel I can pick up with at any time and be right on track. One of these is Joe Stowell, the former president of Moody Bible Institute. Another was Kip Jordan from Word Publishing, who died tragically a few years ago.

I continue to miss Kip deeply. He became for me the kind of friend I'd always wanted. Kip was a fantastic conversationalist, and he and I and our wives shared a love for reading. We once took a trip together to the Grand Cayman Islands, and while our wives went snorkeling, Kip and I spent a whole day reading and talking, trading off reading passages from several books. I can't express the pleasure we had that day as we exchanged knowledge, wonder, beauty, and joy.

God has given me terrific friendships all over the world. I can go to just about any airport and call someone, and they'll meet me to share a meal. I think of marvelous friends in Singapore, India, Oxford, New Zealand, and the Middle East—people whom I know would do anything for me.

And there have been wonderful surprises in latter years—the kinds of moments that cause me to step back and marvel at the wonders God has worked.

Some years ago, I was speaking to a filled auditorium at LeTourneau University in Longview, Texas. After the meeting, a man came up, pushing his way through the well-wishers in the front. "There's a gentleman here in a wheelchair who would like to shake your hand," he said. "Would you be able to come to the back for just a moment, please?"

I followed him to the back of the auditorium, where the man in the wheelchair extended his hand to me. "It's really nice to meet you, my brother," he said. "My name is Leonard Ravenhill."

I almost fell on my knees. I now had the opportunity to tell this man what his book, *Why Revival Tarries*, had meant to me. He was quite moved and invited me to his house in Lindale for tea the next day. What a day that was!

Now, virtually every major engagement I have brings about some event in the present that ties to the past. I could link so much in one anecdote after another. And I keep always in mind that it's important to see these connections as a design that God has woven. He alone knew what was coming, and, in bringing it to pass, He has taken me into the future with *His* design in mind, not mine. In doing so, He causes me to see this design His way, and that is the best way. His story always has a greater plot than ours, and His surprises make the story continuous and not fragmented.

In 1989, as I was speaking in England at a conference, I mentioned that Malcolm Muggeridge was one of my heroes and that his books were among my favorites. A man in the audience came to me afterward and said that Muggeridge lived just fifteen miles up the road from where we were. Unable to pass up the opportunity, I got Muggeridge's telephone number and phoned him—and the next day, I was at lunch with Malcolm and Kitty Muggeridge! We spent about three hours together, hours I have treasured since then. What stories he had—from Gandhi to Stalin to the great figures of the mid-twentieth century. That afternoon was a gift from God to my heart. Muggeridge agreed to write the introduction to my book *The Real Face of Atheism*, but to my great regret, he passed away before my manuscript was complete. He and I exchanged notes on the tragedy of the West as it flirts with atheism but also celebrated the reality that truth has a long reach and will triumph in the end. His encouragement to me was momentous. Meeting him was another reminder that God was at work, putting everything together for me over the years.

I was in my office in Atlanta one day when a young man from Russia showed up at our ministry. He asked if he could see me. I welcomed him in and kept staring at him, knowing that he looked familiar.

"I am a military chaplain now," the grinning man told me. He was the young military officer whose courage had remained so vivid in my memory. Now he had come to thank me for speaking to the Lenin Military Academy.

"You didn't know it then, but your lecture had a great impact on the officers," he said, and he proceeded to describe to me the wonderful things that had happened. Then he urged me, "Please don't give up doing what you're doing. It is making a difference."

He could not have known what his reflection meant. People like me find courage from watching what God has done in others who heard truths that came through you. I remember well the lives that God used to keep *me* on the path, and now I rejoice to hear about how the impact that once was made on me has been transferred to another.

India continues to hold so much of my heart at this stage in my life. I go back two or three times a year to fulfill key invitations. I could mention many experiences. But a very recent one stands out—once again to complete a story. In 2004, I was invited to speak at a dinner in Mumbai, and when I arrived, the host extended a hand in greeting.

"Dr. Zacharias, my name is Sunil Dutt. I will be your host."

I paused. "Sunil Dutt? The famous actor?" The man I had admired as a moviegoing youngster, whom I'd seen in the epic Indian film *Mother India*?

He turned red and answered, "You know who I am then?"

"I certainly do, sir, and what an honor to meet you!"

"The honor is mine," he interjected. "I really want to hear what you have to say as a son of India who is now speaking to audiences the world over."

He had no idea how strange those words sounded to me, coming from him. And he couldn't have imagined my first encounter with him, on-screen in a Delhi movie theater, my feet kicked up alongside my buddies' in the cheap seats. Now we sat side by side in a hotel as he introduced me and then requested that all the speakers—who were prepared to do the pleasantries in typical Indian fashion, taking up long spans of time—please forgo all of that so I could have all the time I needed to speak to them. After my speech, he stood to his feet, and with hands folded, he thanked me for what I said. He then invited me back so that more in his profession could hear this message.

I couldn't help but think of the irony. I had gone to the movies to escape my desperation; now I was being invited by those who made the movies to speak about what meaning in life really is and where it comes from.

One of the great thrills in these years has been to meet the man from whose lips I first heard the gospel—Sam Wolgemuth. Here was the man whose careful sermon in a hot auditorium in Delhi had led me down an aisle and into a decision that would change everything for me. After I moved to the West, our paths crossed many times. I cannot count the number of times Sam would show up when I was speaking in the United States. Invariably, from the front row, he would gaze with a look of parental pride as I presented the talk for the evening. He and his wife, Grace, used to take an annual trip on which they visited their children, who were scattered around the country, and they always managed to fit Margie and me into that schedule as they drove through Atlanta. He always held my arm as he walked by my side—like a father would hold the arm of a son he loved. The last time I saw him before he passed away, he walked from the pastor's office at the famed Willow Creek Church in South Barrington, Illinois, to the auditorium where I would speak, with his arm in mine. In his other arm he held a bag full of my books and tapes that he had bought from the church's bookstore. I have no doubt he already had them at home, but this was just more for the keeping, in the gratitude that filled his heart for my life. I took him with me then so that he could have the front row one more time and be my seniormost cheerleader. Little did I know, the first time I met him, that his son Robert, an author himself, would one day become my close friend, my adviser in the vocation of writing, and my literary agent. God knew it long before. He just saved the story lines.

As I talk about "seniormost," one of the greatest friends I could have had in the last twenty years was D. D. Davis. It was so fitting that I had met this man at a laymen's conference, because he was to me the ultimate example of what a lay contributor to the gospel could be.

In November 2003, just two days after we had been together, D. D. went into the hospital for a pain in his leg. It was exactly twenty years before, almost to the day, that we had met. In this instance we had just finished our annual event, which D. D. always funded to enable us to move forward for another year. It had been a wonderful weekend. But now he had suddenly taken ill. When I phoned him from Dallas, where I was attending a meeting, I reached him in his hospital room. His response was characteristic: "Why are you wasting your nickel on this call?"

I did not know it would be my last conversation with my dear friend and cofounder of this ministry. Something went wrong in the immediate treatment a young doctor had given him. I shall not go into the details because it was quite upsetting to his family and to all of us; what was done ought never to have been done. D. D. died on the operating table. He had gone to the hospital, complaining of a pain in his leg, and he ended up undergoing a heart procedure from which he never recovered. As painful as it has been to think of that, D. D. was a firm believer in the sovereignty of God. He would always say to me, "There are no accidents in life—just incidents that remind us who is boss."

D. D. Davis gave millions to RZIM over the years, in so many generous ways. RZIM was not the only ministry D. D. supported, and I know that others can testify as we can, that each time he gave, it reflected the spirit of the gospel. And he never asked for anything in return. "All I want," he said to me time and time again, "is your integrity."

He was one of the finest human beings I had ever met in my life. His life was about right things, and he wanted only that from others—all for the sake of Christ. What a privilege it is now to have his daughter Beverly playing the role in the ministry that he did. And now one other businessman and his wife have come alongside to model their lives after what D. D. did for us. Together they pour into my life the affirmation of D. D. Davis. Yet, I should say that what I miss most in his absence is the fatherlike figure he was to me. He really loved me and believed in my calling. This is so individual in its expression that no one ever replaces that individuality. Each one brings their irreplaceable individuality to make life a pattern of diversity with a pursuit of unity.

So has it all been worth it? Yes, and more. Add to this the thousands who have come to know Jesus Christ through this ministry and the incredible team that now works with me, supporting, doing their part, preaching the gospel with heart and mind—many of them half my age. The board of this ministry has been a blessing that I cannot gainsay. And to have the joy of my family working so closely with me is the biggest thrill of all.

In one sense, the family becomes larger. There is one such person from many years before who has come near in later years. His appearance was perhaps the greatest surprise of all. Yes, God was in the shadows here as well.

I was in Vancouver for a lecture when my phone rang late at night. "Hello?" I answered.

"Brother Ravi."

With that one sound, I knew immediately who it was—Hien.

After Vietnam, I hadn't known whether my young interpreter friend was even still alive. Now, as my excitement gushed forth, he explained, "I am in San Francisco."

"What are you doing here, Hien?"

"Have you got time to listen?"

If ever I had the time for anything, it was this.

After Vietnam fell, Hien was captured by the Vietcong and imprisoned. They accused him of collaborating with the CIA, since he had worked with missionaries. In prison, they worked him over, telling him again and again that he had been brainwashed by Westerners. They took away his Bible and forbade him to speak English, the language he had loved, permitting him to use only Vietnamese or French.

"There is no such thing as God," came the refrain from his captors, day after hellish day.

The hour finally came when Hien wondered, "Maybe they are right. Maybe there *is* no such thing as God." As he thought back to some of my sermons and the shared blessings we had enjoyed, he wondered if perhaps I had been deluded too. That night he went to bed, muttering to himself, "I'm through with God. When I wake up in the morning, no more God, no more prayer."

The new day dawned, and the commanding officer of the prison barked out the assignments for the day. Hien was to clean the latrines. He cringed when he heard it. It was the ultimate form of indignity for the prisoners. The latrines were the absolute dregs of human filth, and Hien spent the entire day in those inhospitable surroundings.

His final task was to empty the trash cans, which were filled with soiled toilet paper. All day long, he labored with reminders to himself—"No God today." But as his work was coming to an end, something in the last trash can happened to catch his eye. It was a piece of paper with printed type. As Hien looked closer, he saw it was in English. Hungry to read this language again, he looked around to make sure nobody was watching. He hastily rinsed off the filth and tucked the paper into his pocket.

That night, after everyone had fallen asleep, he carefully took out his flashlight and removed the still damp paper from his pocket. In the upper right-hand corner of the page were the words "Romans 8." *Thư Rôma*

Hien, in a state of shock, began reading.

"And we know that in all things God works for the good of those who love him, who have been called according to his purpose."

He read on.

> What, then, shall we say in response to this? If God is for us, who can be against us? He who did not spare his own Son, but gave him up for us all — how will he not also, along with him, graciously give us all things? Who will bring any charge against those whom God has chosen?... Who shall separate us from the love of Christ? Shall trouble or hardship or persecution or famine or nakedness or danger or sword?... No, in all these things we are more than conquerors through him who loved us. For I am convinced that neither death nor life, neither angels nor demons, neither the present nor the future, nor any powers, neither height nor depth, nor anything else in all creation, will be able to separate us from the love of God that is in Christ Jesus our Lord.

Hien began crying. Of all the Scripture verses he had known, these were the ones he most needed to hear, and now they had come back to him. "Lord," he realized, "you would not let me out of your reach for even one day." He turned over in his bed that night and prayed.

The next morning, when he saw the commanding officer, Hien asked him, "Sir, would you mind if I cleaned the latrines again?"

The officer stared at him, quite puzzled. Thinking Hien was being rather arrogant, he decided to assign him to the latrines indefinitely. "You are going to clean them every day, until I tell you to stop," he commanded.

Hien did not know it in the beginning, but the officer himself had been tearing out those pages from the Bible and using them for toilet paper. Now, each day, Hien rinsed them clean, hid them in his pocket, and used them for his devotions at night. He ended up collecting numerous passages from the book of Romans, as well as from other books of the Bible.

After a while, he was let out of prison, and he started to plan his escape from the country. Some fifty others, including a high-powered political family, were involved in this attempt, Hien's third after two failed previous attempts. As the days passed, they worked to build a boat that would be able to navigate the high seas.

A few days before they were to leave, two Vietcong confronted Hien. "Are you planning to escape?" they demanded.

"No."

"Tell us the truth."

"I am telling you the truth."

"Are you lying to us?"

"No."

As they left, Hien was filled with remorse. He'd felt he had no choice but to lie, especially since it would have put the others at risk. Now he prayed, "Lord, I want you to be in control of my life again. I am sorry that I lied. Here I am again, depending on my own wisdom. If you want me to tell those men the truth, send them back to me. I promise I will tell the truth."

They did come back—just hours before the group's departure time. Only now, there were four Vietcong, and they grabbed Hien, pushing him against a wall.

"We know you're going to leave," they said.

"Yes, I am," he admitted, "with fifty-two others. Are you going to put me back in prison?"

"No," they whispered. "We want to go with you."

Hien was rendered speechless. At first, he wondered if it was a trap. But it wasn't—the four Vietcong did go with them.

Once they hit the high seas, the boat was rocked by a terrible storm. "Brother Ravi," Hien told me, "if it weren't for those four men, we would not have made it. They had a tremendous ability to sail."

Days later, they arrived safely in Thailand, and Hien was free. Eventually, he made it to San Francisco, and, after earning a degree from the University of California (Berkeley), he now ran a financial planning firm.

"Brother Ravi, I am getting married," he said, "and I wanted to ask if you would officiate at my wedding." I was overjoyed when my friend later visited our home in Atlanta and spent time with my family. His words carried real weight as he spoke tenderly to our children about what real intimacy with God means, and what it means to live a successful life.

People sometimes have the illusion that success is the tangible result from a plan or effort put to work, or some material gain accomplished through genius or expertise. I would answer that those things should bring the right kind of enjoyment, but only if you are undergirded in life itself by what is true and of ultimate value. Otherwise, if you are merely a pragmatist, success and possessions bring only the wrong kind of enjoyment.

I am asked about this on occasion with regard to whether I've found greater fulfillment through the larger organization of RZIM. On a very practical level, the answer is *no*. As the ministry has grown larger, so have the demands, and that has never suited my personality. Managing those things has always gone against the grain for me.

On a personal level, the answer also is *no*. To me, there has never been any greater fulfillment than in being where God wants me to be. And that fulfillment isn't any greater now, because I was fulfilled from the beginning, knowing that God had me in the right place at all times. If anything, I had more of a comfort level in the early years—with a normal, day-to-day life with my wife and children—than I do now.

I would prefer to rephrase the question: is there fulfillment in knowing you're where God wants you to be? Does that bring satisfaction? The answer is *yes*, absolutely!

A few years ago, I was writing on the subject of the cross and found it difficult to bring the Lord's suffering into focus. The more I pondered it, the more I thought about his words on the cross: "My God, my God, why have you forsaken me?" So I prayed, "Lord, help me to understand the agony of what you went through."

I had just gotten up from my computer to ponder this in my mind. How and why did the Son of God pray such a prayer? Suddenly a truth came into sharp focus. At the very moment that Jesus cried those words, at the height of his sense of desolation, he was, in actual fact, in the very center of his Father's will.

This epiphany turned my thoughts in a small way back to my own moment of desperation—my suicide attempt as a teenager in Delhi. At the very moment I had thought I was farthest away from God, the Lord had his appointment with me. It was an appointment of *life*, and not of death.

I was speaking at Oxford a few years ago when a colleague and son in the ministry, Michael Ramsden, told me, "A young man is traveling here to meet you. He's taking a train, and he's coming a long way."

"What is it about?"

"I'll let him tell you the story."

When I met this strapping young fellow, he shook my hand heartily. "I can't tell you what it means to see you and put a face to your voice," he said.

He was a university student, and at one point in the previous year, he had been lying on his bed, ready to commit suicide. His life had gotten onto the wrong track, and he had decided to end it.

"I had made up my mind, and I had everything planned," he said. "I was going to slit my wrists. But I was afraid that I might cry out and that someone might hear me. So I needed some noise to shut out the sound if I were to shout in pain.

"On the nightstand next to me, there was a tape recorder my father and I had shared. I turned it on, expecting one of my rock music tapes to start blaring. Instead, out of the blue came a sermon of yours, titled 'The Illusions of Our Culture.' My dad must have been listening to it."

I had preached that message almost twenty years before. In it, I shared the story of my suicide attempt.

"I thought, 'I cannot believe this,'" the young man said. "I just could *not* believe it." It was a message about disillusionment on many levels of life, and the young student connected with it.

"Instead of ending my life," he said, "I got up out of bed and got down on my knees."

He committed his life to Jesus Christ that day, and he is now actively involved in his university with missions for the cause of Christ.

"I just wanted to come and say thanks," he said. His face shone with joy.

I've lost count of the number of people who have spoken to me or written to our ministry, saying that they heard a tape or one of our radio programs at the very moment when they were contemplating suicide—and they turned to the Lord instead. Others who had a hatred for Christianity—Muslims, Hindus, atheists, disillusioned academics—tell the same story of hearing a message and committing their lives to Christ.

One day, I was at the bedside of a friend who was a Muslim convert to Jesus Christ. He was in the hospital to have a leg amputated. Some years later, he would pay with his life for his commitment to Christ. But before I left his hospital bed that day, I prayed with him. With tears of joy, he said one sentence that I will never forget: "Brother Ravi, the more I study other beliefs and religions, the more beautiful Jesus becomes to me."

He is right. Even in ministry, the same applies. Through all of the visitations of life—successes or failures—it is not how well you are known or not known. It is not how big your organization is or isn't. It is not even how many sermons one has preached or books one has written or millions of dollars one has accumulated. It is *how well do you know Jesus?* That's it. That is what shapes how you view everything else. Successes are hollow if you do not know the author of life and His purpose. To me, with each passing year, Jesus has only become more beautiful.

I am reminded of the story of a man who was a devout church member, who also happened to love golf. Any opportunity to play golf he would leap at and enjoy doing. Then the day came when it was cutting into every other commitment. Every Sunday, he just felt the urge to play, although he knew there were responsibilities at the church. He nevertheless leaped out of bed, got dressed, and took off for the golf course. As the story goes, Peter and Paul in heaven were talking about this man's out-of-control appetite, and they agreed, "We've got to trim this back." So Peter said, "Leave it to me."

As the man took a massive swing from off the tee, the ball sailed into the air. Peter blinked his eyes, and as the ball descended, it rolled into the hole with a precision never before experienced by this player. Paul, rather aghast at this result, chided Peter and said, "What did you do *that* for?" Peter grinned and said, "Who's he going to tell?"

A funny, imaginative story indeed. But life's joys are joys *only* if they can be shared. Even more, joys multiply when they can be shared with honor and purpose. That is what makes the walk with God so beautiful. It is the ultimate form of sharing and the ultimate imperative to share. The family has grown larger, and the joys have multiplied. After all these years, the ministry that began in our small apartment in Toronto has multiplied into many tracks. But it has still led to one destination.

PART 3

WEST TO EAST

Chapter 16

RETURNING:
GOD IN THE SHADOWS

INDIA IS MY HOMELAND. KERALA AND TAMIL NADU ARE MY HERITAGE. Delhi is the place of my youth.

I make trips to the land of my birth now several times each year, and it looks different each time I return. But in my heart, my love for India only grows deeper with the years. Its people, its colorful pageantry—all add to the mix within my soul. It is a country blessed with enormous intellectual and artistic strength. At this moment in world history, India is rising to the top with incredible accomplishments and skills in computer technology that promise a prominent role in the world for its young minds. At the same time, the past casts a long shadow across the sociocultural landscape that makes for genuine nostalgia. In fact, one of the most dramatic discoveries I made while doing some research on my roots as I began to write this book was found in a statement made by a Hindu historian writing about the impact of Christianity in India. Here are his words: "There is no doubt as to the tradition that Saint Thomas came to Kerala and converted a few families of Nambudiris, some of whom were ordained by him as priests."

That statement gave me pause to mutter a prayer of gratitude that my caste was mentioned alongside the name of this great apostle! So the seeds of the conversions that took place among my forebears were sown in Keralite soil, within the very generation of our Lord's walk on this earth. Heaven will bring further light from this work of God in the shadows.

On *this* trip, I will travel to both cities of my youth—Chennai (yes, Madras, where it all began for me) and Delhi. In Chennai, our RZIM office is holding a groundbreaking ceremony for the building of a new training center. When I arrive, I am surrounded by the smiling friends who do the hard work of RZIM in India: Shalini, our administrator for sixteen years; our apologists, Sudhakar, a former university zoology professor who specializes in scientific subjects and hosts dialogues and open forums with Muslims; Ajoy, our biblical and devotional specialist; and Prakash Yesudian, the prominent evangelist who has just retired from decades of service as our ministry director in India.

As I stand before the group that has gathered for the ceremony, preaching the message I have brought, I am fully aware that I am only a few kilometers from the house on the narrow street where I was born. Two giggling little girls live there now —

Oh, Auntie! Auntie! We love your blue eyes.

— children who have dreams, as I did when I lived there. Perhaps they even have the same dreams I had, and perhaps they'll see those dreams fulfilled. Their day may come when they are among those who benefit from Wellspring International, which is our outreach — including the offering of scholarships to needy students in the name of Christ — to women and children around the world, particularly in Asia. One student is studying law in a restricted country, two are young women working on their bachelor's degrees in Chennai, others are pursuing medicine — and RZIM is helping to make it all happen. In this part of the world, it's not nearly as expensive as in the West. Some students can get through college for around fifteen hundred dollars a year.

I believe that those two little girls' day will come.

I will never forget the street where I was born, never forget the country where I was raised, never forget the mean times our family struggled through. I remember years ago reading the biography of John Newton. His life was punctuated by tragedy. He was beaten; he was involved in the slave trade. And, at one time, he was himself enslaved. Then, rescued by God, he penned these immortal lines: "Amazing grace — how sweet the sound — that saved a wretch like me!" In his study in Olney, England, are the words to remind him never to forget from whence he came. I also think of Charles Dickens, returning to his hometown after years of being away. He said he remembered it being much bigger than it actually was. He started to write that the city had changed, and then he paused and thought, "Maybe it is more because *I* had changed."

Both are true about my trips back to India. Like the gigantic mango tree, once a sapling, that now shades the backyard of our former house in Delhi, so the years have gone by, and the branches of God's reach through my life seem much more extensive than I ever thought they would be. But through it all, one great lesson stands out: the shadows were not as dark as I thought they were at the time, because His light was always there.

I am an official lecturer at Oxford now, teaching there once a year. Yet, it doesn't matter if I'm speaking there—in the halls of academia—or here at a groundbreaking ceremony for RZIM India; I still go into every meeting, never forgetting my roots. God can shape us in any way he pleases. He raised Moses in a palace in order to use him in a desert; he raised Joseph in a desert in order to use him in a palace. For me, the best thing that ever happened culturally was the intersection of East and West. While the languages of the tongue and the anguish of experience may vary, the language of the soul is the same all over the world.

That is why I feel more confident all the time that, outside of the gospel, there are no answers for humanity's most fundamental questions. And I feel a special calling to speak in *any* arena, for which I am always grateful.

We had launched our Wellspring initiative just prior to my trip. As I have mentioned, the mission was primarily to come alongside existing ministries that reach out to women in Third World countries who have been sexually abused or victimized, or who have been caught up in the brutal sex-trafficking industry in Asia. But there is much more to this mission now, as needs have become known. In Thailand, we're helping an orphanage that provides a home for children orphaned or victimized by AIDS, and we're carrying out a ministry that reaches women who have been sold into prostitution. In India, we are working with a ministry that provides housing and medical attention for destitute elderly people, and we've come alongside a ministry in Mumbai that works with prostitutes and provides both the message and means out of that horrific lifestyle, helping them to build their lives on a different foundation. We have been able to buy fishing boats and nets to give to the fishing families near Chennai who lost everything in the tsunami of December 26, 2004. In Indonesia, we are working with a ministry that prepares disadvantaged young people to compete for jobs, as well as with different agencies and ministries providing life-giving sustenance to tsunami survivors. Beyond this, there are numerous individuals we met as we have traveled all over the world, to whom we have the joy of being able to give some financial assistance.

On my flight from Chennai to Delhi, I read a startling headline in the newspaper: "17 Suicides in Kerala." It had been exam week at the university, and grades were about to be posted. The article narrated the stories of two students who killed themselves, one of whom left a note saying he didn't want to be a burden to his parents. That's exactly who *I* had been.

Four decades later, it is still difficult for me to put myself back in those shoes, yet I know that's why I keep coming back here. I keep coming back because there are thousands of young people who are that close to annihilation — as close as I was. I believe if they could be guaranteed that there is nothing beyond the grave — that when they finish off their lives, that would be the end of it — thousands, if not millions more, would do it. They are in that kind of despair.

I turn my attention away from the newspaper to work on my speech to the ambassadors to the United Nations, whom I'll address in another month. The topic will be "Navigating with Absolutes in a Relativistic World." At this time in world cultural history, when East and West seem to be getting closer and closer through communication and travel, you would think our understanding of each other would be better, but it isn't. It's as if we have been able to bridge the distances but not cross the differences.

As I work on the speech, some old familiar but fleeting feelings come back: "I am so unfit for this. I am unsure of myself. Why do these people want to listen to me? I would never have wanted this. It's not my natural inclination."

Slowly, those thoughts are aligned into the right perspective: "Only the Lord could have put these pieces together. No human being could have engineered this."

Thirty days from now, I will have delivered the speech about the four absolutes we all have in our minds: love, justice, evil, and forgiveness.

We know what it means to have a loving parent, or to love our spouse, or to love our children. *Love* is a motivating, guiding concept in life.

Beyond love, we all cry for *justice*, I will tell the ambassadors. The UN exists as a body to make sure that justice is applied to global situations.

But the third area is a nebulous one called *evil*. Even though we may not like to use the term, we know what it is. If somebody deceives or cheats or betrays or hurts us, we know it is morally wrong. We're more likely to talk of the fact of evil when we're on the receiving end of it.

Finally, the fourth absolute is *forgiveness*, and any one of us who has ever done wrong recognizes the grace that's expressed when someone says, "I forgive you."

I will give the ambassadors the illustration of a little boy I saw wearing a helmet as he played soccer on the campus of the college where I once taught. As I got closer to the boy, I saw that there was something radically wrong with his face and hands. When I asked a colleague about it, he said, "That's the son of a science professor. The family was rear-ended when the boy was a baby, and the car burst into flames. He was covered from head to toe with bad burns. And the truck driver who ran into them got away. He jumped out of his truck and eluded capture."

Almost twenty years later, the truck driver was stopped on the highway during a routine license check, and the case came to trial. The boy was now a college graduate and was doing well in life, despite having suffered so much. During the trial, he was allowed to confront the man who had done this to him. The young man said to the man who caused his disfigurement, "I want you to look at me. Look at what you've done to my life." But the man kept his head down the whole time.

The young man then unfolded the story of a lifetime of pain, suffering, and deformity. He demanded one more time that the truck driver look him in the eye. As the man looked up, the young man said, "Now that you see me, I want you to know that because of Jesus Christ, I forgive you." At that, the courtroom fell silent.

I will conclude with these words to the UN ambassadors: "When you can see horror and grace put together, you realize there is no place, humanly speaking, where we can find an absolute way to understand these things. Only on the cross of Jesus Christ do love, justice, evil, and forgiveness converge. Evil, in the heart of man, shown in the crucifixion; love, in the heart of God who gave his Son; forgiveness, because of the grace of Christ; and justice, because of the law of God revealed."

That speech has now been delivered. At its close, there was silence among the ambassadors. Afterward, the president of the United Nations asked me to come to his office to pray for him. Also, an ambassador from an Eastern European country confided in me. "When I came here, I wondered why I was ever brought to a position like this," he said. "I am very lonely out here. I don't like all that is involved. But today, I have been given an answer. God has a cause greater than we have, and unless we find out his course, we will not be able to solve our problems. I come from an atheistic country, but today God has spoken to me." He embraced me in tears.

THE INTERSECTION OF THE STREETS WHERE WE USED TO LIVE IN DELHI— Cornwallis Road and Wellesley Road—has different names on the street signs now—named after Indian patriots. I can see the desire for that kind of honor, but a nation should not forget its history either. People also need to remember what a place was before, especially after you're on peaceful terms.

As I pass the park where we used to play cricket, my old passion rises up with wisdom for today. In cricket, there is a saying, "You have to 'get your eye in' "—which means that when you go to bat, you don't start flailing away at the beginning. You've got to watch the ball carefully at first and see how the bowler is moving the ball. You've got to see the ball "big," to recognize how it's going to take its turn off the ground, how it's going to come up into the air in front of you. That's "getting your eye in."

Life is like this. There are times when you really have to "get your eye in" to see what's going on—to train your eye to have discernment, insight, understanding.

A second lesson from cricket is to be careful of a "sticky wicket." This refers to the unpredictable bounce the ball can take after the rains. It is the equivalent of a knuckleball in baseball, when the batter has no clue what the ball is going to do, which way it will turn or dip. Life often presents a sticky wicket, but we know the One who guards the soul through all of it. None of us know what tomorrow holds. In fact, at this point of writing, my wife has just found out that her dad has been diagnosed with an untreatable cancer, and his days are suddenly numbered. None of us know the hour we will be called, but called we will be. In this sticky wicket of life, we must know the One who controls all things.

Cricket has yet another term—we call it "being stumped." It is a terrible way to get out—you are trapped by the wicket-keeper (the equivalent of the catcher in baseball), and he tags you as you are out of position. The best analogy is being picked off when you're getting ready to steal a base. In other words, in life there are lines and boundaries. If caught outside the lines while the ball is in play, you are out. It is a helpless feeling to turn around and find yourself out of position and tagged. We must ever remember that the game is not there to protect the rules; the rules are there to protect the game. Cricket, like all sports, has many life lessons to teach.

Now I come to Sweets Corner, with its little candies of pure milk, reduced until there is nothing but sweetness and then wrapped in thinly pounded silver paper. When Margie and I came here a decade ago, it had been twenty-seven years since I'd walked through those doors. Naomi and Nathan were with us at the time, and as soon as our family walked in, I noticed that the owner was there but was on the phone. Assuming that he wouldn't recognize me, I just escorted my family in to find a table. But as we walked passed him, with his other arm he reached out and grabbed me, putting the phone aside, and said, "Ravi, *baba*! (little boy!), how are you?" My children were amazed. He ordered that the tables be thoroughly cleaned (which, being interpreted, means please spread the dirt with a greasy cloth) because one of his favorite customers was here "with foreigners."

Soon I arrive at the Cathedral Church of the Redemption, where over the past decade I have visited every couple of years just to sit and meditate. I thank the Lord that, even though things were so wrong in my life here, I finally was brought to a realization of what all those struggles were about. There are some wonderful things from your painful past, things with a beauty you may not have realized at the time. As I sit here now, I remember the names of the people, the homes we went to, the food we ate, the young people I met. Now it all seems like a chapter far in the past, and it causes me to remember that my life didn't begin yesterday. I can hear my father's voice in the choir loft.

Several years ago, Margie and I were visiting Delhi, and she suggested we try to find my grandmother's grave. I had not been there since the day she was buried.

"We'll never find it," I said.

"Let's just go," she insisted.

At the time of my grandmother's burial, there was only one Christian cemetery in Delhi, and because I could remember its name, the taxi had no trouble getting us there.

As we entered the cemetery office, a man I took for the attendant sat puffing on a bidi, a self-rolled cigarette made of strong tobacco and a dried leaf. He just kept staring at Margie and me as he puffed away. I thought maybe it was because my wife was a Westerner, so I broke the ice by saying, *"Kya hal hai,"* which means, "How are you?"

He nodded, broke into a quizzical look, and asked, "Did you arrive in Delhi at one o'clock this morning?"

I was floored. "Yes," I answered. "How did you know that?"

"I was the immigration officer who stamped your passport when you came in."

I had to grin. That's India for you! He had come to visit the manager of the cemetery. So I turned to the manager and said, "Do you think you can help us? We want to find my grandmother's grave."

"Her name, sir?"

"Manickam. Agnes Manickam."

"What year did she die, sir?"

"I wish I knew, but I was a little boy. Why don't I guess at 1955?"

"Let's start at 1950," he said.

"No, that's too early."

He insisted that there was no point arguing, and he brought out a massive register, about two-and-a-half-feet wide and one-and-a-half-feet tall. He motioned for us to sit down across from him while he ponderously studied each page written in fountain-pen ink, approximately ten names per page, with all the details. He kept moistening his finger and turning page after page. I could tell this was going to take an eternity, so I finally convinced him to start at 1955.

Suddenly, there it was! Agnes D. Manickam; Officiant: Rev. Father Ernest T. John. He summoned the gardener.

"He will take you," he said.

The gardener arrived carrying a little can of water and a broom, and gestured for us to follow him. As we walked through the rows of stones, surrounded by tangles of growth and vines, I muttered to Margie, "I can't believe we'll be able to find it in all this dirt."

We located the plot amid a bushy overgrowth. The gardener knelt and began working, clearing away the caked on dirt, the rubble collected over years of no one taking care of it.

I recalled the day I had stood on this very spot as a child and sung the hymn that has stayed so close to my heart, a hymn I still believe is one of the greatest ever written — "Abide with Me." I hadn't understood then the significance of my sweet grandmother's faith.

As the gardener brushed away the last of the vines and dirt, I strained to see the dates of my grandmother's life on earth. Then suddenly, Margie grabbed my arm. "Look, Ravi!" she said. "I don't believe it! I don't believe it!"

Her name, the dates she was born and died, and then the words carved into my grandmother's stone: "Because I live, ye shall live also" — John 14:19.

I was astounded. *The words in the hospital — the Bible passage that Fred David shared.* They were the very words that had rescued me when my mother read them to me. The very words I had put on my mother's grave when she died.

What a closure to the story of a life and a verse! God was no longer in the shadows. He was reading me like a book in the light. This was no grave. This was the resurrection reminder.

In that swirling moment, the connections all came into focus: the simple exchange between Jesus and Thomas; the apostle's impact on the Indian culture; my own life being shaped by the verse as I lay in the hospital near death. For the first time, I thought that my precious grandmother had probably prayed for me in her own way; I do know that somewhere deep in her heart, she was a godly person.

Hidden gold.

I tipped the gardener for his service of cleaning off the stone, telling him in Hindi, "I'm going to give you a larger sum, because I want you to do me a favor. I want you to tend this grave as long as you work here."

He nodded.

"I want you to brush away the dirt regularly. And I want you to water the plants around it."

He gave me his word that he would. I have contracted for a gravestone that is upright, so it is more visible. My parents could not afford that at the time, but we can now do our part.

Coming to India was a cultural journey for each of my children. I think they didn't know how to relate to the Indian side of their heritage. Our middle child, Naomi, came with us for the first time when she was about fifteen, and it was a terrible shock to her system. She got an eye infection from the pollution in the air, and she was taken aback when a leprous man reached his hand through our car window to ask for money. But she seemed to gain her footing after a few days, and on the day we were scheduled to leave India, she asked if we could go again to my grandmother's grave.

"Of course we can do that, honey. Why do you want to go there?"

"I want to put some flowers on her grave."

Paradoxically, maybe her great-grandmother's grave represented a birthplace of sorts in Naomi's mind—a beginning place, a place that did as much to explain her roots as anyplace else. Now our kids love to go back, and they plead to be taken to visit India as often as they can.

I think of another child's magnetic attraction to a loved one's grave. Just before I made this recent trip back to my homeland, I answered a letter from a young woman named Martina. Here's part of what she wrote me: "I heard you speak in Burlington, Ontario, last month. I wish I could have stolen you away and sat across the table from you to talk to you about my dad."

Martina's father was my friend—Koos Fietje.

"Seeing you was like seeing my dad," she went on to write, "and because I hardly knew him, I wanted to talk to somebody who knew him."

Martina told me that after her father was killed, her Uncle Bill, Koos's younger brother, signed up to take his place in Thailand. I knew Bill as well. He became a missionary in Thailand until he returned to Canada some years later.

She concluded her letter, "I want one day to go and see his grave in Thailand."

I have told her we will make sure that happens. She is now expecting her first child, and when she is ready to travel, we will make the visit to her father's grave a reality.

AFTER OUR DAD DIED, THERE WAS NO GLUE LEFT FOR US KIDS, NO PLACE TO go home for Christmas. So, in the succeeding years, we took turns, with each of us hosting the entire family for the holiday. Everyone lives in the Toronto area now—except for my family, having made Atlanta our home, and my sister Prem, who lives in St. Catherine's, Ontario. For twenty years we gathered together at Christmas, the five families, and spent several days together. It doesn't happen much anymore, with our children all grown-up, but we keep in touch, of course, by phone or through family letters, on special occasions and on birthdays.

Whenever we're together, the difficult early days rarely come up. But every once in a while, something will.

"Remember the couple above us who sang Hindu chants after a terrible fight the night before?" I ask.

"I sure do," Ajit says. Then I sing the hymn as I remember it, and remember also the total disjunction of it.

"Ahh," Ajit says with amusement. "I don't know how you remember even those words." But that's me; I've always had a strong memory for lyrics.

Sunder is family now, after marrying my sister Sham. But then, Sunder had always felt like family, and I had always felt like a son in his family.

A few years ago, when Sunder's dad was in his late seventies, he went into the hospital quite ill. As his Hindu friends gathered around him, Mr. Krishnan sat up in bed and spoke to them about what was most important to him.

"All these years we have been friends, and we've gone to the temple," he said. "Now I'm dying. I want you to know that I have been asking myself a question: Who is the answer to life's questions? I have pondered this for seventy-some years. I now want to share the answer with you." In the presence of his wife, his Hindu friends, my sister, and Sunder, he paused and raised his voice: "The answer is Jesus."

That shocked everyone, especially his devout Hindu wife. Sunder said it was the best parting gift he could have received from his father.

Not only was it a dramatic deathbed conversion; it was a dramatic deathbed evangelistic message, and a glorious ending to a wonderful man's life.

My parents are buried in Toronto, side by side. They have been gone for twenty-five and thirty years now, and I often wonder what they would think, had they lived to see where God has taken me to this point in life.

I know my mother would be delighted at my calling and with her grandchildren. And I think my father would tilt his head back in gratitude to God at what has become of my life. I am keenly aware that the race is not over yet, and caution laced with wisdom and commitment must always be the key to an onward step. But even this far, none of us were deserving of what we received, and yet ultimately God shone his light in our home. I believe both of my parents would have rested in the consolation that sometimes, as hopeless as things may look, God has a greater plan and is always working in the shadows on our behalf. I know they would marvel at the legacy the Lord has given them.

Sarah, our oldest, is a gifted writer; indeed, she has already authored her first book, *Confessions of an Honest Wife: On the Mess, Mystery, and Miracle of Marriage*. The loyal, quiet little girl who used to leave her mother notes on her nightstand has blossomed in her art of expression and is married to a young man who practices law. She is a lovely, statuesque young lady with an artistic bent and a creative mind. She started her career with CNN in the marketing department and now uses her creativity to do marketing for RZIM.

Naomi, a marvelous combination of passion and energy, also has chosen to work with her family in RZIM, directing the Wellspring International work, after some exciting stints with Coca-Cola and then in the Bush White House as an events coordinator. A keen mind with a loveliness to match, she wants to take on the world.

When I look at my son, Nathan, today—how he chums around and chats with me, how he puts his arm around me and sees me as a friend—I think of the distance God has brought me to have such a relationship after my own childhood with my dad. Nate is a tenderhearted gentleman and a diehard Atlanta Braves fan, and he now follows cricket as closely and well as I do after seeing only one match. Our son loves the Lord deeply and shares Sarah's gift for writing, working for Focus on the Family.

I know our kids' grandfather would have been proud.

The demands that are made on a spouse who is linked in a calling like mine are greater than you could imagine. The hours alone at home; the willingness to move forward whenever God calls; the trust required to live solely on love offerings in the early days, unsure where the next meal will come from — all these are enough to cause constant tension, and worse. Yet Margie has never, ever complained about the calling we have shared. The cost extracted from us has been beyond what we might have endured were it not for the Lord's grace; yet the blessing that has come has been beyond our imagining.

Many times, I have said to my wife (and *not* in jest), "You know, your life would have been so much easier if you had married someone without all of these challenges and demands." Her response is so sweet every time — with words of fond commitment, playfully rapping my knuckles or grabbing my hand and squeezing, sending such powerful signals of love through her simple touch that only a partner of thirty-three years could understand them all. I will never forget the first time we met, and that sweet face is always in my mind as I travel, ever longing to be back home.

As I reflect on these things now, I recall being touched by the biography of David Livingstone years ago. As a young man, he had studied diligently for the ministry, and as he looked toward Africa he declared, "The haunting specter of the smoke of a thousand villages in the morning sun is burned within my heart." Livingstone then prayed this famous prayer: "Lord, send me anywhere, only go with me. Lay any burden on me, only sustain me. Sever any ties but the ties that bind me to your service and to your heart."

His story is well known. He was attacked by a lion, blinded in an eye when he walked into a tree branch, had a shoulder torn. He lost so much along the way, even having to bury his wife in Africa. By her grave he prayed, "My Jesus, my King, my life, my all, I again consecrate my life to You. I shall place no value in anything I possess, except as it relates to Your kingdom and to Your service." He later testified, "Through it all came the words of Christ to me, 'Lo, I am with you always, even unto the end of the age.'"

David Livingstone carried on, going from village to village and making a profound impact for the gospel. When he died, two African men who loved him carried his body fifteen hundred miles to place it on a boat bound for England, so he could be buried in his homeland.

When I think of a life like this man's, I am inspired also to pray, "Lord, send me anywhere, only go with me. Lay any burden on me, only sustain me. Oh, my Jesus, my King, my life, my all, I again consecrate my life to You." If you've committed your life to Christ from the beginning and you make new commitments all along the journey, in the end you will see that He has been with you always.

God is in the shadows in many ways, but He is also in the bright light of what His servants do every day. My prayer is that He will find me faithful, and that until He calls me home I'll be willing to go anywhere, to bear any burden for Him, and to recommit to Him afresh. It's a tall dream, and without His strength it cannot be done. Yet with His strength, all things are possible.

When I look at the life I've had and at what the Lord has given me—my calling, my friendships, my beautiful wife and children—it is what dreams are made of. I have seen the world. I have walked with great leaders. I have slept in the villages and homes of the poor. I have had to stop at moments along the way and say, "I can never believe this is what the Lord had in mind for me when He started to rebuild my life." Only as you keep in perspective your roots, your ordinary day-to-day life, and the grace that called you, are you able to see clearly the extraordinary privilege of speaking to people who make a difference in our world.

To try to begin to take it all in is to dip your toe into an ocean that's too deep to fathom. It is nothing less than a tapestry woven skillfully and mysteriously by father and son—the elder nodding and the younger responding—a work whose beauty is revealed in fullness only upon its completion.

T. S. Eliot once wrote:

> *We shall not cease from exploration,*
> *And the end of all our exploring*
> *Will be to arrive where we started*
> *And know the place for the first time.*

Life is not merely a geographical journey—not just east to west, or north to south. There is also an up and a down—God's way, or our way. My prayer for you the reader is that you, too, will see it His way, both in the shadows and in the light. There is no greater discovery than seeing God as the author of your destiny.

I can hardly wait for heaven to put it all together—yes, even more.